Planner's Estimating Guide

Projecting Land-Use and Facility Needs

By Arthur C. Nelson, FAICP

PLANNERS PRESS
AMERICAN PLANNING ASSOCIATION
Chicago, Illinois • Washington, D.C.

Copyright 2004 by the American Planning Association
122 S. Michigan Ave., Suite 1600, Chicago, IL 60603

ISBN (paperback edition): 1-884829-76-7
Library of Congress Catalog Control Number: 2004104879

Printed in the United States of America
All rights reserved

Interior composition and copyediting by Joanne Shwed, Backspace Ink
Title and cover design by Peter Katz

To
Maria Abadal Cahill, Tom Beck,
Charles Gauthier, and Dave Jordan
for advancing good public land-use planning
in the face of special interest politics

Acknowledgements

This book was many years in the making. It began when I was a land-use planner in Oregon trying to estimate land-use needs for small local governments to comply with statewide growth management policies. It continued when I was a newly minted assistant professor at Kansas State University where, with support from Mark Lapping (now at the University of Southern Maine), John Keller, and Al Keithley, I was able to hone some of the methods for application to both stagnating rural Kansas communities and the burgeoning Kansas suburbs of Kansas City, Missouri. The journey leading to this book continued at Georgia Tech, where I received important insights from David Sawicki, Bill Drummond, Steve French, and Zhong-Ren Peng (now at the University of Wisconsin–Milwaukee).

Along the way, numerous people dropped me hints, insights, data, and simple encouragement. I fear missing someone but the list includes at least Gerrit Knaap at the University of Maryland, Uri Avin of HNTB, Terry Moore of ECONorthwest, Rosalind Goldstein of the Lincoln Institute of Land Policy, David Russ (formerly of the Florida Department of Community Affairs (DCA) and now in private legal practice), Jim Mirley (formerly of 1000 Friends of Florida and Secretary of the Florida DCA and now at Florida Atlantic University), Steve Pfeiffer (former Florida DCA Legal Counsel and now in private practice), Tom Pelham (former Secretary of the Florida DCA and now in private practice), Jim Nicholas of the University of Florida, Sam Seskin of Parsons Brinkerhoff, Ed Kaiser, David Godschalk, and Ray

Burby of the University of North Carolina, and to the presenters at conferences of the American Planning Association, Urban Land Institute (ULI), Lincoln Institute of Land Policy, and others who gave me bits of information and insights along the way.

I also acknowledge the hundreds of students over the years at Georgia Tech and in continuing education programs who suffered through earlier stages of the book and workbook but, in doing so, made it more accessible to everyone else.

Finally, the people at the American Planning Association are to be given special acknowledgement for several reasons. First, to Frank So for supporting its development and especially for insisting on a method to estimate the land-use and facility impacts associated with development that is not anticipated in local land-use plans (Chapter 11). Because Frank's request delayed the book by about six years in order to craft and test something that's never been done in a textbook, acknowledgement also goes to Sylvia Lewis for encouraging me to see it through. Thanks also to Joanne Shwed of Backspace Ink for editorial assistance.

This book and the accompanying workbook have been in the works for 20 years and it is still a work in progress. I hope you see how it can be improved, and do so.

—Arthur Christian (Chris) Nelson, FAICP
Virginia Polytechnic Institute and State University
Alexandria, Virginia

Contents

Contact the Author

Users of this book and accompanying CD-ROM workbook
should contact the author directly with questions or comments.

E-mail: acn@vt.edu

See the CD-ROM workbook introduction

for details.

List of Figures

List of Tables

List of Acronyms

BEA	Bureau of Economic Analysis		ITE	Institute of Transportation Engineers
CBD	Central Business District		LOS	Level of Service
CBECS	*Commercial Buildings Energy Consumption Survey 1999*		MEGA	Massively Enlarged, Growth-Accelerated
DCA	Department of Community Affairs		MGD	Million Gallons Per Day
E & S	Elementary & Secondary		MPO	Metropolitan Planning Organization
EMS	Emergency Medical Services		na	not applicable
FAR	Floor Area Ratio		NAIOP	National Association of Industrial and Office Properties
FAY	Floor Area Yield		NRPA	National Recreation and Parks Association
FIRE	Finance, Insurance, and Real Estate		*RIMSII*	*Regional Input-Output Multipliers II*
GIS	Geographic Information System		Sq. Ft.	Square Feet
GLA	Gross Leasable Area		TCU	Transportation, Communication, and Utilities
GPD	Gallons Per Day		ULI	Urban Land Institute
I-O	Input-Output			

1

The Challenge Ahead

OVERVIEW

The U.S. population is projected to reach 375 million in 2030, a third more than in 2000. They will live in about 154 million housing units, almost 40 million more than in 2000. Yet, nearly 60 million new housing units will need to be built because 20 million units existing in 2000 will be replaced.

Proportionately more growth will be seen in the space needed to accommodate employment. By my calculations, there will be more than 230 million jobs in 2030, 68 million or 40% more than in 2000. These jobs will require more than 50 billion additional square feet of nonresidential space than existed in 2000. Counting the more than 40 billion square feet to be replaced, about 100 billion square feet of nonresidential space will need to be constructed between 2000 and 2030.

To accommodate growth to 2030, I estimate that the U.S. will construct 50% more residential units and 90% more nonresidential space than existed in 2000. Most of this new growth will occur in the South and West, but parts of the Northeast and Midwest will also grow substantially.

The bottom line is that half of all development in 2030 will be built since 2000. These projections are even higher in the South and West, approaching two-thirds in many rapidly growing metropolitan areas.[1]

Assuming these projections hold, why should we be interested in them? They show in general terms the magnitude of change facing this nation. They show that, for those who fear we cannot change current development patterns, there is hope. There is an opportunity to reshape the built environment. The paved parking lots can become infill and redevelopment sites. Sensitive landscapes can be protected if we know how much new development needs to be steered away from them. Better urban forms can still be achieved in just one generation. To get there from here, however, is a considerable challenge.

Let us examine current trends reflected by development patterns observed during the five-year period of 1992 to 1997. During this period, developed land—as defined by the *National Resources Inventory* (Natural Resources and Conservation Service 1999)—grew by almost 6 million acres, from 92.4 million to 98.3 million acres or 6.4%.[2] At the same time, the nation's population grew by about 12 million people or about 5%. This indicates that land consumption for development is growing 30% faster than population growth. At this pace, the U.S. would lose about 40 million undeveloped acres to development between 2000 and 2030—roughly the size of Oklahoma.

What is the overall magnitude of change we may anticipate as planners, engineers, architects, and others interested in the built environment over the next generation?

Overall, I estimate that total built space in this country will grow from an estimated 290 billion square feet in 2000 to 420 billion square feet in 2030. This increase of 130 billion square feet is on top of the 80 billion square feet that will be replaced because of age, natural disasters, and conversions.[3] Thus, new built space will total 210 billion square feet, more than 70% of the space existing in 2000. Put differently, about half of all development in 2030 did not exist in 2000. Over the 30-year period, more than $20 trillion will be spent on new construction, assuming a modest $100 per square foot excluding land and infrastructure.[4] Counting public and private infrastructure investments, total investment in new development may exceed $25 trillion, perhaps averaging $1 trillion annually (Figure 1-1).

The challenge facing planners, engineers, architects, public officials, and the public generally is where to put this new and replaced development. Some would argue that it should all go to built-up urban areas. This may be problematic because of insufficient infrastructure, brownfields, ownership and development patterns making redevelopment inefficient, inflexible development codes, and neighborhood opposition. Others would argue that much of it will go into greenfields because that is where the land is cheap; ownership and development patterns are conducive to large-scale, master-planned developments; local regulations are favorable; and the public is willing to accept it, at least to some extent. Still others argue for a balance that directs much of the new demand to urban areas and the rest into greenfields in new-urbanism configurations.

Figure 1-1
Future U.S. Development Needs, 2000-2030

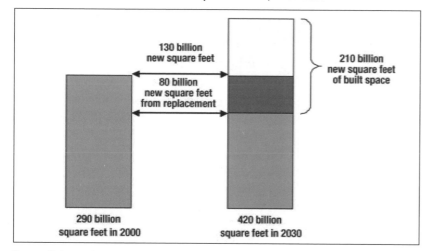

130 billion new square feet

80 billion new square feet from replacement

210 billion new square feet of built space

290 billion square feet in 2000

420 billion square feet in 2030

Source: Estimates by author.

The purpose of this book is not necessarily to advocate one development scenario over another, but rather to present a reasonably straightforward method in which land-use and facility needs of the future may be estimated for a variety of scenarios. The book is written principally for practitioners—not as a prescriptive solution to estimating local land-use and facility needs, but as a way in which to frame land-use and facility needs as a point of departure for long-range planning. It is also written for students, perhaps as a supplement to Kaiser, Godschalk, and Chapin's *Urban Land Use Planning* (1995) and Klosterman et al.'s *Hypothetical City Workbook* (1999).

The text is a guide to using the accompanying workbook, which is an Excel-based program.[5] The workbook should be viewed as a device to gather a first impression of future land-use needs. It does not allocate land uses to the land, nor does it say where development should or should not go. It also does not account for any local development constraints such as publicly owned land, hazardous landscapes, or historically significant areas.

As a first-impression device, it allows one to see a first-cut estimate of land-use and facility needs. If the landscape in question has limitations and the land-use estimations exceed land supply, for instance, one can change assumptions in the workbook to make second and subsequent rounds of estimates. In this way, the workbook can reflect local limitations. Moreover, the workbook is designed to show the user the implications of growth based on standard or rule-of-thumb assumptions. The wise user will change the assumptions as needed to reflect local constraints—including public input—to see how the outcome changes. The workbook is thus a glorified model for testing sensitivities with respect to land supply constraints and changes in policy assumptions. It cannot tell you what to do, but it can tell you the numerical implications of different scenarios.

The worksheets comprising the workbook and the discussion in this book deal with a 20-year planning horizon for a fictitious entire county. The user can manually change the projection period. One could, for example, consider land-use and facility needs in five-, 10-, and 15-year intervals. In this way, the user can create a series of worksheets for five-year intervals out to 20 years or beyond, changing some assumptions between each of the five years to account for known changes (such as increasing elderly households) or speculate on others (such as more people working at home, thereby reducing demand for commercial office space) for several scenarios.

The user can also change the scale of analysis. A fictitious county is used—Yukon—as the basis for analysis in the book, but one could apply and adapt the approach to subcounty areas or other smaller scales.

More qualifications about this book and workbook are necessary. It is not intended to be a book on planning processes or even on "best practices." It is a tool to inform the planning process of the implications of different growth scenarios and planning and development assumptions. It cannot predict local or even national political or legal changes. Oregon's statewide land-use planning program, for example, comes under regular political and legal challenge. Maryland's "smart growth" laws may be revised or the zeal of their implementation may be altered with changing governors. If Florida voters were asked whether they would accept more growth, it is possible the majority would vote for growth caps.

The national scene is even more unpredictable. Although the Supreme Court sanctioned the idea of zoning in the 1920s, there is no certainty that it will not change its mind. The federal tax reform act of 1981 led to a glut of office and other commercial space that was not absorbed by the market in many metropolitan areas until well into the 1990s. The high-tech boom of the 1990s, which led to office and research parks at the fringes of many metropolitan areas, fizzled in the early 2000s, leaving millions of square feet of empty space and half-finished projects in many metropolitan areas.

Finally, as my friend and professional colleague Richard B. Peiser (now at Harvard's Graduate School of Design) once quipped, estimating future land-use needs makes projecting the gross domestic product look like child's play. True enough, but when one needs to raise billions of dollars to pay for new or expanded water, wastewater, drainage, education, transportation, and other facilities to meet the development needs of the future, one should also have at least a general understanding of how much land will need to be served under different scenarios. That is the purpose of this book and accompanying workbook.

YUKON COUNTY

At 159,000 square miles—larger than the State of California—Alaska's Yukon–Koyukuk County is the largest in the United States; it is also its least densely settled county and is in no danger of being overrun by development. When it comes to planning for development, it is an unpainted canvas. In honor of this, I apply the book and workbook examples to "Yukon" County.

Why use a fictitious name at all? I think a name is better than "the subject county" or "the subject jurisdiction." If a name is to be used, which should it be? Washington and Jefferson Counties are probably the most prevalent names, so using them would afford the luxury of generalizability by frequency of use. The trouble is that readers may want to associate the book and numerical examples to a real county they know. I could be clever and use Wobegon County (after Garrison Keillor's Lake Wobegon) but this is not satisfying. I could be even more clever by using something like Halcyon County in the State of Paradise. In the end, I use the writer's license to apply the book and workbook to Yukon County, in some unspecified state.

What kind of a county is our fictitious Yukon? Its population, employment, growth rates, and related characteristics are given in the text. It is large but not too large; it is fast growing but not too fast. It could be in the Sunbelt or the West or the Mountains, or it could be in the growing fringes of some large midwestern and northeastern metropolitan areas. It is mostly suburban, dominated by low-density residential development with a growing employment base.

In a scheme devised by Robert Lang[6] for "metropolitan growth counties," Yukon County would fall in the category of "edge counties" between large, urban counties that he calls "MEGA" (for "massively enlarged, growth-accelerated," such as all the coastal counties in southern California) and the "new metropolis" counties that have claimed metropolitan status since the 1990 census. By his count, there are 54 edge counties in 26 metropolitan areas in 22 states from Florida to Washing-ton, and California to New Hampshire, with stopovers in such states as Illinois, Michigan, Minnesota, Missouri, and Ohio. Representative counties include Ventura County (California), Boulder County (Colorado), Pasco County (Florida), Gwinnett County (Georgia), Lake County (Illinois), Johnson County (Kansas), Anne Arundel County (Maryland), Anoka County (Minnesota), Rockingham County (New Hampshire), Ocean County (New Jersey), Durham County (North Carolina), Clackamas County (Oregon), Bucks County (Pennsylvania), Galveston County (Texas), Prince William County (Virginia), and Snohomish County (Washington).

As a group, "edge counties" average about 250,000 in population, grow at twice the national average, and approach 75% homeownership with two-thirds of the housing being detached. While accounting for less than 10% of the total population, they will account for a quarter of the nation's growth over the next generation. "New metropolis" or MEGA counties will account for about a quarter of the nation's population but will absorb about two-thirds of its growth. Together, these counties may account for 90% of the nation's growth over the next generation.

The principles of this book and workbook are not limited to these kinds of counties, however. The seeds of this book were sewn when I was a planning director in an exurban, slow-growing county in Oregon. They were refined while observing development trends in a central Kansas university town (Manhattan, home of Kansas State University) and refined further in studies of suburbanizing Florida and Georgia. For the most part, the principles of estimating land-use needs do not vary by location or even growth rate—provided there is some growth.

Alas, Yukon County is a county (or borough or parish) and not a city (or township). The county is used as the level of analysis for some very practical reasons:

- Counties are the smallest unit of measure for which the broadest array of projections and data is available.
- Cities vary considerably in their growth patterns, no doubt influenced by state annexation laws.
- Many counties are more influential in establishing land-use patterns than other forms of government because they provide road systems and often water and wastewater services.

Nonetheless, as noted earlier, the methods presented here can be applied to subcounty areas such as cities and townships or, more generally, "planning areas." Subcounty applications could be stitched together and refined further to create an overall land-use and facility plan for the county as a whole. The worksheet can also be applied to multicounty regions so that the mosaic of individual county land-use and facility needs could compose a picture, or series of pictures, for the region as a whole.

DATA NEEDS AND USE

This book and workbook have been designed to make use of data that are readily available usually through published sources. Other data available locally, such as property assessor data, may also be used albeit with some manipulation. The data requirements are thus moderate but hopefully not unreasonable. Test versions of this book have been used by local governments throughout the country over the past decade, thanks to those requesting it from the Planning Advisory Service of

the American Planning Association with my permission. My students have also field-tested many of the estimation techniques over the past decade. Further help refining the workbook was provided by Uri Avin and his staff at HNTB. Obviously, in any given circumstance, not all data needed are available, but it may be hypothecated based on the user's local knowledge and experience, or the knowledge of others such as local realtors and market users. In other cases, the land-use categories used in this book may not be applicable to any given situation, and others may be needed or existing ones modified. The principles developed in this book should allow one to tailor them to local conditions.

The user should keep in mind that this is a book about estimating land-use and facility needs. Estimates are not precise figures, even though some figures in this book are taken to many decimal places. The apparent precision should not hide the fact that all this book does is present a more refined way of estimating general needs and impacts. It is not supposed to predict those needs and impacts with precision.

TABLES

This book includes three types of tables:

- *Informational tables* (found in the body of the text, such as Table 2-1): They include such tables as share of developed land devoted to residential land uses, vacancy rates by growth rates, and market factor adjustments to developed land needs.
- *Calculation tables* (marked with a ⊙ symbol and found in the body of the text as well as on the CD-ROM that accompanies this book, such as Table 2-2): The CD-ROM includes

a Microsoft Excel workbook composed of several individual worksheets and an introduction. There is only one Excel file. It is assumed that the user knows how to use Excel. The worksheets follow the exact order of the chapters and are numbered identically to the book's tables. The worksheets also relate to one another, so a change in one can affect one or more other worksheets. The shaded areas are those where the user can input local numbers, assumptions, scenario parameters, or other data. It is recommended that users make a master copy of the workbook for safekeeping. Also, I anticipate that users will adapt the workbook for their purposes because, after all, one size does not fit all.

- *Reference tables* (found in the body of the text, such as Table 4-7): These tables provide the user with a variety of alternative assumptions that may be applied to several calculation steps. For example, alternative space needs of employees that are different from those assumed for Yukon County are offered as an appendix to Chapter 4.

Finally, while assumptions used throughout the book and workbook are based on data and analysis from published sources, or rules of thumb, the user should be mindful that things change and what may be appropriate generally is not appropriate locally. The user may be more knowledgeable of particular aspects of land-use and facility planning than I and should use assumptions based on this knowledge. The bottom line is that the book and workbook present a framework to estimate land-use and facility needs for comprehensive plans. Users can and I hope will modify the framework to fit local circumstances or include more refined assumptions than presented in the book and workbook examples.

ORGANIZATION

This book has 12 chapters including this one. The next nine chapters address specific issues relating to estimating land-use and facility needs, including estimating capital facility investment needs. The individual chapters and associated worksheet tables cover:

- **Data, Trends, and Baseline Conditions** (Chapter 2) with Baseline worksheet tables
- **Residential Land-Use Needs** (Chapter 3) with Residential Land-Use Needs worksheet tables
- **Employment Land-Use Needs** (Chapter 4) with Employment Land-Use Needs worksheet tables
- **Functional Population Adjustments for Public Facilities** (Chapter 5) with Functional Population Adjustments for Public Facilities worksheet tables
- **Public Facility Space and Land-Use Needs** (Chapter 6) with Public Facility Space and Land-Use Needs worksheet tables
- **Educational Facility Space and Land-Use Needs** (Chapter 7) with Educational Facility Space and Land-Use Needs worksheet tables
- **Water and Wastewater Utility Land-Use Needs** (Chapter 8) with Water and Wastewater Utility Land-Use Needs worksheet tables
- **Summary Land-Use Needs and Market Factor Adjustment** (Chapter 9) with Summary Land-Use Needs and Market Factor Adjustment worksheet tables

- **Capital Facility Cost Implications** (Chapter 10) with Capital Facility Cost Estimations worksheet tables

Chapter 11 (**Estimating Land-Use and Facility Needs of Unanticipated Development**) presents a method to estimate the land-use and facility impacts of unanticipated development, such as a major planned development. The workbook includes a series of worksheets that estimates these unanticipated impacts.

Chapter 12 (**The Canvas Beckons**) concludes with a call for planners to consider the future as a canvas yet to be sketched.

Keep in mind that this book is about numbers, not configurations. Planners may begin with the numbers—the "demand"—but their work becomes vastly more complex when dealing with the allocation of land-use and facility needs to the landscape. In some cases, some of the land-use needs estimated in this book can be combined: some of the residential demand, for example, can be combined with some of the demand for office and retail in mixed-use configurations that economize on total land consumed. I do not include mixed-use, land-use categories in this book. The user could create a new mixed-use building category that absorbs a share of total estimated development for a given area, or adjust individual categories to reflect the share of mixed uses the land use represents.

Finally, because I do not wish to advance a particular configuration of land uses, the whole area of transportation facility demand is not addressed here. I included this component in previous versions of the approach only to find reasoned objection by reviewers: it is better to estimate land-use and facility needs associated with different scenarios than to presuppose how they are stitched together with a given or even hypothetical transportation system. Nonetheless, the land-use and facility estimates include a gross land area adjustment factor to account for land that may be needed for transportation facilities.

ROLE IN THE PLANNING PROCESS

Where does the book and workbook fit in the local land-use and facility planning process? Probably in the beginning, the middle, and the end. Consider first the overall planning process. Although there are as many different ways of viewing the planning process as there are planners, Figure 1-2 presents a simplified version.

The book and workbook can be initially applied to the step that estimates trends and their consequences. This would be what I call the "first-impression" step. Assuming that local conditions and desires warrant an improvement over the trend, the next step where this book and workbook may be useful is in evaluating ways to achieve a preferred vision. In particular, if estimated land uses in one category are different from a consensus vision, assumptions may be changed and the workbook rerun to see the outcome. An iterative process can be used as different assumptions are tested until one set proves capable of achieving the vision consistent with development pressures.

For example, if the trend shows 100,000 acres of detached residential housing, but there are only 50,000 acres available, assumptions (such as on units per acre, housing mix, and land needed for roads and rights-of-way) can be changed until a mix of assumptions is achieved consistent with the vision but within the constraint. The book and workbook should also be used at the end (i.e., some years after the plan is implemented) to help evaluate and assess progress toward achieving the

Figure 1-2
Generalized Land-Use and Facility Planning Process

Inventory and Assess Current Conditions

↓

Estimate Trends and Their Consequences

↓

Establish a Vision for the Future

↓

Adopt Goals Consistent with the Vision

↓

Evaluate Ways to Achieve the Vision

↓

Establish a Plan to Guide Development

↓

Implement the Plan

↓

Evaluate and Assess Progress

vision. This last step can lead back to the first step in a plan update process.

ROLE OF PROFESSIONAL JUDGMENT

I am confident that the formulas and worksheets presented in this book and accompanying CD workbook will make the job of estimating land-use and facility needs much quicker and easier for individual planners and their communities. However, please understand that the book and workbook are tools, not a prescription. The tool can be used accurately only if the numbers being plugged into the formulas are accurate. Each user is responsible for her or his own numbers—and therefore for the estimates that will ultimately result. Finally, we professional planners are keenly aware that output from computer programs may not always reflect local conditions or circumstances. They give us an initial or first impression. Some professional judgment may be needed to interpret or refine analysis for any given community or application.

NOTES

1. Nelson (2003).
2. Calculated from U.S. Bureau of the Census (2002).
3. The national average of 0.58% annual average loss in residential units converts into a life span of about 170 years (1/0.0058). I assume that the life span of commercial and institutional space is about 75 years and manufacturing space is about 50 years.
4. The projections used in this report are very general, employ many simplifying assumptions, and are subject to important limitations explained in Nelson (2003).
5. I prefer Lotus 1-2-3, which can read the Excel workbook on the CD-ROM accompanying this book.
6. Lang (2002).

REFERENCES

Kaiser, Edward, David R. Godschalk, and F. Stuart Chapin, Jr. *Urban Land Use Planning*. Urbana, IL: University of Illinois Press, 1995.

Klosterman, Richard E. with Edward J. Kaiser, David R. Godschalk and Ann-Margaret Esnard. *Hypothetical City Workbook: Exercises, Spreadsheets and GIS Data to Accompany Urban Land Use Planning, Fourth Edition*. Champaign, IL: University of Illinois Press, 1999.

Lang, Robert E. "Metropolitan Growth Counties," *Post Suburbia: Examining the New Metropolitan Form*. Washington, DC: Fannie Mae Foundation, November 2002.

Natural Resources and Conservation Service. *National Resources Inventory*. Washington, DC: U.S. Department of Agriculture, 1999.

Nelson, Arthur C. *Reshaping America: The Opportunity to Build America's Future: 2000 to 2030*. Alexandria, VA: Metropolitan Institute, Virginia Polytechnic Institute and State University, 2003.

U.S. Bureau of the Census. *Statistical Abstract of the United States*. Washington, DC: U.S. Bureau of the Census, 2002.

Data, Trends, and Baseline Conditions

OVERVIEW

Chapter 1 addressed the general purposes, limitations, and applications of the book and workbook. In this chapter, we begin the process of building a method to estimate land-use and facility needs over a long-term planning horizon. A natural first question is: What data are needed to make the workbook work? Generally speaking, we need data on existing land uses and facilities, and projections of population, households, and employment. The methods of acquiring these data are reviewed first. This is followed by a review of how land-use patterns are changing and suggestions as to the reasons why. The end of the chapter presents the baseline worksheets for Yukon County showing past, present, and projected population, households, and employment.

POPULATION AND EMPLOYMENT DATA

To the maximum extent possible, this book and workbook require only the use of readily available data principally from secondary sources combined with some local data that are reasonably accessible. Because it is a book about estimating future land-use and facility needs, projections are needed about population, households, and employment. Fortunately, data for past, present, and projected future population and employment are provided by a large number of agencies and private sources, such as:

- the U.S. Bureau of the Census
- the U.S. Bureau of Economic Analysis (BEA)
- state population centers, usually affiliated with a major university

- state departments of commerce, labor, or economic development
- regional Councils of Government, many of which are required by state law to provide "official" estimates for planning purposes
- Metropolitan Planning Organizations (MPOs), many of which provide metropolitan area projections for transportation planning and related purposes
- utility companies
- Woods and Poole Economics, a private firm that generates population, employment, and economic projections out to 25 years

Often, there is little need to perform local population and employment projections since there are already so many projections from which to choose. Indeed, the larger problem is deciding which projection to use for land-use planning purposes. Some states, such as Florida and Oregon, require the use of projections prepared by specific state agencies. Other states, such as Georgia, acquire privately prepared projections (such as that from Woods and Poole Economics) but do not require local governments to use them. Most states do not dictate the use of any particular projection; indeed, in the states that do, there are procedures that allow local governments to use substitute projections. This book assumes that the community has already selected a set of projections on which it will base land-use and facility planning.

This is not to say that one should rely exclusively on projections others make for the community. Professor Andrew Isserman of the University of Illinois argues for locally generated projections using a combination of recent growth and local judgment (Isserman 1993). Klosterman (1990) offers a variety of off-the-shelf techniques for projecting local population and employment. Sometimes faculty in college programs of planning and economics may be able to provide projections. I recommend consideration of locally developed projections; in their absence, secondary sources are usually sufficient for "first-impression" purposes.

Other data needed to perform estimations come from local sources. These include tabulations of housing units by land-use category, estimates of vacancy rates, and characteristics of community facilities. These data may come from local property tax records, the U.S. Postal Service (for vacancy rates), and local market analysis firms, which I usually find quite willing to help with local planning processes.

LAND-USE DATA

Land-use data may not be so easy to gather. One problem is that land-use data are not usually available centrally (i.e., there are no states that keep a record of past or present land uses, let alone project them into the future). Even the two states with the longest history of the most aggressive efforts to facilitate local planning—Florida and Oregon—do not compile land-use data statewide and certainly not at the local level.

Another problem is that local governments often do not keep good records of land uses or change over time, at least until recent years. The advent of electronic data systems for property tax assessment have improved local information, as have geographic information systems (GISs), but the variation in local government data collection and reporting protocol is considerable. There is certainly room for consensus in this area.

Nonetheless, reasonably good albeit not precise data are typically available at the county level through local property tax assessor offices and sometimes from local market, engineering, and planning analysis firms.

CHANGING LAND-USE PATTERNS

Times change and so do land-use patterns. The combination of liberal home purchase financing, subsidized infrastructure, improving technology, and especially rising incomes—I estimate, based on U.S. BEA data, that incomes have risen by about a factor of three in real buying-power terms since 1950—has given people more opportunity to choose where they live. This is a good thing. On the other hand, the range of residential choices in many suburban communities has declined since 1990, in my view through exclusionary zoning in suburbs that prevent housing options. This is a bad thing. The overall effect is that land-use patterns have changed considerably, especially over the past half century. Table 2-1 shows this change for urban areas under about 100,000 population. Figure 2-1 and Figure 2-2 illustrate this trend for large and small urban areas, respectively.

Table 2-1 is instructive because it shows the order of magnitude of land-use distribution seen just as suburbanization began to reshape the American landscape at the end of World War II. The pre-war period is nowadays considered the basis for "neotraditional" or "new urbanism" planning. In other words, if one wanted to create a local land-use pattern that reflected neotraditional parameters across a large area, one may look to land-use patterns existing before that war.

Figure 2-1
Changing Land-Use Ratios Over Time for Large Cities

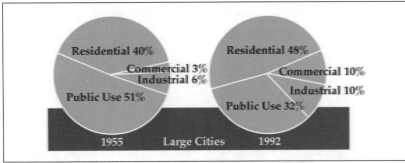

Source: Harris (August 1992), for communities over 100,000 population.

Figure 2-2
Changing Land-Use Ratios Over Time for Small Cities

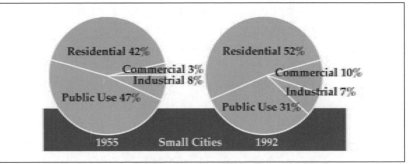

Source: Harris (August 1992), for communities under 100,000 population.

Table 2-1
Changing Land-Use Ratios Over Time

Year	Residential	Workplace	Civic	Other and Rights-of-Way
1992	52%	17%	15%	16%
1983	48%	15%	18%	19%
1955	42%	10%	21%	27%

Source: Adapted from Harris (August 1992). Analysis applies to communities under 100,000 population. Civic includes parks. Civic estimates for 1983 and 1992 by author.

As we can see, the share of the urban/suburban landscape used by residential land uses has grown by about a quarter, and workplace land uses by two-thirds, in just the quarter century from 1955 to 1992. Losing share are civic, right-of-way, and other land uses, principally parks and open space within cities. Why is this? It is mostly a shift from attached and small-lot residential land uses to detached and large-lot uses, and from compact commercial configurations to land-extensive ones characterized by suburban shopping centers and low-rise office/business/industrial land uses. Although the amount of land in public parks and open space, and rights-of-way, have certainly increased, their share of the urban/suburban landscape has declined as residential density and commercial land-use intensity has declined.

WORKBOOK BASELINE TABLES

With these considerations in mind, let us establish baseline conditions for Yukon County. The planning horizon for Yukon County is the period 2000 to 2020, but it could just as well be 2005 to 2030, or 2005 to 2010, or any number of other horizons. In our example, baseline data for 1980, 1990, and 2000 for population and households come from the census while baseline employment data come from the Regional Economic Information System of the BEA. Data for 1990 to 2000 allow us to observe trends over the past decade. Although past patterns of development do not necessarily predict the future, they nonetheless influence it. Figures for 2020 come from a state population data center; most states provide population, household, and employment projections for all counties.

When the planning area is smaller than a county, county-level data will need to be disaggregated to that area. If the planning area is reasonably coterminous with census tracts or block groups, census data can match those planning area boundaries. The Census Transportation Planning Package for 1990 and 2000 is based on transportation analysis zones and provides population, household, housing type, and employment data to this level for most metropolitan areas. A "constant share" adjustment to allocate countywide projections to subcounty planning areas can be used to project population, households, and employment into the future (see Klostermann 1990), but considerable judgment is necessary to consider development constraints and opportunities in subcounty planning areas (see Isserman 1993).

Baseline population and employment data for Yukon County as a whole are presented in Table 2-2 and Table 2-3. Table 2-2 shows population and household figures and Table 2-3 shows employment figures. Notice that while population figures appear precise (to the nearest whole person), employment data are rounded (to the nearest 100). This is customary since population data are usually based on actual census counts while employment data are often estimates. These tables will drive many of the subsequent land-use and facility estimation tables throughout the book and workbook.

The next two chapters (Chapters 3 and 4) on residential and employment land-use needs will be derived substantially from the baseline tables. Subsequent chapters will be derived from a combination of the baseline tables and the tables reported in those two chapters.

Table 2-2
Baseline Population and Household Data

Population Data Category	1980	1990	2000	2020	Change 1990-2020	Percent Change 1990-2020	Annual Rate 1990-2020
Year-Round Population	169,212	363,344	558,528	744,360	381,016	104.86%	2.42%
Institutionalized	780	920	1,160	1,250	330	35.87%	1.03%
Other Group Quarters	3,404	5,780	8,700	22,300	16,520	285.81%	4.60%
Total Group Quarters	4,184	6,700	9,860	23,550	16,850	251.49%	4.28%
Permanent Population	165,028	356,644	548,668	720,810	364,166	102.11%	2.37%
Permanent Households	55,194	130,800	209,000	283,000	152,200	116.36%	2.61%
Average Household Size	2.99	2.73	2.63	2.55		−6.59%	
Hotel/Motel Peak Population							
Hotel/Motel Residents, Peak Season	24,850	53,354	93,177	133,000	79,646	149.28%	3.09%
Total Peak Population	194,062	416,698	651,705	877,360	460,662	110.55%	2.51%

Table 2-3
Baseline Employment Data

Employment Data Category	1980	1990	2000	2020	Change 1990-2020	Percent Change 1990-2020	Annual Rate 1990-2020
Nonurban Related*							
Agriculture, Forestry, Fishing	600	500	400	200	(300)	-60.00%	-3.01%
Mining	200	2,000	100	100	(1,900)	-95.00%	-9.50%
Total Nonurban-Related Employees	800	2,500	500	300	(2,200)	-88.00%	-6.82%
Urban Related							
Construction	4,800	7,200	12,400	15,300	8,100	112.50%	2.54%
Manufacturing	11,700	19,000	22,300	25,500	6,500	34.21%	0.99%
TCU	2,200	3,200	10,000	19,800	16,600	518.75%	6.26%
Wholesale	10,900	17,800	20,000	23,600	5,800	32.58%	0.94%
Retail	14,700	23,600	31,600	46,500	22,900	97.03%	2.29%
FIRE	4,100	7,600	15,500	24,700	17,100	225.00%	4.01%
Services**	12,700	28,900	55,200	82,100	53,200	184.08%	3.54%
Group Care Employment	800	1,400	2,200	4,700	3,300	235.71%	4.12%
Hotel/Motel Employment	3,350	7,200	12,600	17,700	10,500	145.83%	3.04%
Government	7,200	16,200	25,800	37,900	21,700	133.95%	2.87%
Total Urban-Related Employees	72,450	132,100	207,600	297,800	165,700	125.44%	2.75%
Total Employment	73,250	134,600	208,100	298,100	163,500	121.47%	2.69%

*   Not used in employment-based land-use and facility needs calculations.
** Excludes group care, hotel/motel, and government workers.

REFERENCES

Harris, Christopher. *PAS Memo*. Chicago, IL: American Planning Association, August 1992.

Isserman, Andrew M. "The right people, the right rates: Making population estimates and projections with an interregional cohort-component method." *Journal of the American Planning Association* 59,1:45-64, 1993.

Klosterman, Richard. *Community Analysis and Planning Techniques*. Savage, MD: Rowman and Littlefield, 1990.

CHAPTERY

3

Residential
Land-Use Needs

OVERVIEW

As noted in Chapter 2, housing consumes the largest share of land of all major land uses and its share has grown steadily since the 1950s. It is also among the most flexible of land uses in which to accommodate demand. Unlike some land uses, such as many retail and manufacturing activities that have relatively rigid space requirements, housing needs can be accommodated along a wide spectrum of arrangements. Many efforts in planning to contain urban sprawl, prevent development of important resource lands, or create more compact urban forms focus primarily on influencing the use of land for housing.

This chapter presents a framework for estimating residential land-use needs. In keeping with the orientation of the book, only the basic steps of estimating residential land-use needs are presented and applied to arrive at a "first impression." Issues of housing affordability, fair-share housing allocations, and the link between nonresidential development and housing are not addressed but, of course, need to be in any final land-use planning scheme. In a word, this chapter generates the numbers to be considered to meet broad housing needs, but not the configuration.

The approach used here is not a housing market analysis, which focuses on housing requirements based on income, household life cycle, and housing preferences of market segments. Market analyses often require data that are not available at the local government level, and such data are often not developed for use beyond about five years. Instead, land-use planning requires estimating needs out to 10, 20, and more years.[1]

The basic steps involved in estimating future residential land-use needs are:

- inventorying residential land uses and analyzing trends
- estimating occupied units and residents
- estimating residential acres and units lost
- estimating residential units needed
- estimating residential land-use needs

Residential land-use needs are estimated for rural residential, urban detached, urban attached, group care (including nursing homes and assisted living units), and hotel/motel land uses. For many communities, the estimation of residential land uses must also consider second homes, condominiums, and campgrounds. For simplicity, "hotel/motel" housing needs are estimated for hotels and motels only. If second homes are a substantial element of the land market, the user may create "second home" residential categories comparable to those used to estimate needs of permanent residents.

INVENTORYING RESIDENTIAL LAND USES AND ANALYZING TRENDS

An inventory of existing residential land-use patterns and trends is needed. This involves two efforts: establishing existing patterns affecting the entire housing stock and determining land-use patterns observed during a recent interval of time, in this case the 1990s. Both efforts entail organizing housing data in a manner useful for land-use planning. In the case of Yukon County, there are tens of thousands of housing units on lots ranging from farms over 20 acres in size to apartments.

What are the appropriate land-use categories in which to organize housing data? Although local planning offices have their own categories, I prefer those shown in Table 3-1. The cat-

Table 3-1
Residential Land-Use, Density, and Housing Type Categories

Residential Land-Use Category	Density Category	Housing Type Category	Comments
20+ Acres Per Unit	Resource Density	Detached	Characteristic of resource-based land uses such as agriculture and forestry. (This is not to be confused with such designations as "rural residential" or "agriculture residential" since, at this density, the primary function of land is for agriculture, forestry, mining, or related resource activities.)
5-20 Acres Per Unit	Rural Residential Density	Detached	Normally on septic and private well; found at urban fringe and throughout exurbia. Most problematic for resource land preservation and efficient long-range urban planning.
1-5 Acres Per Unit	Very Low Density	Detached	Normally on septic and sometimes on central water; often dominating the urban fringe. Least efficient urban density.
1-2 Units Per Net Acre	Low Density	Detached	Normally lowest density on public sewer and central water, although some units may be on septic systems and/or use water wells. Most costly density on public facilities. Not efficient density for most modes of public transit.
3-5 Units Per Net Acre	Low Density	Detached	Lowest density on public sewer and central water. Not efficient density for most modes of public transit.
6-8 Units Per Net Acre	Moderately Low Density	Detached, Cluster, and Zero Lot Line	Most efficient detached housing. Also typical of manufactured housing developments. Lowest density that justifies bus service with 15-minute commuting headways over large area.
9-14 Units Per Net Acre	Moderate Density	Townhouse and Garden Apartment, Condominium	Single-floor and/or walk-up configurations with common walls. Lower end of range justifies bus service throughout day at 15-minute headways over large area; higher end of range justifies light rail service over large area. Surface parking provided.
15-25 Units Per Net Acre	Moderately High Density	Garden and Low-Rise Structures	Garden apartments (one to two floors) and low-rise structures (up to three floors). Surface parking can be provided.
26-40 Units Per Net Acre	High Density	Low-Rise Structures	Three- to six-floor apartments and condominiums. Parking often underground or off site. Typical of transit station areas.
40+ Units Per Net Acre	Very High Density	High-Rise Structures	High-rise apartments and condominiums. Parking is restricted and located underground, off site, or not provided.

Source: Adapted from American Public Health Association (1960); U.S. Department of Health and Human Services (1962); ULI (1990); Pushkarev and Zupan (1977).

egories are reasonably reflective of important engineering and planning implications associated with each density pattern. Table 3-1 also comments on the utility of each category in estimating residential land-use needs.

It is my view—based on professional practice and research—that these residential land-use categories are perhaps the most reasonable for long-range planning purposes for urban and urbanizing areas. Each category represents resource land use, fiscal benefit and cost, infrastructure planning and finance, and urban form implications that are substantially different from each other. On the other hand, as will be evident, aside from accounting for the rural residential population, we do not include a "rural residential" category (homes on parcels of more than 5 acres) in estimates of urban land-use and facility needs. Planning for rural residential land uses is perhaps the least understood of all land-use planning fields and worthy of separate treatment.

An inventory of existing residential land uses is prepared and organized into these land-use categories. For Yukon County, the distribution of housing units by residential land-use category is shown in Table 3-2 (the first residential land-use calculation table). Although Table 3-1 shows additional higher density residential land-use categories than reported in Table 3-2, those shown in Table 3-2 reflect current categories of residential development observed in Yukon County in 2000.

If a detailed land-use inventory is not already available, which is very often the case, it can be done by sorting property tax assessor records of improved residential property into the residential land-use categories up to a base year, which is June 1990 in the case of Yukon County. Property tax records usually include the lot area, either in acres or in square feet. This makes the task of sorting records into land-use categories reasonably efficient.

Sorting can be done by hand, which can be time-consuming, or digitally through reasonably simple reprogramming of assessor records. This was done in the analysis of Yukon County. (Many planning offices have digitized property tax records, which greatly economizes the task of inventorying and analyzing residential land-use patterns.) Total land area within each residential land-use category must also be computed. This is the sum of all lot sizes developed for residential use within each category with the result showing both the total residents units and total net acres developed for residential uses, which is easily converted to an average number of residential units built per net residential acre.

In Table 3-2, the number of residential units on tracts of land of less than 5 acres is shown. Some of these tracts will be redeveloped into higher density uses as shown in other tables. For the most part, tracts larger than 5 acres are considered resource or rural residential. The user may decide to add this category especially if substantial conversions from large rural tracts into urban development are anticipated.

The next step is to determine recent residential development trends. This will allow local planners to estimate trends in housing demand. While future trends do not necessarily replicate those of the past, recent trends may nonetheless guide planning to accommodate future needs. In the case of Yukon County, trends for the period 1990 to 2000 are shown in Table 3-2. Note the following:

Table 3-2
Residential Land-Use Baseline Conditions

Residential Land-Use Category	Units 1990	Share of Units 1990	Existing Acres 1990	Units Per Net Acre 1990	Units 2000	Share of Units 2000	Existing Acres 2000	Units Per Net Acre 2000	Units Added 1990-2000	New Units Per Net Acre 1990-2000	Percent of New Units 1990-2000	Acres Added 1990-2000	Percent of Acres 1990-2000
Detached													
1-5 Acres Per Unit	8,837	6.56%	13,289.00	0.6650	13,697	6.50%	20,584.00	0.6654	4,860	0.6662	6.39%	7,295.00	24.87%
1-2 Units Per Net Acre	45,673	33.90%	25,691.00	1.7778	66,481	31.55%	37,721.00	1.7624	20,808	1.7297	27.38%	12,030.00	41.00%
3-5 Units Per Net Acre	20,076	14.90%	4,874.00	4.1190	43,253	20.52%	11,288.00	3.8318	23,177	3.6135	30.49%	6,414.00	21.86%
6-8 Units Per Net Acre	10,701	7.94%	1,495.00	7.1579	22,085	10.48%	3,450.00	6.4014	11,384	5.8230	14.98%	1,955.00	6.66%
Subtotal Detached	85,287	63.30%	45,349.00	1.8807	145,516	69.05%	73,043.00	1.9922	60,229	2.1748	79.25%	27,694.00	94.40%
Attached													
9-14 Units Per Net Acre	32,902	24.42%	2,575.00	12.7775	46,429	22.03%	3,960.00	11.7245	13,527	9.7668	17.80%	1,385.00	4.72%
15+ Units Per Net Acre	16,553	12.28%	696.00	23.7830	18,800	8.92%	955.00	19.6859	2,247	8.6757	2.96%	259.00	0.88%
Subtotal Attached	49,455	36.70%	3,271.00	15.1192	65,229	30.95%	4,915.00	13.2714	15,774	9.5949	20.75%	1,644.00	5.60%
Total Residential	134,742	100.00%	48,620.00	2.7713	210,745	100.00%	77,958.00	2.7033	76,003	2.5906	100.00%	29,338.00	100.00%
Group Care													
Nursing Home Beds	5,370	65.89%	162.00	33.1481	5,500	64.71%	224.00	24.5536	130	2.0968	37.14%	62.00	47.69%
Assisted Living Units	2,780	34.11%	128.00	21.7188	3,000	35.29%	196.00	15.3061	220	3.2353	62.86%	68.00	52.31%
Total Group Care	8,150	100.00%	290.00	28.1034	8,500	100.00%	420.00	20.2381	350	2.6923	100.00%	130.00	100.00%
Hotel/Motel Units													
Low Rise (1-3 Floors)	18,476	51.88%	445.00	41.5191	28,040	50.09%	722.00	38.8366	9,564	34.5271	46.97%	277.00	55.96%
Mid Rise (4-7 Floors)	9,411	26.42%	168.00	56.0179	15,210	27.17%	315.00	48.2857	5,799	39.4490	28.48%	147.00	29.70%
High Rise (8+ Floors)	7,729	21.70%	122.00	63.3525	12,730	22.74%	193.00	65.9585	5,001	70.4366	24.56%	71.00	14.34%
Total Hotel/Motel Units	35,616	100.00%	735.00	48.4571	55,980	100.00%	1,230.00	45.5122	20,364	41.1394	100.00%	495.00	100.00%

Note: The rural residential land-use category is not considered here (see text for discussion).

- The number and share of lower density residential units rose. This indicates the presence of low-density, single-purpose residential development. Literature tells us this is the most costly pattern of development to serve.

- Although the number of attached units rose, its share of all housing units fell. This is indicative of several factors: (1) many older suburban areas have an abundance of attached housing often mixed among detached housing areas; (2) a natural outcome of suburbanization is movement of higher income households from closer-in areas outward, or attraction of suburbs to in-migrants into the region from other regions; and (3) over time, suburban communities attempt to change their mix of housing and, by implication, their mix of residents toward more affluent ones. Exclusionary housing practices are thus used, such as increasing minimum lot sizes, reducing attached housing densities, and even deflating the supply of land zoned for attached housing. Whether this is the case in Yukon County cannot be said for certain, but the data show that attached housing is a smaller share of total housing in 2000 than it was in 1990.

- The share of housing in the 3-5 and 6-8 units per net acre categories rose while that for housing in the 1-2 units per net acre category fell, though the number of units has risen. Development on public water and wastewater at a density of 1-2 units per net acre is the most expensive of all residential development types, and perhaps of all development types. Higher densities are less costly and more efficient, especially in reducing inflow and infiltration. Trends indicate probably both public and private sector sensitiv-

ity to these considerations, although development in the 1-2 units per net acre category absorbed the most land of all land uses during this period.

Trends could be extrapolated into the future. For example, if 27.4% of the new population projected lives in the 1-2 units per net acre category, Yukon County will need another 24,000 acres from 2000 to 2020 (27.4% × 152,000 new households @ 1.73 units per acre trend during 1990 to 2000). Counting land needed for rights-of-way, easements, and so forth (the 20% "Gross Acre Adjustment Factor" shown in Table 3-7), more than 47 square miles of land would be needed to accommodate this need based on "trend."

Will this projection of the "trend" actually occur? Probably not. As Professor Robert Burchell of the Center for Urban Policy Research at Rutgers University observes, trend "learns" in the sense that changing demographics and rising costs associated with distance from services and jobs probably mean that densities in the future will be somewhat higher than observed now; however, this is not a certainty.

ESTIMATING OCCUPIED UNITS AND RESIDENTS

The second step is to estimate occupied units and the population residing in each of the residential land-use categories. This is shown in Table 3-3 (the second residential land-use calculation table) and entails making two assumptions—the first involving vacancy rates and the second the assumed percent of residents occupying each land-use category.

Consider vacancy rates. Some amount of vacant residential units is needed to facilitate the free movement of population

Table 3-3
Occupied Units

Residential Land-Use Category	Units 2000	Vacancy Rate 2000	Occupied Units 2000	Estimated Household Size 2000	Estimated Residents 2000
Rural Residential					27,260
Detached					
1-5 Acres Per Unit	13,697	3.10%	13,272	2.80	37,163
1-2 Units Per Net Acre	66,481	3.10%	64,420	2.80	180,376
3-5 Units Per Net Acre	43,253	3.10%	41,912	2.75	115,258
6-8 Units Per Net Acre	22,085	3.10%	21,400	2.75	58,851
Subtotal Detached	145,516		141,005	2.78	391,648
Attached					
9-14 Units Per Net Acre	46,429	6.35%	43,481	2.30	100,006
15+ Units Per Net Acre	18,800	6.35%	17,606	2.25	39,614
Subtotal Attached	65,229		61,087	2.29	139,620
Total Residential	210,745	4.11%	202,092	2.63	531,268
Group Care					
Nursing Home Beds	5,500	2.50%	5,363	0.60	5,237
Assisted Living Units	3,000	2.00%	2,940	0.40	3,463
Total Group Care	8,500	2.32%	8,303	1.00	8,700
Hotel/Motel Units					
Low Rise (1-3 Floors)	28,040	6.50%	26,217	0.50	46,672
Mid Rise (4-7 Floors)	15,210	6.50%	14,221	0.27	25,317
High Rise (8+ Floors)	12,730	6.50%	11,903	0.23	21,189
Total Hotel/Motel Units	55,980	6.50%	52,341	1.00	93,177

and choice of reasonable alternatives. The number of vacant units, usually expressed as a percent of total habitable units, varies by such things as growth rates and tenure characteristics of renters and buyers. Table 3-4 shows the range of vacancy rate assumptions that may be used based on a number of states and other authorities under "normal" market conditions. Vacancy rates in excess of normal ranges are considered "surplus" vacancy rates, which indicate a failure of the market to properly

Table 3-4
Alternative Residential Vacancy Rate Assumptions

Source	Detached (Owner-Occupied)	Attached (Renter-Occupied)
State of California[a]	2.00%	6.00%
State of Florida[b]	3.00%	8.00%
State of New Jersey[c]	2.50%	8.00%
State of Oregon[d]	1.75%–2.00%	5.00%–6.00%
Readings in Market Research for Real Estate [e]	4.00%	7.00%
Federal Housing Administration[f]	5%+ Annual Growth 1.50%–2.00%	5%+ Annual Growth 6.00%–8.00%
	1%-5% Annual Growth 1.00%–1.50%	1%-5% Annual Growth 4.00%–6.00%
	Below 1% Annual Growth < 1.00%	Below 1% Annual Growth < 4.00%

a. Office of Planning and Research (1978), p. 67.
b. Florida Department of Community Affairs (1987), p. 35.
c. New Jersey Department of Community Affairs (1991), p. 183.
d. Housing Division (undated, circa 1985).
e. Singer (1985), pp. 92-93; *Readings in Market Research for Real Estate*, pp. 85-101.
f. Federal Housing Administration (undated).

regulate the amount of residential units needed. Consumer choice may improve with higher vacancy rates, but this usually also means that home values are falling and the value of investment portfolios are declining.

Vacancy rates can vary by growth rate. The lower the growth rate, the fewer the number of vacant habitable units needed to provide sufficient alternatives and facilitate free movement. For this reason, I sometimes calculate vacancy rates that correspond to the average annual household growth rate projected over the planning horizon, as suggested by the Federal Housing Administration. For detached (normally owner-occupied) residential units, the estimated vacancy rate for land-use planning purposes is equal to one-half the average annual household growth rate. For cluster, zero-lot line, or lower density townhouse developments, the estimated vacancy rate for land-use planning purposes is assumed to be equal to the average annual household growth rate. For attached (normally renter-occupied) residential units, the estimated vacancy rate for land-use planning purposes is assumed to be up to twice the average annual household growth rate. For group care and hotel/motel units, normal vacancy rates given growth will need to be estimated based on information provided by knowledgeable people of those residential sectors.

In the present case, actual vacancy rates observed are shown in Table 3-3. Because only one vacancy rate per major land-use category is available, this is the one used here. It comes from a local real estate information service for detached, attached, group care, and hotel/motel units. This information is used to estimate occupied units for each category.

The second step is estimating the percent of residents occupying each residential land-use category. This is the estimate of the percent of residents within each group (permanent, group care, and hotel/motel) based on local knowledge. Normally, household sizes do not vary much among detached housing unit types. Cluster housing may have smaller household sizes than other detached types, although in some metropolitan areas this is not the case. Household sizes for attached housing are usually lower than for detached types.

Generally speaking, because the census provides information on the population living in detached and attached units, this exercise can be completed by distributing the detached and attached populations proportionately based on detached and attached housing unit share (from Table 3-1).

Table 3-3 shows the estimated residents by residential land-use category for Yukon County. The calculations necessary for this step are:

Units 2000: From Table 3-2.

Vacancy Rate 2000: Detached unit vacancy data come from local realtors or real estate tracking services, postal records, and water and wastewater billing records.

Occupied Units 2000: Calculated as

$$[(UNITS\ 2000) \times (1 - VACANCY\ RATE\ 2000)]$$

Estimated Household Size 2000: This is the assumed percentage distribution of residents within each group (permanent, group care, and hotel/motel) for planning purposes.

Estimated Residents 2000: Calculated as

[(OCCUPIED UNITS 2000) × (ESTIMATED HOUSEHOLD SIZE 2000)]

The result of this step is an estimate of existing occupied housing units by type and persons per such unit. This information will be used later to estimate future housing units needed by type based on occupants per units type.

There is one important adjustment here. Note that total permanent population (from baseline Table 2-2) less estimated urban residential population is the default estimate of the rural residential population. In substantially urbanized counties, there may not be a significant number of rural residential land uses or residents.

ESTIMATING RESIDENTIAL UNITS AND ACRES LOST

Throughout the planning horizon, existing residential units will be removed from the inventory and usually replaced either with residential units of greater density or entirely different land uses. There are of course instances when someone buys two or more homes, razes them, and builds a "monster" home. There are no good data on this and I suspect it represents a small share of all residential conversions.

The first reason for the removal of existing units is that a certain number of units may be lost normally throughout the planning period through fire, natural disasters, and obsolescence due principally to aging. It is customary for planners to assume that about one-half of one percent (0.5%) of conforming residential units will be lost during the planning horizon for these reasons. In older communities that continue to grow, the loss rate may be higher; in new communities that are beginning to stabilize, the rate may be lower. However, I have found that, for the most part, residential units lost are not included in long-range planning. In this analysis, we use a slightly higher figure than the rule of thumb because data from the *American Housing Survey* (U.S. Department of Housing and Urban Development, 1989 and 1999) indicate that the average national annual loss rate is about 0.58%. The user can use different assumptions.

The second reason for losing housing units is related to nonconformity, which means that certain existing units are in areas designated for different densities or different land uses altogether. Within the planning horizon, many if not all such units will be expected to be removed. However, it is only when plans explicitly show certain areas converting from one kind of land-use activity to another that losses due to nonconformity are important.

The third kind of loss is attributable to conversion from one kind of land use to another because of planning policies. These are called "planned conversions." These are the losses that long-range planning should attempt to estimate. There is no formula for estimating these losses. Instead, local planners through the planning process should identify those areas presently occupied by residential land uses that must give way to higher density housing or different kinds of land uses to facilitate plan implementation.

In the case of housing, this is typically seen as converting a series of large acreage tracts developed at a range of 1 unit to 5, 10, 20, or more acres into subdivisions, cluster homes, planned communities, high-density housing, or perhaps to other kinds

Table 3-5
Residential Acres and Units Lost

Residential Land-Use Category	Existing Acres 2000	Planned Acres Converted	Units Lost From Planned Conversion	Units Remaining From Planned Conversion	Units Lost, Average Annual Loss Rate @ 0.58%	Total Units Lost	Acres Remaining	Units Remaining
Detached								
1-5 Acres Per Unit	20,584.00	2,500.00	1,664	12,033	1,396	3,059	18,084.00	10,638
1-2 Units Per Net Acre	37,721.00	2,500.00	4,406	62,075	7,201	11,607	35,221.00	54,874
3-5 Units Per Net Acre	11,288.00	1,000.00	3,832	39,421	4,573	8,405	10,288.00	34,848
6-8 Units Per Net Acre	3,450.00	0.00	0	22,085	2,562	2,562	3,450.00	19,523
Subtotal Detached	73,043.00	6,000.00	9,901	135,615	15,731	25,633	67,043.00	119,883
Attached								
9-14 Units Per Net Acre	3,960.00	500.00	5,862	40,567	4,706	10,568	3,460.00	35,861
15+ Units Per Net Acre	955.00	0.00	0	18,800	2,181	2,181	955.00	16,619
Subtotal Attached	4,915.00	500.00	5,862	40,885	4,743	12,749	4,415.00	52,480
Total Residential	77,958.00	6,500.00	15,764	176,500	20,474	38,381	71,458.00	172,364
Group Care								
Nursing Home Beds	224.00	0.00	0	5,500	638	638	224.00	4,862
Assisted Living Units	196.00	0.00	0	3,000	348	348	196.00	2,652
Total Group Care	420.00	0.00	0	43,885	5,091	986	420.00	7,514
Hotel/Motel Units								
Low Rise (1-3 Floors)	722.00	200.00	7,767	20,273	2,352	10,119	522.00	17,921
Mid Rise (4-7 Floors)	315.00	0.00	0	15,210	1,764	1,764	315.00	13,446
High Rise (8+ Floors)	193.00	0.00	0	12,730	1,477	1,477	193.00	11,253
Total Hotel/Motel Units	1,230.00	200.00	7,767	48,213	5,593	13,360	1,030.00	42,620

of land uses. Conversions can also occur among higher density residential land uses, especially in older or blighted areas. The housing units located in areas targeted for conversion in land-use plans are often made up, although not necessarily so, at comparable densities. On the other hand, the number of units lost is normally a relatively small share of all units presently existing that will survive through the planning process. Table 3-5 (the third residential calculation table) shows the acres planned for conversion from their current land-use categories to others, associated units lost, net acres remaining, and units remaining.

There is one pitfall with estimating conversions and one practical solution. The pitfall is that one usually does not know exactly which units will be removed from the inventory (e.g., which ones will burn down, flood away, or collapse from inattention). Even when one assumes large tracts with just one home may be ripe for conversion over the planning horizon, will such tracts actually be converted?

The practical solution is that, with GIS, local planners can often carve out an existing home on a large tract, calling it "developed" but classifying the remaining land as "vacant." If this can be done, there may be little reason to assume any of the large tracts per se will be converted.

Finally, the user will see that only residential land is considered for any conversion and not employment-based or facility land uses. Why? We assume that it is more likely that nonresidential development will be replaced with other nonresidential land uses, but residential development could be replaced with residential or nonresidential land uses. If nonresidential con-

version to residential land use is considered to be a significant probability, the user can adapt the worksheets to estimate this.

These adjustments to current housing supply associated with conversions are made in the following way:

Existing Acres 2000: From Table 3-2.

Planned Acres Converted: This is the assumed acres in land-use category to be converted over the planning horizon to another residential category or nonresidential land use. It is based on local knowledge, or left blank.

Units Lost From Planned Conversion: Calculated as

[(PLANNED ACRES CONVERTED) × (UNITS PER NET ACRE 1990)]

where UNITS PER NET ACRE 1990 comes from Table 3-2.

Units Remaining From Planned Conversion: Calculated as

[(UNITS 2000) − (UNITS LOST FROM PLANNED CONVERSION)]

where UNITS 2000 comes from Table 3-2.

Units Lost, Average Annual Loss Rate @ 0.58%: This is the assumed rate of loss for units not otherwise subject to planned conversions. This assumption is based on the national average and may be refined based on local knowledge. It also applies to all residential land uses. Users may be able to refine this figure for individual residential land uses based on analysis of local property assessor data. The formula for estimating losses of units remaining from planned conversion is:

$$\{(\text{UNITS REMAINING FROM PLANNED CONVERSION}) \times [(\text{UNITS LOST, AVERAGE ANNUAL LOSS RATE @ 0.58\%}) \times \text{PLANNING HORIZON YEAR}_{2020} - \text{PLANNING BASE YEAR}_{2000})]\}$$

keeping in mind that the 0.58% figure is an assumption subject to change by the user and the different in years (the horizon year being 2020 and the base year being 2000, as suggested in Table 2-2) is subject to change based on the planning horizon selected.

Total Units Lost: Calculated as

[(UNITS LOST FROM PLANNED CONVERSION)
+ (UNITS LOST, AVERAGE ANNUAL LOSS RATE @ 0.58%)]

Acres Remaining: Calculated as

[(EXISTING ACRES 2000) – (PLANNED ACRES CONVERTED)]

Units Remaining: Calculated as

[(UNITS 2000) – (TOTAL UNITS LOST)]

where UNITS 2000 comes from Table 3-2.

This step thus estimates the units existing in 2000 or the beginning of the planning horizon estimated to be lost over the planning horizon, in this case to 2020.

ESTIMATING RESIDENTIAL UNITS NEEDED

The fourth step is estimating residential units needed to meet residential development needs to 2020. A pair of assumptions is required: the percent of residents apportioned to each land use for each residential category (permanent residents, group care, and hotel/motel) and the assumed household size of occupied units. Apportioning population to residential land-use categories requires a combination of analysis of trends,

assessment of demographic shifts, and a clear vision of the preferred future land-use pattern. Let us consider each element.

In the case of Yukon County, as elsewhere, there is a trend toward higher density where full urban services are present. The reasons are obvious. With growing awareness of the need for more affordable housing options, combined with increasing awareness of the fiscal cost of lower densities when the full range of urban services are available, local governments are increasingly willing to raise densities albeit perhaps not to the highest market-feasible levels. A side benefit to local governments is that costs per residential unit fall with increasing density for many facilities. The development community usually welcomes higher density because it gives them more flexibility to meet housing needs.

The next reason relates to demographic changes and hence changing market conditions toward more flexible housing options, higher densities, and mixed land uses. *Emerging Trends in Real Estate 1999*, prepared by PriceWaterhouseCoopers (1999), describes several long-run national trends that may affect the real estate market throughout most metropolitan areas:

- Cities should benefit from demographic trends. Young professionals and aging baby boomers are migrating back to urban cores—young people for excitement and empty nesters for convenience and amenities. The suburbs are less attractive to these groups because single-family homes are more trouble to maintain than apartments, townhouses, and condominiums, and suburban traffic congestion has become more aggravating.

- More people than in the past may want to live closer to where they work and play. Hectic lifestyles demand convenience. Commercial real estate markets may thrive if they have attractive adjacent residential districts. Areas cut off from good neighborhoods, or showing residential deterioration, will suffer.
- Lifestyle trends will encourage redevelopment of obsolete or underutilized space in desirable core city or inner-ring suburban areas. More developers will convert aging malls into multiuse projects with urban features (such as apartments, stores, restaurants, and offices) or turn past-its-prime central business district (CBD) offices into lofts and condominiums. Some 1960s-era corporate campus sites may be rebuilt. Smart local governments should encourage this activity with tax and other incentives, fostering environments that seamlessly meld residential with commercial uses.

The Joint Center for Housing Studies of Harvard University and the Massachusetts Institute of Technology analyze the ways in which housing policy and practices are shaped by economic and demographic trends.[2] According to my review of information provided by the center, the important demographic trends that will shape housing demand over the next decade are the increasing diversity of the population, the aging of the baby boomers, the higher propensity of people to live alone, and the growth of the elderly population. Specifically, between 2000 and 2010:

- The aging population, and aging baby boomers in particular, will drive changes in the age distribution of households. As the leading edge of the baby boom enters the 55-64 age range, the number of households in this age group will grow by about 7 million by 2010. Meanwhile, the trailing edge of the baby boom will add approximately 3.5 million households to the population of 45- to 54-year-olds. With life expectancies rising, the number of 65- to 74-year-old household heads will increase by about 2 million, and the number of over-75 household heads by more than 1 million between 2000 and 2010.
- Baby boomers now reaching their 50s have moved, or are about to move, into the "empty nest" stage of life when their children leave home. As a result, couples without children under the age of 18 will be the fastest growing family type in the years ahead. Assuming that the share of households aged 45 to 64 without children at home remains constant, the number of empty nesters will increase by about 3.2 million over the next decade.
- The number of people living alone will also increase. The average age at first marriage continues to increase, and the share of single-person households with persons born after 1940 is climbing. The number of single-person households age 65 and over will grow by 1.7 million. At the same time, the number under the age of 45 will decline by over a quarter million in the next decade as the baby-boom generation moves into its late 40s and early 50s.
- Single-parent households are headed for a slowdown. With the number of women in their mid-20s to mid-30s declining by nearly 2 million between 1995 and 2005, growth of this household type will decrease before picking up again after 2005.

- Married couples with children under age 18 will also decrease in number, both because fewer women will be in their late 20s and early 30s, and because the last of the baby boomers will be leaving their childbearing years.
- With the over-85 population growing by 1.3 million during the first decade of the 21st century, housing suited to the health-related needs of the frail elderly will be increasingly in demand. By the time people reach their late 60s and 70s, about one in 10 of those living in the community (outside of nursing homes and group quarters) requires assistance in performing the activities of daily life. As they advance into their 80s and 90s, disabilities become much more common and the share needing help increases to one in three.

These demographic trends have important implications for housing markets at the national level. According to the Joint Center for Housing Studies, household growth should average close to 1.1 to 1.2 million units annually in the first decades of the 21st century—about the same as seen in the 1990s. Because the number of households is the primary determinant of housing demand, the expected stability of household growth should translate into residential construction rates that are roughly comparable to rates seen in the 1990s and early 21st century.

Although it is difficult to predict how housing demand will sort itself out by structure type, the age and regional distribution of the population suggest gains in the multifamily and manufactured housing shares. With demand for multifamily and manufactured housing strengthening, the single-family share of new construction is likely to decrease slightly in the years ahead. Another analysis, conducted by ECONorthwest, based on data from the *Current Construction Reports* (U.S Bureau of the Census 2002), found nationally that between 1987 and 1997 the median lot size decreased from 9,295 square feet to 9,100 square feet, or about 2%.[3]

The final area of consideration is changing attitudes toward residential land-use patterns. Neotraditionalism and smart growth, for example, are changing the public's perception of desirable land-use patterns from one geared solely to segregating land uses—especially residential land uses—to one that integrates them with higher density development as the usual consequence. This is occurring amidst a growing desire to preserve open space, create greenspaces, and contain urban development.

Table 3-6 (the fourth residential calculation table) reflects these trends, shifts, and changes in attitude by apportioning population to each residential land-use category in a manner that decreases new, rural residential development and new development at 1-2 units per net acre relative to recent trends, and increases share of development in all other permanent residential land-use categories. It also takes account of rising demand for nursing home and group care opportunities. For hotel/motel land uses, the apportionment includes hotel/motel residents and employees in those land uses.

The second of the pair of assumptions concerns the assumed household size by residential group in 2020. This comes from a variety of sources such as the U.S. Bureau of the Census, state population centers, and MPOs. Household size assumptions for Yukon County come from the MPO for its region.

The calculations involved in this step include:

Table 3-6
Residential Units Needed

Residential Land-Use Category	Plan Percent Residents 2020	Estimated Residents 2020	Share of All Peak Residents 2020	Employment Share 2020	Assumed Household Size 2020	Occupied Units Needed 2020
Rural Residential	2.00%	14,416	1.67%			
Detached						
1-5 Acres Per Unit	4.00%	28,832	3.35%		2.75	10,485
1-2 Units Per Net Acre	20.00%	144,162	16.73%		2.75	52,423
3-5 Units Per Net Acre	20.00%	144,162	16.73%		2.70	53,393
6-8 Units Per Net Acre	18.00%	129,746	15.06%		2.70	48,054
Subtotal Detached	64.00%	446,902	51.86%		2.72	164,354
Attached						
9-14 Units Per Net Acre	23.00%	165,786	19.24%		2.35	70,547
15+ Units Per Net Acre	13.00%	93,705	10.87%		2.20	42,593
Subtotal Attached	36.00%	259,492	30.11%		2.29	113,141
Total Residential	100.00%	706,394	81.98%		2.55	277,495
Group Care						
Nursing Home Beds	45.00%	10,035	1.16%	60.00%	1.75	5,734
Assisted Living Units	55.00%	12,265	1.42%	40.00%	1.25	9,812
Total Group Care	100.00%	22,300	2.59%			15,546
Hotel/Motel Units						
Low Rise (1-3 Floors)	50.00%	66,500	7.72%	50.00%	1.90	35,000
Mid Rise (4-7 Floors)	25.00%	33,250	3.86%	25.00%	1.90	17,500
High Rise (8+ Floors)	25.00%	33,250	3.86%	25.00%	1.90	17,500
Total Hotel/Motel Units	100.00%	133,000	15.43%			70,000
Grand Total		861,694	100.00%		2.37	363,041

Note: The rural residential land-use category is not considered here (see text for discussion).

Plan Percent Residents 2020: This is the local planning target for the percent of population that will reside in each land-use category in 2020 within each residential group (permanent, group care, and hotel/motel). It also includes the percent of 2020 population estimated to choose rural residential locations.

Estimated Residents 2020: Calculated as

[(PLAN PERCENT RESIDENTS 2020) × (PERMANENT POPULATION)]

where PERMANENT POPULATION is from Table 2-2 for the year 2020.

Note that this land-use category is split between the residential and employment-based analyses. This is because, in some parts of the country, some households spend a considerable amount of time locally during peak seasons occupying hotels, resorts, townhouses, condominiums, and the like. Hotel/motel workers will be employed to tend to the needs of hotel/motel residents. Therefore, hotel/motel housing will include land-use needs associated with residential development but employment-based facility and associated land-use needs associated with jobs.

Share of All Peak Residents 2020: The above calculation involves estimating the population living in urban areas permanently (rural residential residents are excluded) plus hotel/motel residents occupying hotel/motel units during peak occupancy. This column divides the estimated residents in 2020 for all residential land uses by the grand total of all residents from Table 3-6. Note that the grand total population figure from Table 3-6 includes permanent rural residential population and urban residential population plus peak hotel/motel population, but does not include residents noted in Table 2-2 living in institutions (such as prisons) and group quarters (such as dormitories).

Employment Share 2020: This is the distribution of employees within the group care and hotel/motel residential groups assigned to each land-use category within each group. For group care facilities, representatives from the nursing home and assisted living industry can be used to help estimate this distribution. For hotel/motel housing, local hospitality industry representatives may be useful.

Assumed Household Size 2020: Estimated household size for each land-use category. It is assumed to be the same for detached types, smaller for low-rise attached housing, and lowest for high-density attached housing. Household size information comes from population projection services, MPOs, utility companies, and state population centers.

Occupied Units Needed 2020: Calculated as

[(ESTIMATED RESIDENTS 2020) / (ASSUMED HOUSEHOLD SIZE 2020)]

This step estimates total housing units needed by type and density category at the end of the planning horizon.

ESTIMATING RESIDENTIAL LAND-USE NEEDS

The final step is estimating net and gross land needs for residential land uses. This involves three assumptions with associated calculations (see Table 3-7, the fifth residential calculation table). Those assumptions are future vacancy rate, density of new development, and the gross area factor to account for rights-of-way, easements, drainage ways, and other property-serving land not included in the net developed land calculations. Vacancy rate assumptions shown in Table 3-7 reflect the earlier discussion as well as current vacancy rate patterns; they vary little from the current rates because it is assumed here that current market conditions are not unusual for Yukon County.

The next assumption concerns the density of new development for each land-use category. In Table 3-6, the population

Table 3-7
Residential Land-Use Needs

Residential Land-Use Category	Vacancy Rate 2020	Total Units Needed 2020	Total Units Lost	Total New Units Needed 2020	Plan New Unit Net Density 2020	New Net Acres Needed	Plan Net Acres Needed	Gross Acre Adjustment Factor	Gross Plan Acres Needed
Detached									
1-5 Acres Per Unit	3.00%	10,809	3,059	171	0.500	342.40	18,426.40	10.00%	20,473.78
1-2 Units Per Net Acre	3.00%	54,044	11,607	(830)	1.750	(474.49)	34,746.51	20.00%	43,433.14
3-5 Units Per Net Acre	3.00%	55,045	8,405	20,196	4.500	4,488.07	14,776.07	25.00%	19,701.42
6-8 Units Per Net Acre	3.00%	49,540	2,562	30,017	7.500	4,002.28	7,452.28	30.00%	10,646.11
Subtotal Detached		169,438	25,633	49,554	5.929	8,358.26	75,401.26		94,254.46
Attached									
9-14 Units Per Net Acre	6.00%	75,050	10,568	39,189	12.750	3,073.68	6,533.68	35.00%	10,051.81
15+ Units Per Net Acre	6.00%	45,312	2,181	28,693	25.500	1,125.21	2,080.21	40.00%	3,467.02
Subtotal Attached		120,362	12,749	67,882	13.973	4,198.89	8,613.89		13,518.83
Total Residential	4.25%	289,800	38,381	117,436	9.352	12,557.15	84,015.15		107,773.28
Group Care									
Nursing Home Beds	2.00%	5,851	638	989	32.000	30.92	254.92	40.00%	424.86
Assisted Living Units	2.00%	10,012	348	7,360	24.000	306.68	502.68	40.00%	837.79
Total Group Care		15,864	986	8,350	20.939	337.59	757.59		1,262.65
Hotel/Motel Units									
Low Rise (1-3 Floors)	6.00%	37,234	10,119	19,313	45.000	429.18	951.18	40.00%	1,585.30
Mid Rise (4-7 Floors)	6.00%	18,617	1,764	5,171	60.000	86.19	401.19	45.00%	729.44
High Rise (8+ Floors)	6.00%	18,617	1,477	7,364	75.000	98.18	291.18	50.00%	582.37
Total Hotel/Motel Units		74,468	13,360	31,848	45.309	613.55	1,643.55		2,897.10
Grand Total		380,132	52,727	157,634	11.669	13,508.29	86,416.29		111,933.03

was apportioned to reflect trends, demographic shifts, and changing community attitudes about development patterns; here, the density within each land-use category is geared to help achieve the same objectives.

Generally speaking, the densities indicated are 75% of the difference between the highest and lowest of the range (a ratio used for years in Dade County, Florida, for example), but the actual density "yield" can vary dramatically. For example, in the land-use category for 6-8 units per net acre, the difference is 2 units per net acre—75% of which is 1.5. When added to the base of 6, this comes to 7.5 units per net acre. For group care and hotel/motel land uses, densities are based in part on local experts knowledgeable of those housing groups.

The final assumption concerns the adjustment from net acres (reflecting land on which development occurs) to gross acres (reflecting all developed land including that used for streets, easements, drainage ways, and other property-serving purposes). The factors shown in Table 3-7 reflect recommendations and experience from several sources for affected land-use categories.[4]

The particular calculations involved are as follows:

Vacancy Rate 2020: This is assumed to be the vacancy rate for 2020. In this case, the assumed rate is slightly less than the current rate.

Total Units Needed 2020: Calculated as

[(OCCUPIED UNITS NEEDED 2020) / (1 − VACANCY RATE 2020)]

where OCCUPIED UNITS NEEDED 2020 is from Table 3-6.

Total Units Lost: From Table 3-5.

Total New Units Needed 2020: Calculated as

[(TOTAL UNITS NEEDED 2020) − (UNITS 2000) + (UNITS LOST)]

where UNITS 2000 is from Table 3-3.

Plan New Unit Net Density 2020: Local planning target for the density of residential development within each land-use category. Lower densities mean much more land will be needed to accommodate future development than higher densities, as will be seen when lower densities are applied to this example.

New Net Acres Needed: Calculated as

[(TOTAL NEW UNITS NEEDED 2020) / (PLAN NEW UNIT NET DENSITY 2020)]

Plan Net Acres Needed: Calculated as

[(ACRES REMAINING) + (NEW NET ACRES NEEDED)]

where ACRES REMAINING is from Table 3-5.

Gross Acre Adjustment Factor: Planning assumption for the amount of total developed land that is used for roads, drainage, utility easements, and other property-serving purposes. This is based on local planning knowledge and planning targets (the higher the factor, the less efficient will land be used and the more costly development becomes).

Gross Plan Acres Needed: Calculated as

[(PLAN NET ACRES NEEDED) / (1 − GROSS ACRE ADJUSTMENT FACTOR)]

SUMMARY OBSERVATIONS

Of all land uses, residential is the most malleable. Small fluctuations in interest rates, local land-use regulations, and growth rates can affect this land use more than perhaps any other for the simple reason that it is the most consuming of space and demanding of services. From a planning perspective, this is the one land use that can lead to sprawl or compact development, and all the consequences that either development characterization evince.

Suppose the user wishes to steer a community toward a more compact development pattern than trends indicate. Also suppose there is some opposition to this for fear of the unknown among citizens. In my view, the user can offer two suggestions that many, if not most, citizens would accept at least in principle.

The first is what Robert Burchell advises: Raising density by just 1 unit per acre can have the greatest influence on changing land-use patterns in ways that are imperceptible. For example, raising densities from 3 to 4 units per acre will hardly be noticed and certainly not perceived as forcing people to live on top of each other.

A second suggestion would be to facilitate accessory dwellings in detached housing units, perhaps subject to house size, access, design, and occupancy conditions. Conceptually, accessory units can be important opportunities for the elderly, empty-nester, temporarily dislocated, or single-person households. In the case of Yukon County, if just 10% of all future detached homes would be allowed to have accessory units, about 17,000 households could be accommodated in this manner. Assuming those households would otherwise occupy units in the attached residential land-use category, the savings could approach about 2,000 acres or about 3 square miles of land, not to mention savings in infrastructure costs.

There is one more consideration. It appears that demand for neotraditional housing, cluster housing, lofts, and the like exceeds supply.[5] This should signal to the user that much more needs to be done to facilitate these changes in housing demand.

It would seem that perhaps estimating the future gross domestic product would be easier than estimating land-use needs, especially for residential land uses. Yet, it must be done, otherwise the community has no road map to follow when making infrastructure investment decisions, let alone trying to shape the future built environment to achieve multiple planning objectives.

NOTES

1. This is not to say that housing market analysis has no place in land-use planning. Long-range land-use planning sets forth the general land-use allocations. As communities develop, particular areas will undergo development that is responsive to market needs. Housing market analyses may be used to refine long-range analysis during community build-out. However, caution is made that housing market claims by some need to be independently verified. There are too many examples in which developers proposed projects based on market analysis only to have the built product result in overbuilding (see Nelson and Duncan 1995). Moreover, housing market analyses generally project existing trends into the near term, but a community plan may have important long-range objectives such as preserving important rural, resource, and environmentally sensitive land from urban sprawl. Where housing market analysis may suggest low-density development of such lands, for example, the community is within its planning obligations to prevent it and to redirect housing demand (see Knaap and Nelson 1992). Finally, because housing market analysis is driven by recent trends (see, e.g., Carn et al. 1988), important housing alternatives are not usually considered. The neotraditional community of Seaside, Florida, for instance, was not consistent with conventional market analysis wisdom and instead included small lots, restricted parking, and 19th-century platting patterns. The result is one of the most successful resort and second-home communities ever built (see Duany and Plater-Zyberk 1991, and Mohney and Easterling 1991).

2. The report can be found at www.gsd.harvard.edu/jcenter.

3. These conclusions are interpreted from ECONorthwest (January 2000).

4. Percent of gross developed land used for public facilities and street rights-of-way associated with each residential land-use category is adapted from American Public Health Association (1960), Real Estate Research Corporation (1974), Wisconsin State Planning Office (1975), and selected *Project Reference Files* for the period 1981 to 1996 from the ULI.

5. Based on Eppli and Tu (1999).

REFERENCES

American Public Health Association. *Planning the Neighborhood.* Chicago, IL: American Public Health Association, 1960.

Carn, Neal, Joseph Rabianski, Ronald Racster, and Maury Seldin. *Real Estate Market Analysis: Techniques and Applications.* Englewood Cliffs, NJ: Prentice-Hall, 1988.

Duany, Andres and Elizabeth Plater-Zyberk. *Towns and Town-Making Principles.* Cambridge, MA: Harvard University, 1991.

ECONorthwest. *Density, Development Patterns, and Definition of Alternatives, Research Report No. 1.* Eugene, OR: ECONorthwest, January 2000.

Eppli, Mark J. and Charles C. Tu. *Valuing the New Urbanism: The Impact of the New Urbanism on Prices of Single-Family Homes.* Washington, DC: Urban Land Institute, 1999.

Federal Housing Administration. *Techniques of Housing Market Analysis.* Washington, DC: U.S. Department of Housing and Urban Development, undated.

Florida Department of Community Affairs. *Model Housing Element.* Tallahassee, FL: State of Florida, May 1987.

Housing Division. *Memo: Housing Report—2000 Commission.* Salem, OR: State of Oregon, undated, circa 1985.

Knaap, Gerrit J. and Arthur C. Nelson. *The Regulated Landscape.* Cambridge, MA: Lincoln Institute of Land Policy, 1992.

Mohney, David and Keller Easterling. *Seaside: Making a Town in America.* Princeton, NJ: Princeton Architectural Press, 1991.

Nelson, Arthur C. and James Duncan, et al. *Growth Management Principles and Practices.* Chicago, IL: American Planning Association, 1995.

New Jersey Department of Community Affairs. *Draft State of New Jersey Comprehensive Housing Affordability Strategy (CHAS).* Trenton, NJ: State of New Jersey, August 21, 1991.

Office of Planning and Research. *Economic Practices Manual.* Sacramento, CA: State of California, 1978.

PriceWaterhouseCoopers. *Emerging Trends in Real Estate 1999.* New York, NY: PriceWaterhouseCoopers, 1999.

Pushkarev, Boris S. and Jeffrey M. Zupan. *Public Transportation and Land Use Policy.* Bloomington, IN: Indiana University Press, 1977.

Real Estate Research Corporation. *The Costs of Sprawl.* Chicago, IL: Real Estate Research Corporation, 1974.

Singer, Bruce Sheldon. "A Systematic Approach to Housing Market Analysis." In *Readings in Market Research for Real Estate*, James D. Vernor, editor. Chicago, IL: American Institute of Real Estate Appraisers, 1985.

Urban Land Institute. *Residential Development Handbook—Second Edition.* Washington, DC: Urban Land Institute, 1990.

___. *Project Reference Files.* Washington, DC: Urban Land Institute, selected from 1981-1996.

U.S. Bureau of the Census. *Current Construction Reports.* Washington, DC: U.S. Bureau of the Census, 2002.

U.S. Department of Health and Human Services. *Environmental Health Planning Guide.* Washington, DC: Public Health Service, 1962.

U.S. Department of Housing and Urban Development. *American Housing Survey.* Washington, DC: U.S. Department of Housing and Urban Development, 1989 and 1999.

Wisconsin State Planning Office. *Public Service Costs and Development.* Madison, WI: State of Wisconsin, 1975.

Employment
Land-Use Needs

OVERVIEW

Communities need to estimate land-use requirements associated with private and public sector employment over five- to 20-year planning horizons. In my view, they often fail to do so adequately. Problems include the lack of good information about land-use parameters, the quality of data that is available, and the changing trends. For example, largely because of automation in manufacturing and computerization of office functions, the average square feet of space per employee has risen during the past three decades (see Table 4-1). It is difficult to say whether this trend will continue. One mitigating factor is that high technology may have achieved saturation in workspace, especially among service industries.

This chapter presents a method for estimating employment-based land-use requirements principally using secondary data or locally derived data together with planning decisions. Issues reviewed include land-use ratios for workers in different land-use categories, adjustments to account for gross floor area and gross land area, and adjustments to account for normal vacancy rates. The result is a set of employment-based land-use demand coefficients that may be applied to local employment projections.

Unlike the estimation of land-use needs for residential development, in which total residential unit demands were estimated and allocated among different density categories, the estimation of land-use needs for employment-based development starts with coefficients per employee by broad land-use category. This difference is attributable more to custom than to the need to be consistent, yet the results are based conceptually on the same steps.

Table 4-1
Manufacturing and Office Space Trends

Year	Sq. Ft. Per Office Employee[a]	Sq. Ft. Per Manufacturing Employee[b]
1942	110	
1958	121	
1961		389
1979	199	
1980	209	
1990	252	
1991		495
2000[c]	280	546

a. Adapted from: Armstrong (1972); Building Owners and Managers Association International (1980); Price Waterhouse Real Estate Group (1991); NAIOP (1990).
b. Adapted from: Nez (1961, pp. 3-8) (for light industry); ITE (1991) (for light industry); NAIOP (1990) (for general manufacturing).
c. Extrapolation of trends.

The coefficients developed in this chapter can be used for "first-impression" land-use needs estimation. Results can be compared to the buildable land inventory of the community. If adequate land supply exists to accommodate employment land-use needs generated from the first-impression outcome, perhaps little further work is needed except for allocating land uses accordingly. If, however, inadequate land supplies exist, further analysis will be needed to refine the model. For example, higher floor area ratios (FARs) for office workers may be assumed but probably not more efficient use of space. Many other assumptions employed in the model can be similarly manipulated to generate results that are more appropriate to particular landscapes or otherwise consistent with local planning policies, such as:

- gross square feet of building space per employee by major employment-based land-use category; and
- net and gross acres needed to accommodate future nonresidential, employment-based land uses.

For Yukon County, the employment projections for the period 2000 to 2020 are shown in Table 2-3. These data happen to be provided by the MPO for Yukon County's region. The land-use needs of employment-based activities are estimated in two steps.

STEP 1: DETERMINE GROSS SQUARE FEET OF BUILDING SPACE PER WORKER

The starting point for this analysis is an estimate of square feet of building space consumed by workers in each major employment-based land-use category. Averages are calculated. The averages used here are based in part from studies conducted by the National Association of Industrial and Office Properties (NAIOP) (1990), the Institute of Transportation Engineers (ITE) (1997), and Price Waterhouse Real Estate Group (1991). These studies are perhaps the most reliable on space consumption per employee by major industry category for general land-use planning purposes. The NAIOP study in particular was based on a survey of more than 2.5 million firms.

Generally, space needs of most major employment groups are reasonably constant across regions, different-sized cities, and different-sized firms. This is mostly attributable to standardization of technologies and employee productivity across most major economic sectors. Some users may view office workers as an exception because of the possibility that:

- office space consumption will be less among firms in large cities and more among firms in small cities;
- firms in CBDs will have less office space consumption per employee relative to firms outside CBDs; and
- firms with fewer employees will consume more office space per employee than firms with many employees.

The NAIOP (1990) study addresses those concerns in its national study and found little variation among office employees. Firms with more than 250 employees in CBDs averaged 229 square feet per employee, compared to firms of fewer than five employees in the most rural locations that averaged 269 square feet per employee. While there is more variation among all firms and all employees (262 square feet among the largest CBD firms to 455 among the smallest rural firms), they really reflect the differences in land-use activities between CBDs and rural areas. CBDs have higher concentrations of office workers, while rural areas typically have higher concentrations of manufacturing, distribution, and natural resources workers. It is my view that the national average figures can be used with confidence.

Three other studies may be used to determine space consumption figures. Recht Hausrath & Associates (1981) surveyed downtown and near-downtown San Francisco businesses to determine space consumption per employee for a large range of employment types. The Metropolitan Service District (1980) of metropolitan Portland, Oregon, determined workers per net developed acre among the 20 two-digit Standard Industrial Classification code manufacturing industries for the Portland metropolitan region. The third is provided by the U.S. Department of Energy's Energy Information Administration through the *Commercial Buildings Energy Consumption Survey*

1999 (CBECS) (2002). This occasional national survey of commercial and public buildings shows space consumption per worker for a wide range of specific activities. It is not directly applicable in estimating land-use needs because the categories of building use differ from categories of land use, but the figures are illuminating nonetheless. These studies are summarized in this chapter's appendix.

The figures used to estimate future employment land-use needs are shown in Table 4-2 (the first employment land-use calculation table). Some categories of employment are excluded, such as agriculture, fishing, forestry, and mining. These activities are found usually in rural and resource areas, and are not typically considered urban land uses.

The manufacturing land-use category combines light and heavy manufacturing and durable and nondurable goods manufacturing. The reason is that these manufacturing activities are becoming more alike in their space consumption per employee. For example, the appendix shows that employee space consumption and land-use densities are similar across these manufacturing categories. However, if a community has an inordinately large share of a particular manufacturing industry with extraordinarily low or high employee densities, local figures should be used. Employment for retail and office land uses are given in more detail since they are increasing in prominence in the share of required land.

Most studies of space consumed by workers are net of building space used for halls, lavatories, lobbies, and other common areas. To adjust for the total building space actually used per employee, "efficiency ratios" (the percent of net to gross square feet) must be used. In many malls, the open walk-ways and other open areas (excluding food courts and retail carts) will often use 20% of the total enclosed space. The efficiency ratio conversion factor to bring net to total space is thus 0.75. The efficiency ratio of strip shopping centers, however, is usually 0.90. Low-rise office buildings have efficiency ratios of about 0.90, while high rises can have efficiency ratios of 0.85 or lower. Table 4-2 uses the mid-range efficiency ratios, where available. The efficiency ratio for industrial buildings tends to close to 1.0, although 0.95 is used in Table 4-2. The appendix reports typical efficiency ratios for a wide range of building types.

A final adjustment is needed to account for vacancy rates among building types. Competitive markets will have a natural vacancy rate reflecting fluidity in firms finding the most suitable space, while assuring reasonably competitive rents. Table 4-2 assumes vacancy rates of 5% for all land-use categories except government. The government vacancy rate is set at 2% on the assumption that, based on personal observation, office space in government buildings or space leased by government agencies is not available for other than government purposes. Moreover, government tends to wait longer than the private sector to expand office space needs, so it tends to use office space more intensively than other users.

Table 4-2 shows the projected employment for each major employment-based land-use category. These figures are used to derive a blended average gross-square-foot figure for all office employees, which is used later.

In review, gross building area per worker and total workers for each employment land-use category are calculated as follows:

Table 4-2
Gross Building Space Occupied Per Employee

Employment Land-Use Category	Net Sq. Ft. Per Employee	Efficiency Ratio	Adjusted Net Sq. Ft. Per Employee	Vacancy Rate	Gross Sq. Ft. Per Employee	Employee Share	Projected Employment 2020
Industrial							
Construction	260.00	95.00%	273.68	5.00%	288.09	18.17%	15,300
Manufacturing	550.00	95.00%	578.95	5.00%	609.42	30.29%	25,500
TCU	250.00	95.00%	263.16	5.00%	277.01	23.52%	19,800
Wholesale Trade	630.00	95.00%	663.16	5.00%	698.06	28.03%	23,600
Subtotal Industrial	449.00	95.00%	472.63	5.00%	497.51	100.00%	84,200
Retail Trade							
Neighborhood	510.00	85.00%	600.00	5.00%	631.58	40.00%	18,600
Community	510.00	80.00%	637.50	5.00%	671.05	30.00%	13,950
Regional	510.00	75.00%	680.00	5.00%	715.79	20.00%	9,300
Super Regional	510.00	70.00%	728.57	5.00%	766.92	10.00%	4,650
Subtotal Retail Trade	510.00	80.00%	637.50	5.00%	671.05	100.00%	46,500
Office*							
General Office	280.00	85.00%	329.41	6.00%	350.44	65.00%	94,055
Office Park	280.00	85.00%	329.41	6.00%	350.44	25.00%	36,175
Suburban Multilevel	280.00	85.00%	329.41	2.00%	336.13	10.00%	14,470
Subtotal Office	280.00	85.00%	329.41	4.67%	349.01	100.00%	144,700

*Office includes FIRE, services, and government.

Net Sq. Ft. Per Employee: This is a local planning assumption. In this example, it is based substantially on NAIOP (1990). The government land-use category is assumed to be the same as Finance, Insurance, and Real Estate (FIRE), because these land uses tend to be intermixed in office parks and sometimes in the same buildings more than other land uses.

Efficiency Ratio: Adapted mainly from the ULI (1975, 1980, 1982, 1988, and 2000) and the ULI's *Project Reference Files* (selected from the years 1976-94), and from Canestaro (1989).

Adjusted Net Sq. Ft. Per Employee: Calculated as

[(NET SQ. FT. PER EMPLOYEE) / (1 – EFFICIENCY RATIO)]

Vacancy Rate: This is adapted mainly from NAIOP (1989 and 1990) and Recht Hausrath & Associates (1981).

Gross Sq. Ft. Per Employee: Calculated as

[(ADJUSTED NET SQ. FT. PER EMPLOYEE) / (1 – VACANCY RATE)]

Employee Share: This is the share of total employment projected for a given land-use category based on total employment in its group (land-use category employment divided by total group employment in Table 2-3). There are two exceptions. First, retail employment is assigned to four broad groups representing neighborhood, community, regional, and super regional market areas. This distribution is adapted from studies on retail space and employment distribution among shopping center types including National Research Bureau, *Shopping Center Directions* (Spring 1993, p. 1); Georgia DCA, *Shopping Centers in Georgia* (1987), for both the Atlanta Region and the State of Georgia; and the ULI (1997). Second, office employment is composed of services, FIRE, and government, and

is distributed based on assumptions made by the user in consultation with people knowledgeable about local office patterns.

Projected Employment 2020: This figure is the **Total Urban-Related Employees** for 2020 from Table 2-3.

STEP 2: DETERMINE NET AND GROSS ACRES NEEDED FOR EMPLOYMENT-BASED LAND USES

This step estimates the net and gross acres of land needed to accommodate employment-based land uses. For the most part, employment-based land uses are in low-rise structures. This is especially true of most, if not all, industrial and retail land uses. Even among office land uses, modern high-rise towers in suburban or edge-city locations tend to have considerable amounts of open space around them. Often the FAR in suburban areas is 0.25, which means that, regardless of the number of floors, the land on which a building sits is as large for a one-story building of 200,000 square feet as it is for a 10-story building of 200,000 square feet.

The estimation of new land-use needs for industrial activities is reasonably straightforward. For the most part, industrial land-use needs are the least flexible in terms of land requirements. The "target-effective FARs" selected by local planners in the Yukon County example are adapted from the ITE's average building coverage ratios for similar land uses (see the appendix in this chapter).

At first glance, the demand for retail land uses may seem more complex. The traditional view of planning for retail activities has been to assume up to three (or four) prototypical shopping center types within any given community meeting minimum population requirements. Recent years have seen the emergence of discount centers, especially in remote rural or exurban areas, "power" centers clustering near regional and super regional shopping centers, and concentrated specialty centers such as full-service automobile centers within which separate proprietors would handle specific functions. Nonetheless, for general land-use planning purposes, the differentiation of retail land-use needs by up to three or four general retail shopping center categories remains reasonable.

Table 4-3 reports the land-use planning characteristics of major shopping center types, including such features as population ranges, minimum and maximum center size in square feet and in acres, corresponding FARs, and derived net square feet per acre. It is customary in land-use planning to use such figures to calculate land-use needs of all retail activities, including strip commercial centers, isolated service centers, and to some degree land-extensive retail operations such as car lots.

Since the estimation of land-use needs for retail activities is derived from projections of retail employment, the projected employment in this category must be allocated to each of the applicable retail shopping center types. Studies on the nature of this distribution are summarized in Table 4-4, which includes the recommended distribution for land-use planning purposes. Since not all communities have the population thresholds needed to accommodate all retail shopping center types, Table 4-5 suggests how retail employment forecasts may be allocated among shopping center types depending on population.

To allow for different levels of intensity among office land uses, it may be useful to distribute office employment—FIRE, services, and government—into at least three major intensity

Table 4-3
Land-Use Planning Characteristics of Major Retail Shopping Center Types

Type of Center	Population Range	Typical GLA	Range of Acres	FAR Range	Floor Area Per Acre	Maximum GLA
Neighborhood	3,000-40,000	50,000	3-10	0.23	10,019	100,000
Community	40,000-150,000	150,000	10-30	0.23	10,019	450,000
Regional	150,000+	450,000	10-60	0.34-0.69	30,056	900,000
Super Regional	300,000+	900,000	15-100+	0.34-0.77	33,541	2,000,000

Source: Adapted from the ULI (1999), p. 8.

Table 4-4
Distribution of Employment Among Shopping Center Types

Shopping Center Type	Research Source				
	National Research Bureau[a]	Atlanta Region[b]	State of Georgia[b]	ULI[c]	Recommended For Land-Use Planning
Neighborhood	25.44%	36.20%	38.90%	41.00%	40.00%
Community	44.79%	35.50%	35.50%	31.00%	30.00%
Regional	13.95%				20.00%
Super Regional	15.81%				10.00%
Regional, Total	29.76%	28.30%	28.30%	28.00%	30.00%

a. National Research Bureau (Spring 1993), p. 1.
b. Georgia Department of Community Affairs (1987), for both the Atlanta Region and the State of Georgia.
c. ULI (1999).

Table 4-5
Distribution of Employment Among
Shopping Center Types Based on Population

Shopping Center Type	Population Ranges			
	Less Than 40,000	Less Than 150,000	Less Than 300,000	300,000 or More
Neighborhood	100%	60	45	40
Community		40	35	30
Regional				20
Super Regional				10
All Regional			20	30

Source: Information interpreted by the author. Subject to refinement locally.

configurations representing suburban office and business park developments; office park developments; and suburban, high-density office developments. For each development type, a "target-effective FAR" is selected by local planners. In Yukon County, local planners decided on target FARs of 0.25, 0.42, and 0.84, respectively. Projected office employment is allocated to each of these FARs. The allocation may be made based on analysis of recent or emerging trends, or through another analysis determining the need to pursue different levels of intensity than may be observed in the absence of planning.

While it is possible that more than three FAR targets may be used, as a practical matter the three selected are likely to account for much, if not all, office development during the planning horizon of most suburbanizing communities. An important consideration in choosing these categories is the difference in the effective FAR of total land area developed into offices. According to Stern (1981), an FAR of 1.00 that suppos-

edly allows 43,560 square feet of office space per acre, but that includes surface parking at four stalls per 1,000 square feet plus associated setbacks and landscaping, could only have an effective FAR of about 0.35, or about 15,000 square feet (see the appendix in this chapter). The reason is that, with a parking ratio of four stalls per 1,000 square feet of building space and ground-level parking, it is not possible to achieve FARs over net developed land of more than 0.30 for a 1-acre site. However, by reducing parking ratios and building garages for parking, FARs rise more proportionately than the reduction in stalls. The same effect is observed by placing parking in garages or under the building.

The FARs selected at the 0.25 and 0.42 levels reflect average floor area per acre figures shown in Table 4-6 (the second employment land-use calculation table) as derived from the ITE (1991) (see the appendix in this chapter). The ITE's studies find a land coverage ratio of 0.25 for suburban headquarters offices, and 0.26 for business parks and for research and development centers. These effective FARs are remarkably close to the limits calculated by Stern (1981) for parking ratios of four stalls per 1,000 square feet with surface parking. Because these figures relate to single-floor land uses, they should be reconsidered in situations where the community anticipates a large share of development in a particular employment land use in multilevel structures. For example, an FAR of 0.84, or twice the ITE office park findings, would require either a parking ratio of two stalls per 1,000 square feet, or placement of parking in garages or underneath buildings. Thus, an effective FAR of 0.84 would naturally result in high-rise, more compact, suburban

Table 4-6
Employment-Based Land-Use Needs

Employment Land-Use Category	Employee Share	FAR	Gross Sq. Ft. Per Employee	Gross Sq. Ft. Per Net Acre	Employees Per Net Acre	Projected Employment 2020	In-Place Employee Percent	Planned In-Place Employees 2020	Planned Acres Needed 2020	Existing Acres 2000	New Acres Needed	Gross Acre Adjustment Factor	Gross Acres Needed
Industrial													
Construction	18.17%	0.1900	288.09	8,276.40	28.73	15,300	25.00%	3,825	133.14	20.00	113.14	20.00%	166.43
Manufacturing	30.29%	0.2300	609.42	10,018.80	16.44	25,500	100.00%	25,500	1,551.10	250.00	1,301.10	20.00%	1,938.88
TCU	23.52%	0.1900	277.01	8,276.40	29.88	19,800	100.00%	19,800	662.70	200.00	462.70	20.00%	828.37
Wholesale Trade	28.03%	0.2600	698.06	11,325.60	16.22	23,600	100.00%	23,600	1,454.60	900.00	554.60	20.00%	1,818.25
Subtotal Industrial	100.00%	0.2217	497.51	10,154.06	22.15	84,200	86.37%	72,725	3,801.54	1,370.00	2,431.54	20.00%	4,751.93
Retail Trade													
Neighborhood	40.00%	0.2300	631.58	10,018.80	15.86	18,600	100.00%	18,600	1,172.53	800.00	372.53	35.00%	1,803.90
Community	30.00%	0.2300	671.05	10,018.80	14.93	13,950	100.00%	13,950	934.36	620.00	314.36	30.00%	1,334.80
Regional	20.00%	0.3400	715.79	14,810.40	20.69	9,300	100.00%	9,300	449.47	315.00	134.47	25.00%	599.29
Super Regional	10.00%	0.3400	766.92	14,810.40	19.31	4,650	100.00%	4,650	240.79	172.00	68.79	20.00%	300.98
Subtotal Retail Trade	100.00%	0.2630	671.05	11,201.23	16.62	46,500	100.00%	46,500	2,797.15	1,907.00	890.15	30.75%	4,038.98
Office*													
General Office	65.00%	0.2500	350.44	10,890.00	31.08	94,055	80.00%	75,244	2,421.34	800.00	1,621.34	20.00%	3,026.67
Office Park	25.00%	0.4200	350.44	18,295.20	52.21	36,175	80.00%	28,940	554.34	200.00	354.34	25.00%	739.11
Suburban Multilevel	10.00%	0.8400	336.13	36,590.40	108.86	14,470	80.00%	11,576	106.34	40.00	66.34	30.00%	151.92
Subtotal Office	100.00%	0.3515	349.01	13,108.68	46.95	144,700	80.00%	115,760	3,082.01	1,040.00	2,042.01	21.33%	3,917.70
Grand Total						275,400			9,680.71	4,317.00	5,363.71		12,708.61

*Office includes FIRE, services, and government.

office buildings. This is the logic used in the Yukon County example shown in Table 4-6.

In all cases where effective FARs are targeted, zoning ordinances would normally assign higher allowable FARs. Local planners would monitor development patterns to evaluate the extent to which target FARs are actually achieved.

This final set of calculations converts net acres needed to gross acres needed to accommodate employment-based land-use needs. The gross area conversion factor is required to account for land needed to serve development such as rights-of-way, utility easements, and drainage. In general, the less intense a land use, the less land is needed to support it in terms of streets and public facilities. Unfortunately, there is no reliable information on the relative shares of land area needed for streets and public facilities for different nonresidential land uses. A typical rule of thumb assumes that 25% of gross land area is needed for public rights-of-way including streets and public facilities. The figures reported in Table 4-6 are based on a sample of nonresidential developments reported in the ULI's *Project Reference Files* for the period 1976-1994. This analysis involved evaluating project site plans, determining the nature of public access, identifying streets that may bound one or more sides of the project, and estimating the total public right-of-way that may be allocated to the project.

Finally, because not all workers work at their place of business address and many work full time from their home, an adjustment is needed. For example, recent studies have shown that only about 25% of all construction workers work in offices, which is sensible (Otak, Inc., et al. 1999). Full assignments are assumed for all other industrial categories as well as all retail categories, although research would be welcome to refine these figures. For office employment, the estimate of 80% assigned to the place of business is used. These jobs are in FIRE, services, and government, with services comprising the bulk of employment. Many service workers, and other office workers, have no offices per se, but work in the field (such as realtors, salespeople, and repair people) or at home.[1]

Table 4-6 also shows the total existing land area allocated for these land uses in current plans or otherwise used for these activities based on assessor records. Subtracted from the inventory would be those areas targeted by local planners for conversion to different land uses. The table shows total net and gross land area needed to accommodate nonresidential, employment-based land-use needs through the planning horizon.

In review, the calculations needed to estimate net and gross acres for employment land uses are:

Employee Share: From Table 4-2.

FAR: FAR appropriate for each land-use category. The higher the FAR, the less land is needed to accommodate needed development.

Gross Sq. Ft. Per Employee: From Table 4-2.

Gross Sq. Ft. Per Net Acre: Calculated as

$$[(FAR) \times (43,560 \text{ SQ. FT. PER ACRE})]$$

Employees Per Net Acre: Calculated as

$$[(GROSS \text{ SQ. FT. PER NET ACRE}) / (GROSS \text{ SQ. FT. PER EMPLOYEE})]$$

Projected Employment 2020: From Table 2-3 with adjustments from Table 4-2.

In-Place Employee Percent: This is the assumed percent of workers actually working at their location of business.

Planned In-Place Employees 2020: Calculated as

[(PROJECTED EMPLOYMENT 2020) × (IN-PLACE EMPLOYEE PERCENT)]

Planned Acres Needed 2020: Calculated as

[(PLANNED IN-PLACE EMPLOYEES 2020) / (EMPLOYEES PER NET ACRE)]

Existing Acres 2000: This is based on data estimated from archived property tax assessor records, Pittmon fire insurance maps, aerial photography with overlain property boundaries, land-use inventories, or traffic analysis zone data assembled by the local MPO or other transportation planning organization. This figure excludes land area designated for conversion to other than employment land uses.

New Acres Needed: Calculated as

[(PLANNED ACRES NEEDED 2020) − (EXISTING ACRES 2000)]

Gross Acre Adjustment Factor: Planning assumption for the amount of total developed land that is used for roads, drainage, utility easements, and other property-serving purposes. This is based on local planning knowledge and planning targets (the higher the factor, the less efficient will land be used and the more costly development becomes).

Gross Acres Needed: Calculated as

[(PLANNED ACRES NEEDED 2020)
/ (1 − GROSS ACRE ADJUSTMENT FACTOR)]

SUMMARY OBSERVATIONS

Unlike residential land uses, employment-based land uses are relatively stable in that the space per worker does not change much. For many such uses, single-floor construction is the most efficient, such as manufacturing, wholesale, retail, and related activities. Even office activities, which are conducive to stacking on multiple floors, local land-use regulations combined with higher costs per square foot for multiple floors make much modern office construction single level or low rise. All this does not bode well for shrinking the amount of land that may be needed to accommodate future development needs.

There are two offsetting considerations, however. First, commercial land is a small share of total land needs, so even if all such development is on one level, real land-use savings may be realized in other areas such as residential. Related to this is the steadily shrinking presence of industrial activities. Although manufacturing operations have become very land extensive since World War II, the outward migration of manufacturing from urban areas has probably reached its peak and not much growth is anticipated. Indeed, fewer people worked in manufacturing in 2002.

The second consideration is parking. This is probably where the most savings in land can be made, even if a substantial share of all commercial and industrial construction is on one level. My interpretation of recent studies by the ULI indicates that suburban America is probably "overparked" by about one-third (i.e., we have about one-third more parking spaces around office buildings, shopping centers, and even government buildings than is necessary).[2]

For example, in a metropolitan area of about 2 million people—such as Cincinnati, Ohio; Orlando, Florida; Portland, Oregon; and Sacramento, California—there will be about 1 million people working in single-level or low-rise locations with associated surface parking. Based on the assumptions used in this report, they will work in about 800 million square feet of space. A typical parking ratio, dictated by local zoning standards, calls for about four parking stalls per 1,000 square feet of space; this comes to about 3.2 million parking spaces. One-third or about 1 million of these spaces are not needed to meet normal demands. At about 400 square feet per parking stall,[3] the excess parking area comes to about 400 million square feet or about 10,000 acres, which is roughly 15 square miles.

Redevelopment of this land can make more economical use than parking. Redevelopment into mixed uses may actually reduce overall parking demand. It is possible that, over the next generation, much of these "overparked" areas may be redeveloped. In addition, by relaxing parking requirements, economies of agglomeration may emerge in some settings, whereby the market will support mixed uses and multifloor arrangements simply because activities can be closer together, and money saved on parking land can be reinvested into structures that generate more rent.

Finally, the location dynamics of commercial activities appear to be shifting, albeit slightly. The recession of the early 21st century—fueled in part by the collapse of the high-tech sector, combined with lending restrictions that took effect in the wake of the savings and loan bailout of a decade earlier and which cost the U.S. Treasury about $100 billion in the early 1990s and set the national economy back about one-half trillion dollars—could mean that more central locations may become preferred investment opportunities. In most metropolitan areas, central city and inner suburban vacancy rates are lower than those in outlying areas. Central locations usually offer the advantage of better access to markets throughout metropolitan areas than fringe locations, and are thus better able to weather downturns in the business cycle. This shift in commercial and even retail location strategy by the private sector appears to be underway, and may influence future land-use planning in suburban and exurban areas as a consequence.

NOTES

1. The percent of employment in home-based businesses among the self-employed was 19.2% in 1999 (U.S. Bureau of the Census 2000).
2. The ULI and the International Council for Shopping Centers (1998).
3. A typical stall measures 8 to 9 feet by 18 to 20 feet. Parking lot access lanes and buffer areas, for example, double this area.

APPENDIX

This appendix includes information on nonresidential space consumption and land-use needs synthesized from a variety of sources. Although I tend to use the NAIOP (1990) space consumption figures in my work because its sampling and analysis were generally more rigorous than other sources (with one exception, noted below), the user may decide that other sources work best for their applications.

The NAIOP (1990) data are reported in Table 4-7. For the most part, the NAIOP study included a larger sample size than other studies and, unlike other studies, was used explicitly to project future space needs for a variety of nonresidential land uses. Table 4-8 and Table 4-9 report employees per 1,000 square feet of gross leasable area based on ITE data a decade apart (1987 and 1997).

Table 4-10 is based on the CBECS (2002) published by the Energy Information Administration of the U.S. Department of Energy. It shows the mean square feet per worker for a variety of building uses. Figures for this table are generally higher than reported in other surveys. One reason is that while some studies (such as NAIOP, for example) project future space needs, the CBECS figures include all buildings in use. Another reason is that exurban and rural areas are included, which, because land uses in these areas tend to be more land extensive usually with more space per worker than urban areas, the overall averages are shifted higher.

Table 4-11 summarizes employee space consumption for the financial district of San Francisco. Although conducted in the early 1980s, I have not found a more comprehensive study of any downtown in this format, and I do not suspect that space consumption characteristics for CBDs will have changed much since then. If the user is estimating space and land-use needs for downtowns, this may be the preferred study to use.

Table 4-12 summarizes employee space consumption for industrial activities in a large metropolitan area—Portland, Oregon—conducted by Metro, the regional governing body for Portland, to determine future space and land-use needs for manufacturing and related industrial uses. If the user is estimating space and land-use needs for such activities in metropolitan areas but not exurban or rural ones, this may be the preferred study to use. (A later study published by Metro is not as useful for projecting space and land-use needs.)

The last two tables are included for general background on building efficiency ratios: Table 4-13 is based on work by James C. Canestaro (1989) and Table 4-14 by Richard B. Stern (1981) calculates net land-use needs for specific building proposals.

Table 4-7
National Average Square Feet Per Worker
By Major Industry Category, 1990

Industry Category	Mean Sq. Ft. Per Employee
Agriculture and Mining	380
Construction	259
General Manufacturing	601
High-Tech Manufacturing	466
TCU	248
Distribution and Wholesale Trade	627
General Retail Trade	509
FIRE	279
General Services	550
Business and Professional Services	269

Source: NAIOP (1990).

Table 4-8
Space Consumption Based on Parking Generation Data

Land Use	ITE Code	Employees Per 1,000 Sq. Ft. GLA
General Light Industry < 100k Sq. Ft.	111	2.04
General Light Industry > 100k Sq. Ft.	112	2.10
Industrial Park < 400k Sq. Ft.	131	2.98
Industrial Park > 400k Sq. Ft.	132	2.23
Manufacturing	140	1.99
Warehousing	150	0.47
Government Office Building	730	5.37

Source: ITE (1987).

Table 4-9
Space and Land Consumption Based on the Institute of Transportation Engineers

Land Use	ITE Code	Trips Per Employee	Trips Per 1,000 Sq. Ft.	Trips Per Acre	Employees Per 1,000 Sq. Ft.	Employees Per Gross Acre	Gross Sq. Ft. Per Acre	FAR	Vehicle Occupancy
General Light Industrial[a]	110	3.02	6.97	51.80	2.31	17.15	7,432	0.17	1.30
General Heavy Industrial[a]	120	0.82	1.50	6.75	1.83	8.23	4,500	0.10	
Industrial Park[a]	130	3.34	6.96	63.11	2.08	18.90	9,068	0.21	1.37
Manufacturing[a]	140	2.10	3.82	38.88	1.82	18.51	10,178	0.23	1.20-1.30
Warehousing[a]	150	3.89	4.96	57.23	1.28	14.71	11,538	0.26	1.30
Hospital	610	5.17	16.78		3.25				
Nursing Home (AM peak)	620	0.20	0.40		2.00				
General Office Building[b]	710	3.32	11.01		3.32	7.91	2,240	0.05	
Corporate Headquarters[b]	714	2.27	7.72		3.40	31.07	11,040	0.25	1.20
Medical-Dental Building[b]	720	8.91	36.13		4.05	81.53	21,760	0.50	1.37
Single Tenant Office[b]	715	3.62	11.57		3.20	16.95	4,890	0.11	1.10
Office Park	750	3.50	11.42	195.11	3.26	55.75	17,085	0.39	
Research and Development	760	2.77	8.11	79.61	2.93	28.74	9,816	0.23	1.19
Business Park	770	4.04	12.76	149.79	3.16	37.08	11,739	0.27	

a. Trip and vehicle occupancy data from the ITE (1997). Calculations for employees per 1,000 gross sq. ft., employees per acre, gross building area per acre, and FAR by author.
b. Trip and vehicle occupancy data from the ITE (1997). All other data from the ITE (1991).

Table 4-10
Totals and Means of Floorspace, and Number of Workers, 1999

Principal Building Activity	All Buildings (thousand)	Total Floorspace (million sq. ft.)	Total Workers in All Buildings (thousand)	Mean Sq. Ft. Per Building (thousand)	Mean Sq. Ft. Per Worker
Education	327	8,651	8,927	26.4	969
Food Sales	174	994	980	5.7	1,014
Food Service	349	1,851	4,031	5.3	459
Health Care	127	2,918	6,219	22.9	469
Inpatient	11	1,865	3,350	168.2	557
Outpatient	116	1,053	2,869	9.1	367
Lodging	153	4,521	2,356	29.5	1,919
Mercantile	667	10,398	11,384	15.6	913
Retail (Other Than Mall)	534	4,766	4,668	8.9	1,021
Enclosed and Strip Malls	133	5,631	6,716	42.2	838
Office	739	12,044	28,969	16.3	416
Public Assembly	305	4,393	3,147	14.4	1,396
Public Order and Safety	72	1,168	1,702	16.2	686
Religious Worship	307	3,405	1,654	11.1	2,059
Service	478	3,388	4,554	7.1	744
Warehouse and Storage	603	10,477	6,216	17.4	1,685
Other	102	1,222	1,453	12.0	841
Vacant	253	1,908	261	7.6	na

Source: Figures are gross sq. ft. of total space. Adapted from U.S. Department of Energy (2002).

Table 4-11
Space and Land Consumption Based on
Downtown San Francisco, California, 1981 Study

Business Activity	Employment Density[a]
Management/Technical Office	
FIRE	222
Business/Professional Services	315
TCU	299
Government	266
Trade/Consumer Service Office	
Wholesale	232
Retail Services	178
Branch Banks	240
Retail Trade	
Retail Stores, Shops	442
Restaurants, Bars	200
Short-Term Occupancy	
Hotel/Motel	759[b]
Residence	2,498
Cultural/Institutional/Educational	
Educational Facilities	758
Nonprofits	546
Theatres, Museums, Institutions	828
Industrial/Warehouse/Automotive	
Industrial/Warehouse	661
Automotive	2,335
Overall Average (Weighted)	265

a. Gross sq. ft. of occupied building space per employee, excluding vacant space
b. Hotels average 0.74 employees per room

Source: Recht Hausrath & Associates (1981).

Table 4-12
Manufacturing Employment Density Based on
Metropolitan Portland, Oregon, Urban Growth Boundary Study

Manufacturing Category	Workers Per Net Acre
Light Industry	
Food and Kindred	17.40
Textiles	25.00
Apparel and Leather	12.40
Lumber and Wood	2.50
Furniture, Fixtures	24.75
Printing, Publishing	63.20
Electrical Equipment	28.00
Instruments	12.00
Other	8.30
Heavy Industry	
Paper and Allied	12.44
Chemical and Allied	11.94
Petroleum and Related	na
Rubber and Plastics	12.41
Stone, Clay, Glass	6.75
Primary Metals	6.78
Fabricated Metals	8.25
Machinery	8.26
Transportation Equipment	16.30

Source: Metropolitan Service District (metropolitan Portland, Oregon) (1980).

Table 4-13
Typical Efficiency Ratios

Land-Use Type	Efficiency Ratio
Industrial Buildings; One-Story Office Buildings; Single Tenant Shops/Stores; Row Houses; Townhouses	0.90+
Corporate Mid-Rise Buildings; Multitenant Low-Rise Buildings; Strip Shops/Stores; Low-Rise Walkup Apartments	0.85 to 0.90
Multitenant Mid-Rise Office Buildings; Neighborhood Shopping Centers; Mid-Rise Apartments	0.80 to 0.85
Corporate High-Rise Office Buildings; Community Shopping Centers; Mid-Rise Apartments	0.75 to 0.80
Government Office Buildings; Regional Shopping Centers; Hotels and Dormitories; Hospitals and Health Service Centers; Public Buildings; High-Rise Apartments	< 0.75

Source: Canestaro (1989).

Table 4-14
Determining Net Developed Land Area of Nonresidential Buildings

Step	Formula	Explanation
1	a	Total building area in sq. ft.
2	b	Number of floors in the building.
3	$c = a/b$	Building ground coverage in sq. ft., but only for noncubic buildings.
4	w	Width of building envelope. Many zoning and site planning ordinances require a minimum 6-foot edge exterior to the building line to accommodate sidewalks or fire access around the building. In downtowns, this may exceed 6 ft. and approach 15 ft. to provide sidewalk cafes, vending, landscaping, and related amenities.
5	$d = [(\sqrt{c}+w)^2 - c]$	Calculates the building area envelope in sq. ft., whereby the width of the envelope is the key variable.

Table 4-14 (continued)
Determining Net Developed Land Area of Nonresidential Buildings

Step	Formula	Explanation
6	y	Parking ratio or parking spaces required per 1,000 sq. ft. of building area. This is usually dictated by local parking regulations. The higher the ratio, the greater the total land area needed for the same building space, and the lower the effective FAR per acre of land developed.
7	z	Ground area per parking space, which includes the parking stall, lanes, access ways, sidewalks, and landscaping areas internal to the parking area.
8	$e = [(a/1,000)(y)(z)]$	Parking area coverage in sq. ft. Assumes ground-level parking. If multiple levels are anticipated, the term $[(a/1,000)(y)(z)]$ may be divided by the number of parking levels anticipated. If parking will be completely underneath the building, (z) may be set to 0. If parking will be in decks, then (z) should be divided by the number of decks anticipated; ground level would be (z/1) or simply (z), but a four-level garage separate from the building would be (z/4).
9	s	Width of the open space along the periphery. Many zoning and site planning ordinances require a minimum of 15 ft., but more is often required.
10	$f = [(\sqrt{c}+d+e+s)^2 - (c+d+e)]$	Total area of the open space along the periphery in sq. ft.
11	$g = (\Sigma c+d+e+f)/43,560$	Total land area of the developed site in acres.
12	$FAR = a/g$	Effective FAR of the total developed site.
13	$FAY = a/(g/43,560)$	FAY per acre of the total developed site.

Source: Adapted from Stern (1981).

REFERENCES AND SELECTED BIBLIOGRAPHY

Armstrong, Regina B. *The Office Industry: Patterns of Growth and Location.* New York, NY: Regional Plan Association, 1972.

Building Owners and Managers Association International. *Downtown and Suburban Office Building Experience Exchange Report.* Washington, DC: Building Owners and Managers Association International, 1980.

Canestaro, James C. *Refining Project Feasibility—Third Edition.* Blacksburg, VA: The Refine Group, 1989.

Georgia Department of Community Affairs. *Shopping Centers in Georgia.* Atlanta, GA: State of Georgia, 1987.

Institute of Transportation Engineers. *Trip Generation—Sixth Edition.* Washington, DC: Institute of Transportation Engineers, 1997.

___. *Trip Generation—Fifth Edition.* Washington, DC: Institute of Transportation Engineers, 1991.

___. *Parking Generation—Second Edition.* Washington, DC: Institute of Transportation Engineers, 1987.

Metropolitan Service District. *Urban Growth Boundary Findings.* Portland, OR: Metropolitan Service District, 1980.

National Association of Industrial and Office Properties. *America's Future Office Space Needs.* Washington, DC: National Association of Industrial and Office Properties, 1990.

___. *America's Future Industrial Space Needs.* Washington, DC: National Association of Industrial and Office Properties, 1989.

National Research Bureau. *Shopping Center Directions.* Falls Church, VA: National Research Bureau, Spring 1993.

Nez, George. "Standards for New Development," *Urban Land* 20(5), 1961.

Otak, Inc., Hammer Siler George Associates, and Golder Associates. *Regional Industrial Land Study.* Salem, OR: Department of Land Conservation and Development, 1999.

Price Waterhouse Real Estate Group. *Demand for Office Space in Southern California—Projections Through the Year 2000.* New York, NY: PriceWaterhouseCoopers, 1991.

Recht Hausrath & Associates. *Downtown San Francisco Office Survey.* Redwood City, CA: Townhall Services, 1981.

Stern, Richard B. "Determining a Building's Site Size Requirements," *Urban Land,* May 1981, pp. 12-15.

Urban Land Institute. *Multifamily Housing Development Handbook.* Washington, DC: Urban Land Institute, 2000.

___. *Shopping Center Development Handbook—Third Edition.* Washington, DC: Urban Land Institute, 1999.

___. *Resort Development Handbook.* Washington, DC: Urban Land Institute, 1997.

___. *Business and Industrial Park Development Handbook.* Washington, DC: Urban Land Institute, 1988.

___. *Office Development Handbook.* Washington, DC: Urban Land Institute, 1982.

___. *Downtown Development Handbook.* Washington, DC: Urban Land Institute, 1980.

___. *Industrial Park Development Handbook.* Washington, DC: Urban Land Institute, 1975.

___. *Project Reference Files.* Washington, DC: Urban Land Institute, 1976-1994.

Urban Land Institute and the International Council for Shopping Centers. *Parking Requirements for Shopping Centers.* Washington, DC: Urban Land Institute and the International Council for Shopping Centers, 1998.

U.S. Bureau of the Census. *Statistical Abstract of the United States 2000.* Washington, DC: U.S. Department of Commerce, 2000.

U.S. Department of Energy, Energy Information Administration. *Commercial Buildings Energy Consumption Survey 1999.* Washington, DC: U.S. Department of Energy, 2002.

Functional Population Adjustments for Public Facilities

OVERVIEW

As Yukon County grows, it will need to expand public facilities to meet new needs. Some privately provided facilities and services will also need to be expanded. The next three chapters (Chapters 6, 7, and 8) estimate facility needs including building space, student stations, land area, and water and wastewater provisions. The expansion needs of some facilities, such as water and wastewater, may be estimated using observed demand extrapolated into the future. The expansion needs for other facilities, however, may be more complicated. For example, the demand for police and fire facilities varies by land use in ways that are not always clear. How many "units" of police service are needed to serve commercial, industrial, or single-family residential activities? Only if local police and fire departments collect and maintain detailed records on responses by land use can this question be answered. For other facilities, such as emergency medical and rescue, jails, courts, and general government, it is virtually impossible to allocate demand based on observations.

The traditional way of estimating the current and future demand for certain facilities is to simply use the population as the basis. For example, some states have established a statewide minimum standard of 0.5 square feet of library space per capita based on resident population of communities meeting minimum thresholds. Yet, communities with high volumes of nonresidents who use library services may need more than 0.5 square feet per resident to meet needs. In the case of fire, police, emergency medical, courts, jails, and government administration buildings, the higher the nonresident daytime population, the greater the need for service relative to the resident population. Moreover, it is not enough to simply add resident population to the number of employees, since the service-demand characteristics of employees can vary considerably by type of industry. Using unweighted population and employment data to estimate facility needs may result in substantial error.

For many facilities, there is a convenient way—a method called "functional population"—to rationally attribute demand by land use and estimate aggregate demand for a community. Functional population is the equivalent number of people occupying space within a community on a 24-hour-per-day, seven-day-per-week basis. A person living and working in the community will have a functional population coefficient of 1.0. A person living in the community but working elsewhere may only spend 16 hours per day in the community on weekdays and 24 hours per day on weekends for a functional population coefficient of 0.76 (128 hours presence divided by 168 hours in a week). A person commuting into the community to work five days per week would have a functional population coefficient of 0.24 (40 hours presence divided by 168 hours in a week). A person traveling into the community to shop at stores, perhaps averaging eight hours per week, would have a functional population coefficient of 0.05.

Functional population thus tries to capture the presence of all people within the community—residents, workers, or visitors—to arrive at a total estimate of effective population that needs to be served.

These forms of adjusting population to help measure real facility needs replace the popularly used approach of merely weighting residents two-thirds and workers one-third (Nelson and Nicholas 1992). By estimating the functional population per unit of land use across all major land uses in a community, the user can rationally estimate the demand for certain facilities and services in the present and in a future year.

Estimating residential functional population is considerably easier than estimating functional population attributable to employment. Conceptually, residential functional population is the number of residents who occupy residential space on a 24-hour-per-day, seven-day-per-week basis. How many hours per weekday and weekend day does the average resident occupy residential space? A rule of thumb assumes that half of a person's life is spent in residential space (Chapin 1974; Nelson and Nicholas 1992). This figure could be as high as two-thirds, depending on the population demographics and outdoor opportunities.

For some population groups, such as retired persons, invalids, and prisoners, the figure approaches 100%. For Atlanta, Georgia, James Duncan and Associates (1993) assumed the residential component of functional population was 0.67 during a 24-hour day. This differentiation allows for reasonably refined estimates of needs for particular facilities and associated land uses. For example, public safety facilities serve all residents, workers, and visitors to the community 24 hours per day. This approach has been adopted nationally among several impact fee consultants.

The estimation of the hotel/motel functional population is similar. There are no definitive studies of hotel/motel population characteristics in the planning or engineering literature, and trade association literature is sketchy at best in this regard. Nonetheless, one normally considers a hotel/motel occupant to be a tourist, conventioneer, or a person on business. The time spent in a given hotel/motel is mostly during the evening for sleeping, otherwise the person is outside the facility if not merely passing through the community entirely. For this reason, the estimation of functional population is equated to one-half that of residents.

The estimation of functional population for employment-based land uses is conceptually different. Because it is possible to use trip generation data provided by the ITE in its *Trip Generation* (1997) manual,[1] estimates of functional population for employment land uses can be derived from those data. In addition, the *2000 Nationwide Household Transportation Survey* (Federal Highway Administration 2001) provides information on the average number of occupants per vehicle trip for type of trip. Combined, these two data sources help generate information on total trips, total people including visitors, and total workers by major nonresidential, employment-based land-use category for varying numbers of days during the week.

Here, we consider two variations of functional population.

- "24/7" functional population relates to public safety facilities because they serve the community 24 hours per day, seven days per week. Such facilities include fire and emergency medical facilities, police facilities, and jail and detention facilities.

- "Daytime" functional population relates to facilities serving the public essentially during daylight hours, such as parks, libraries, and community centers. Although they are used at night, many are not open certain days or certain hours on certain days. For daylight functional population, we assume 12 hours of operation daily seven days per week.

Daytime functional population applies to all public facilities other than public safety and government buildings.

More variations are possible, of course, but these seem to be the most generally applicable. The user may modify one or more parameters of these variations or add more variations.

Estimating functional population is done in three tables. Table 5-1 establishes the baseline parameters for calculation of both functional population variations. It combines data from the ITE's *Trip Generation* (1997) handbook with the Federal Highway Administration's *2000 Nationwide Household Transportation Survey* (2001) as follows:

ITE Code: This is the land-use code used by the ITE in its *Trip Generation* (1997) handbook that reflects best the general land-use categories used in this book. Users can use other ITE codes if local conditions warrant.

In-Place Occupant Ratio: This is the **In-Place Employee Percent** from Table 4-6 converted into a ratio. The user will need to assume ratios for group care, hotel/motel, and student activities. (1.0000 is assumed here.)

Hours In Place: This means the number of hours on any given day that a worker or student occupies space in the respective land-use category. (Nine hours are assumed here.)

Trips Per Employee: This is from the ITE's *Trip Generation* (1997) handbook based on the land-use codes and trip figures referenced in Table 5-1. Retail land uses are more complicated, however, because trip generation varies significantly by size of retail center.

For retail land uses, this is calculated as

$$\{[(0.643 \, \text{Ln}(\text{SQ. FT.} / 1{,}000) + 5.866)$$
$$\times (\text{SQ. FT.} / 1{,}000)] \times (\text{EMPLOYEES} / 1{,}000 \, \text{SQ. FT.})\} / 2$$

In Lotus, Excel, and Quatro, the general worksheet formula is:

$$\{[@\text{EXP}((0.643*@\text{LN}(\text{SQ. FT.}/1{,}000)) + 5.866)$$
$$/ (\text{SQ. FT.}/1{,}000)]* (\text{EMPLOYMENT PER } 1{,}000 \, \text{SQ. FT.})\} / 2$$

Because employment is weighted between different types of centers based on market areas, the figure for retail land uses is weighted so that neighborhood centers (at 50,000 assumed square feet) are 40% of retail employment, community centers (at 250,000 assumed square feet) are 30% of retail employment, regional centers (at 500,000 assumed square feet) are 20% of retail employment, and super regional centers (at 1,000,000 assumed square feet) are 10% of retail employment. The figure is thus the sum of each center's trip generation using the above formulas where trip generation for each center is multiplied by the employment share of each center. (This distribution may need to be adjusted for analysis of planning areas with populations under about 300,000 as per Table 4-5.)

One-Way Trips Per Employee: This divides numbers in the previous column by two to avoid double counting trips to and from the land use.

Journey-to-Work Occupants Per Trip: This is from the *2000 Nationwide Household Transportation Survey* (Federal Highway Administration 2001). For all occupations, there was an average of 1.19 occupants per vehicle per journey-to-work trip. This figure does not include public transit, walking, or bicycling to work, but these modes account for fewer than 5% of all such trips in suburban locations.[2] Because the *2000 Nationwide Household Transportation Survey* data are based on occupations of workers in their journey to work and not on land uses, we convert those data to land uses in the following manner:

Table 5-1
Baseline Functional Population Assumptions

Land-Use Category	ITE Code	In-Place Occupant Ratio	Hours In Place	Trips Per Employee	One-Way Trips Per Employee	Journey-to-Work Occupants Per Trip	Daily Occupants Per Trip	Visitors Per Employee	Visitor Hours Per Trip
Permanent Population									
Group Care Population									
Hotel/Motel Population									
Construction	110	0.2500	9.0000	3.0200	1.5100	1.3000	2.0200	1.0872	1.0000
Manufacturing	140	1.0000	9.0000	2.1000	1.0500	1.3000	2.0200	0.7560	1.0000
TCU	110	1.0000	9.0000	3.0200	1.5100	1.3000	2.0200	1.0872	1.0000
Wholesale Trade	150	1.0000	9.0000	3.8900	1.9450	1.3000	2.0200	1.4004	1.0000
Retail Trade	820	1.0000	9.0000	40.6552	20.3276	1.1900	1.9300	15.0424	1.0000
FIRE	710	0.8000	9.0000	3.3200	1.6600	1.1350	1.9150	1.2948	1.0000
Services	710	0.8000	9.0000	3.3200	1.6600	1.1350	1.9150	1.2948	1.0000
Group Care Employees	252			2.6100					
	253	1.0000	9.0000	3.4800	1.7400	1.1350	1.9150	1.3572	2.0000
Hotel/Motel Employees	310	1.0000	9.0000	8.9200	4.4600	1.1350	1.9150	3.4788	1.0000
Government	730	0.8000	9.0000	11.9500	5.9750	1.1350	1.9150	4.6605	1.0000
Students	na	1.0000	9.0000	na	na	na	na	na	na

Table 5-1 (continued)
Baseline Functional Population Assumptions

Trips per employee based on *Trip Generation* (ITE 1997) as follows:

- ITE Code 110 at 3.02 weekday trips per employee, page 90.
- ITE Code 140 at 2.10 weekday trips per employee, page 161.
- ITE Code 150 at 3.89 weekday trips per employee, page 189.
- ITE Code 710 at 3.32 weekday trips per employee, page 1045.
- ITE Code 252 at 2.61 weekday trips per employee, page 457.
- ITE Code 253 at 3.48 weekday trips per employee, page 463.
- ITE Code 310 at 8.92 weekday trips per employee, page 503.
- ITE Code 730 at 11.95 weekday trips per employee, page 1093.
- ITE Code 820 based on blended average of trips by retail center size calculated below, adapted from page 1337.

Trips per retail employee from the following table:

Retail Scale	Assumed Center Size	Trip Rate	Share	Weighted Trips
Neighborhood < 50k Sq. Ft.	50,000	87.31	40.0%	34.92
Community 50k–250k Sq. Ft.	250,000	49.15	30.0%	14.74
Regional 250k–500k Sq. Ft.	500,000	38.37	20.0%	7.67
Super Regional 500k–1000k Sq. Ft.	1,000,000	29.96	10.0%	3.00
Sum of Weighted Trips Per 1k Sq. Ft.				60.34
Projected Retail Space				31,331,560
Projected Retail Employees				46,500
Employees Per 1,000 Sq. Ft.				1.4841
Trips Per Employee				40.6552

For trip rate formula, see text.

Table 5-1 (continued)
Baseline Functional Population Assumptions

- One-way trips per employee for Group Care based on ITE trips per employee for ITE Code 252 plus 260 divided by two.

- Journey-to-work occupants per trip from *2000 Nationwide Household Transportation Survey* (Federal Highway Administration 2001).

- Occupants per journey-to-work trip adapted from *2000 Nationwide Household Transportation Survey* as follows:

  — 1.30 occupants per Construction, Manufacturing, TCU, and Wholesale trip; 1.19 per retail trip;

  — 1.135 per FIRE, Service, Group Care, Hotel/Motel Employee and Government trip.

- Daily Occupants per trip adapted from *2000 Nationwide Household Transportation Survey* as follows:

  — 2.02 occupants per Construction, Manufacturing, TCU, and Wholesale trip; 1.93 per retail trip;

  — 1.195 per FIRE, Service, Group Care, Hotel/Motel Employee and Government trip.

Occupation	Occupants	Land-Use Category
Manufacturing, construction, maintenance	1.3000	Construction Manufacturing TCU Wholesale Trade
Sales	1.1900	Retail
Professional, managerial, technical	1.1300	
Clerical, administrative support	1.1400	
Unweighted average	1.1350	FIRE Services Group Care Hotel/Motel Government

Daily Occupants Per Trip: This is also from the *2000 Nationwide Household Transportation Survey* and includes all other nonjourney-to-work trips. The conversions from occupations to land uses used here are as follows:

Occupation	Occupants	Land-Use Category
Manufacturing, construction, maintenance	2.0200	Construction Manufacturing TCU Wholesale Trade
Sales	1.9300	Retail
Professional, managerial, technical	1.9200	
Clerical, administrative support	1.9100	
Unweighted average	1.9150	FIRE Services Group Care Hotel/Motel Government

Visitors Per Employee: This estimates the number of nonworkers who visit land uses during the day. The number of visitors per employee is estimated in the following formula:

$$\{[(\text{DAILY OCCUPANTS PER TRIP}) \times (\text{ONE-WAY TRIPS PER EMPLOYEE})] - [(\text{JOURNEY-TO-WORK OCCUPANTS PER TRIP} \times \text{ONE-WAY TRIPS PER EMPLOYEE})]\}$$

Visitor Hours Per Trip: This is the assumed length of time a visitor occupies space in a given land-use category. There is certainly a great variation, especially in retail where a trip to the convenience store may take only a quarter hour but a trip to the regional mall could take all day.

Table 5-2 uses the baseline assumptions to establish functional population coefficients or multipliers that are used to estimate functional population in Table 5-3. The calculations are as follows:

24/7 Days Per Week, Daytime Days Per Week: These indicate the number of days per week the land use is occupied. These are all assumptions than can be changed by the user.

24/7 Functional Population Coefficient–Hours @ 168, Daytime Functional Population Coefficient–Hours @ 84: These calculate the coefficient or multiplier to estimate functional population based on these two variations: (1) a week at 24 hours per day for seven days is 184 total hours; and (2) a daytime week at 12 hours per day for seven days is 84 hours. For residential land uses, the coefficients are assumed; the figures shown are those used commonly by the author but can be changed by the user. For nonresidential land uses and the employment part of group care and hotel/motel land uses, the coefficients are estimated by the following formula:

$$\{[(\text{IN-PLACE OCCUPANT RATIO}) \times (\text{HOURS IN PLACE})] + [(\text{VISITORS PER EMPLOYEE}) \times (\text{VISITOR HOURS PER TRIP})] \times (\text{DAYS PER WEEK}_{24/7, \text{DAYTIME}})\} / (\text{HOURS @}_{168, 84})$$

Table 5-2
24/7 and Daytime Functional Population Coefficients

Land-Use Category	24/7 Days Per Week	24/7 Functional Population Coefficient – Hours @ 168	Daytime Days Per Week	Daytime Functional Population Coefficient – Hours @ 84
Permanent Population	7.00	0.6700	7.00	0.5000
Group Care Population	7.00	0.8333	7.00	1.0000
Hotel/Motel Population	7.00	0.3300	7.00	0.2500
Construction	5.00	0.0993	5.00	0.1986
Manufacturing	5.00	0.2904	5.00	0.5807
TCU	5.00	0.3002	5.00	0.6004
Wholesale Trade	5.00	0.3095	5.00	0.6191
Retail Trade	7.00	1.0018	7.00	2.0035
FIRE	5.00	0.2528	5.00	0.5056
Services	5.00	0.2528	5.00	0.5056
Group Care Employees	7.00	0.4881	7.00	0.9762
Hotel/Motel Employees	7.00	0.3714	7.00	0.7428
Government	5.00	0.3530	5.00	0.7060
Students	5.00	0.2679	5.00	0.5357

For students, the formula is:

$$[(\text{IN-PLACE OCCUPANCY RATIO}) \times (\text{HOURS-IN-PLACE}) \times (\text{DAYS PER WEEK}_{24/7, \text{ DAYTIME}})] / (\text{HOURS @}_{168, 84})$$

Table 5-3 multiplies the 2000 and 2020 population, employment, and student figures by the coefficients for both of the functional population variations to estimate total functional population. These figures will be used in Chapter 6 to estimate space and land-use demands for public facilities.

Table 5-3
24/7 and Daytime Functional Population

Land-Use Category	Residents, Employees, Students 2000	Residents, Employees, Students 2020	24/7 Functional Population 2000	24/7 Functional Population 2020	Daytime Functional Population 2000	Daytime Functional Population 2020
Permanent Residents						
Rural Residential	17,400	14,416	11,658	9,659	8,700	7,208
1-5 Acres Per Unit	37,163	28,832	24,899	19,318	18,581	14,416
1-2 Units Per Net Acre	180,376	144,162	120,852	96,589	90,188	72,081
3-5 Units Per Net Acre	115,258	144,162	77,223	96,589	57,629	72,081
6-8 Units Per Net Acre	58,851	129,746	39,430	86,930	29,426	64,873
9-14 Units Per Net Acre	100,006	165,786	67,004	111,077	50,003	82,893
15+ Units Per Net Acre	39,614	93,705	26,541	62,783	19,807	46,853
Total Permanent Population	548,668	720,810	367,608	482,943	274,334	360,405
Group Care						
Residential	8,700	22,300	7,250	18,583	8,700	22,300
Employment	2,200	4,700	1,074	2,294	2,148	4,588
Total Group Care	10,900	27,000	8,324	20,877	10,848	26,888
Hotel/Motel						
Residential	93,177	133,000	30,748	43,890	23,294	33,250
Employment	12,600	17,700	4,680	6,574	9,359	13,147
Total Hotel/Motel	105,777	150,700	35,428	50,464	32,653	46,397
Employment						
Industrial						
Construction	12,400	15,300	1,232	1,520	2,463	3,039
Manufacturing	22,300	25,500	6,475	7,404	12,950	14,808
TCU	10,000	19,800	3,002	5,944	6,004	11,888
Wholesale Trade	20,000	23,600	6,191	7,305	12,381	14,610
Total Industrial	64,700	84,200	16,899	22,173	33,799	44,346

Table 5-3 (continued)
24/7 and Daytime Functional Population

Land-Use Category	Residents, Employees, Students 2000	Residents, Employees, Students 2020	24/7 Functional Population 2000	24/7 Functional Population 2020	Daytime Functional Population 2000	Daytime Functional Population 2020
Retail Trade						
Retail Trade	31,600	46,500	31,656	46,582	63,312	93,164
Office						
FIRE	15,500	24,700	3,919	6,245	7,837	12,489
Services	55,200	82,100	13,956	20,757	27,911	41,513
Government	25,800	37,900	9,107	13,378	18,214	26,757
Total Office	96,500	144,700	26,982	40,380	53,963	80,759
Total Employment	205,400	293,100	75,537	109,135	151,074	218,270
Students	122,360	195,150	32,775	52,272	61,180	97,575
Functional Population Total			519,671	715,691	530,089	749,535
New Functional Population				196,020		219,446

SUMMARY OBSERVATIONS

How do these estimates of functional population compare with other measures of equivalent population used for impact analysis purposes recommended in literature? The most common measure is simply resident population, but this assumes that communities with high numbers of people who commute into work have the same facility demands as those with more balanced jobs-to-housing or resident relationships. Recognizing the limitation of using just resident population for impact analysis purposes, the ULI method (used by Burchell, Listokin, and Dolphin (1994) for the ULI) recommends that the equivalent population be considered residents plus workers. This more accurately reflects real impacts and is fairly easy to estimate. The method recommended here is a refinement on the idea that workers, tourists, and visitors to a community impose burdens in addition to the residents. The principal advantage in the recommended method developed by Nelson and Nicholas (1992) is that it rationally apportions facility impacts and burdens according to the time in which each resident or worker actually demands services from the community.

For example, while the resident population method completely ignores the needs of nonresidential employment-based land uses, in contrast the ULI method may shift a more than proportionate share of the community facility burden to employment-based land uses by essentially considering any worker as imposing the same demand for the full range of community services as residents—who may also be workers in the same community. Because the Nelson and Nicholas method was developed to help development impact fees withstand judicial scrutiny—principally by apportioning people

Table 5-4
Comparing Equivalent Population Methods

Year	Permanent Population Method	ULI Method	24/7 Functional Population Method	Daytime Functional Population Method
2000	548,668	754,068	519,671	530,089
2020	720,810	1,013,910	715,691	749,535

between home, work, and visits—it should be quite suitable for estimating community facility and land-use needs as well. The differences between these methods as applied to the Yukon County case are illustrated in Table 5-4.

NOTES

1. As this book was going to press, the ITE published its seventh edition of *Trip Generation*. The user may wish to recalculate coefficients reported in this book and workbook to reflect ITE's updated edition. However, preliminary review of the newest edition by the author indicates that changes would be minor and would not change overall outcomes substantially.

2. This is based on analysis by the author of *American Housing Survey for the United States 2001* (U.S. Bureau of the Census 2002, Table 2-24).

REFERENCES

Burchell, Robert, David Listokin, and William R. Dolphin. *Development Impact Assessment Handbook.* Washington, DC: Urban Land Institute, 1994.

Chapin, F. S., Jr. *Human Activity Patterns in the City: Things People Do in Time and Space.* New York, NY: John Wiley & Sons, 1974.

Federal Highway Administration, U.S. Department of Transportation. *2000 Nationwide Household Transportation Survey.* Washington, DC: U.S. Department of Transportation (data disk), 2001.

Institute of Transportation Engineers. *Trip Generation—Sixth Edition*. Washington, DC: Institute of Transportation Engineers, 1997.

James Duncan and Associates. *City of Atlanta Impact Fee Study*. Atlanta, GA: Commissioner for Planning, February 19, 1993.

Nelson, Arthur C. and James C. Nicholas. "Estimating and Applying Functional Population." *Journal of Urban Planning and Development*. 118(2):45-58, 1992.

U.S. Bureau of the Census. *American Housing Survey for the United States 2001*. Washington, DC: U.S. Government Printing Office, 2002.

6

Public Facility Space and Land-Use Needs

OVERVIEW

In this chapter, the need for public facilities and associated land-use needs is estimated. Public facilities are perhaps the most idiosyncratic of all land uses to estimate. Each community has its own character and expresses its individual preferences for public facility quantity and quality through variable investments in buildings, land, personnel, and equipment. For example, one community may prefer parks over libraries, and its investment decisions will result in higher-than-average land area for parks, and lower-than-average capital and personnel investment in libraries. For some facilities, such as parks and recreation, standards are recommended by national associations but rarely adopted locally. For other facilities, such as police and fire, there are no recommended national standards applicable to land-use planning per se.

Moreover, the nature of facility and land-use needs of different facilities is affected differently by the same population and employment base. For example, police and fire services must be available on a 24-hour-per-day, seven-day-per-week basis, while library and recreation services are geared to business and early evening hours, five to seven days per week. Demands on public facilities are also affected by all people in the community—not just residents, visitors, or workers. It is therefore necessary to estimate land-use and facility needs based on some accounting of all residents, workers, and visitors.

The estimation of public facility space and associated land-use needs depends in part on three elements: (1) there should be some understanding of the appropriate level of public facilities based on standards recommended by national organizations, national studies, or other authoritative sources; (2) there

should be an assessment of the current level of service (LOS) provided by the community as compared to authoritative standards; and (3) the community should formally adopt, as a matter of public policy, the LOS that it will achieve by the end of the planning horizon. This step really involves a conscious decision by the community on the quality of life the community desires as measured by the provision of community facilities.

These three steps will be shown for each of 10 major categories of public facilities including:
- public safety facilities
- general government facilities
- community centers
- recreation centers
- library facilities
- major community center facilities
- public parks and open space
- private land-extensive land uses
- miscellaneous support facilities
- religious facility land uses

Addressed separately in the next two chapters (Chapters 7 and 8), respectively, are education and water and wastewater utility facilities. Not addressed here are public health facilities such as public hospitals and clinics. These facilities are highly idiosyncratic and are often limited to only large jurisdictions or entire regions. The user, however, may adapt the workbook to account for these and other facilities.

Before proceeding, a word of caution is necessary. There are few national standards and fewer state standards guiding the planning for many kinds of facilities, although not all. There are no databases compiling standards adopted by local governments, however, for any major facility—whether public or private. This is an area worthy of research so that communities can benchmark themselves and users can help communities provide facilities more rationally. Finally, although professionals engaged in planning individual facilities consider many factors, a basic method for estimating facility needs is presented here, usually based on building square feet and land area per functional or weighted resident. The size, location, and configuration of buildings and land must be left to those professionals.

PUBLIC SAFETY FACILITIES

Public safety facilities include fire and emergency medical facilities, police facilities, and jails and detention facilities. Although there are virtually no planning standards recommended by national organizations,[1] Table 6-1 summarizes results of a variety of studies based on national surveys, and shows a range of service levels based on actual experience among communities in terms of uniformed, sworn personnel per 1,000 residents. These surveys provide rather sketchy information for local planning purposes. On the other hand, the provision of these kinds of facilities depends greatly on local preferences, subject to change over time. Notice, for example, that the number of sworn officers per 1,000 population fell between 1992 and 2003.

While declining crime rates in recent years may help explain reduction in sworn police officers, the situation would seem to be different in the case of fire and emergency medical services (EMS). The provision of fire facilities depends principally on local desires to achieve certain fire insurance ratings made by Insurance Services Offices located in most states. A fire insurance rating of 1 is considered best and carries with it the lowest

possible fire insurance premiums; a rating of 10 indicates there is no fire protection and thus insurance premiums are the highest *if* insurance is available. Most large cities have ratings of 2 to 4, suburban cities and counties have ratings of 3 to 5, and rural communities with volunteer fire departments have ratings of 5 to 7. Lower scores mean better protection and this translates into lower insurance rates. Yet, lower rates are achieved in part with higher ratios of sworn officers per 1,000 population, which have been falling since 1992.

Instead of relying on sketchy national scale information, the local planners of Yukon County inventoried fire and EMS, police, and jail and detention facilities to establish the current LOS for each. Working with officials from those operations, an LOS standard was established to guide future facility planning. These calculations for fire/EMS, police, and jail facilities are shown in Table 6-2, Table 6-3, and Table 6-4, respectively.

For each, the following calculations are made:

24/7 Functional Population: This is from Table 5-3 for 2000 and 2020.

Facility Sq. Ft.: Data for 2000 is provided by local officials.

Sq. Ft. Per Functional Resident: This is calculated for the **Existing 2000** column as:

$$[(\text{FACILITY SQ. FT.}) / (\text{24/7 FUNCTIONAL POPULATION}_{2000})]$$

Adopted Facility Sq. Ft. Per Functional Resident: This is the locally adopted LOS standard for facility space per 24/7 functional resident.

Facility Sq. Ft. Needed to Meet LOS: This is calculated for both the **Existing 2000** and **Needed 2020** columns as:

Table 6-1
Uniformed Sworn Personnel for Public Safety Facilities, 1992 and 2003

Population Category	Police Personnel Per 1,000 Residents[a] 1992	Fire/EMS Personnel Per 1,000 Residents[a] 1992	Police Personnel Per 1,000 Residents[b] 2003	Fire/EMS Personnel Per 1,000 Residents[b] 2003
All Cities	2.65	1.63	1.98	1.48
1,000,000	4.01	1.56	3.10	1.33
500,000-1,000,000	3.01	1.67	2.37	1.69
250,000-499,999	2.90	1.76	2.19	1.42
100,000-249,999	2.43	1.66	1.87	1.41
50,000-99,999	2.37	1.65	1.75	1.35
25,000-49,999	2.29	1.66	1.86	1.53
10,000-24,999	2.32	1.47	2.05	1.51
New England	2.49	2.23	1.89	1.67
Mid-Atlantic	2.98	1.84	1.90	1.43
East North Central	2.78	1.55	1.86	1.39
West North Central	1.97	1.27	1.69	1.07
South Atlantic	3.47	2.03	2.61	1.94
East South Central	2.63	2.14	2.62	2.26
West South Central	2.3	1.6	2.08	1.60
Mountain	2.59	1.44	1.94	1.20
Pacific	2.32	1.28	1.43	1.02

a. International City/County Management Association (1992), Table 3/4.
b. International City/County Management Association (2003), Table 3/3.

Table 6-2
Fire/Emergency Medical Services Facility Space and Land-Use Needs

Measure	Existing 2000	Needed 2020
24/7 Functional Population	519,671	715,691
Facility Space		
Facility Sq. Ft.	70,000	
Sq. Ft. Per Functional Resident	0.13	
Adopted Facility Sq. Ft. Per Functional Resident	0.40	
Facility Sq. Ft. Needed to Meet LOS	207,869	286,276
Additional Facility Sq. Ft. Needed to Meet LOS	137,869	216,276
Land Area		
Land Area Acres	10.00	
Land Area Sq. Ft.	435,600	
Land Area Sq. Ft. Per Functional Resident	0.84	
Adopted Land Area Sq. Ft. Per Functional Resident	2.50	
Land Area Sq. Ft. Needed to Meet LOS	1,299,178	1,789,227
Land Area Acres Needed to Meet LOS	29.83	41.08
Additional Land Area Sq. Ft. Needed to Meet LOS	863,578	1,353,627
Additional Acres Needed to Meet LOS	19.83	31.08

Table 6-3
Police Facility Space and Land-Use Needs

Measure	Existing 2000	Needed 2020
24/7 Functional Population	519,671	715,691
Facility Space		
Facility Sq. Ft.	100,000	
Sq. Ft. Per Functional Resident	0.19	
Adopted Facility Sq. Ft. Per Functional Resident	0.65	
Facility Sq. Ft. Needed to Meet LOS	337,786	465,199
Additional Facility Sq. Ft. Needed to Meet LOS	237,786	365,199
Land Area		
Land Area Acres	15.00	
Land Area Sq. Ft.	653,400	
Land Area Sq. Ft. Per Functional Resident	1.26	
Adopted Land Area Sq. Ft. Per Functional Resident	3.00	
Land Area Sq. Ft. Needed to Meet LOS	1,559,014	2,147,073
Land Area Acres Needed to Meet LOS	35.79	49.29
Additional Land Area Sq. Ft. Needed to Meet LOS	905,614	1,493,673
Additional Acres Needed to Meet LOS	20.79	34.29

Table 6-4
Jail and Detention Facility Space and Land-Use Needs

Measure	Existing 2000	Needed 2020
24/7 Functional Population	519,671	715,691
Maximum Security Facilities		
Beds	500	
Beds Per 1,000 Functional Residents	0.96	
Adopted Beds Per 1,000 Functional Residents	3.00	
Beds Needed to Meet LOS	1,559	2,147
Additional Beds Needed to Meet LOS	1,059	1,647
Minimum Security Facilities		
Beds	500	
Beds Per 1,000 Functional Residents	0.96	
Adopted Beds Per 1,000 Functional Residents	3.00	
Beds Needed to Meet LOS	1,559	2,147
Additional Beds Needed to Meet LOS	1,059	1,647
Juvenile Detention Facilities		
Beds	200	
Beds Per 1,000 Functional Residents	0.38	
Adopted Beds Per 1,000 Functional Residents	1.50	
Beds Needed to Meet LOS	780	1,074
Additional Beds Needed to Meet LOS	580	874
Land Area		
Land Area Acres	20.00	
Land Area Sq. Ft.	871,200	
Land Area Sq. Ft. Per Functional Resident	1.68	
Adopted Land Area Sq. Ft. Per Functional Resident	6.00	
Land Area Sq. Ft. Needed to Meet LOS	3,118,028	4,294,146
Land Area Acres Needed to Meet LOS	71.58	98.58
Additional Land Area Sq. Ft. Needed to Meet LOS	2,246,828	3,422,946
Additional Acres Needed to Meet LOS	51.58	78.58

$$[(24/7 \text{ FUNCTIONAL POPULATION}_{2000, 2020})$$
$$\times (\text{ADOPTED FACILITY SQ. FT. PER FUNCTIONAL RESIDENT})]$$

Additional Facility Sq. Ft. Needed to Meet LOS: This is calculated for the **Existing 2000** column using worksheet programming formulas as:

$$@\text{IF(FACILITY SQ. FT. NEEDED TO MEET LOS}$$
$$> \text{FACILITY SQ. FT., FACILITY SQ. FT.}$$
$$\text{NEEDED TO MEET LOS} - \text{FACILITY SQ. FT., 0)}$$

which means that if the existing supply of facility square feet is more than that needed to meet LOS, there is no existing deficiency, and for the **Needed 2020** column as:

$$[(\text{FACILITY SQ. FT. NEEDED TO MEET LOS}_{2020}) - (\text{FACILITY SQ. FT.})]$$

Land Area Acres: This is the total land area in acres used by the respective facilities based on data from local officials. It does not need to include unused land area.

Land Area Sq. Ft.: This is **Land Area Acres** times 43,560 square feet.

Land Area Sq. Ft. Per Functional Resident: This is calculated for the **Existing 2000** column as:

$$[(\text{LAND AREA SQ. FT.}) / (24/7 \text{ FUNCTIONAL POPULATION}_{2000})]$$

Adopted Land Area Sq. Ft. Per Functional Resident: This is the locally adopted LOS standard for facility land area per 24/7 functional resident.

Land Area Sq. Ft. Needed to Meet LOS: This is calculated for both the **Existing 2000** and **Needed 2020** columns as:

$$[(24/7 \text{ FUNCTIONAL POPULATION}_{2000, 2020})$$
$$\times (\text{ADOPTED LAND AREA SQ. FT. PER FUNCTIONAL RESIDENT})]$$

Land Area Acres Needed to Meet LOS: This is **Land Area Sq. Ft. Needed to Meet LOS** divided by 43,560 square feet. In the **Needed 2020** column, this is the total net land area that needs to be accommodated in the comprehensive plan for these facilities.

Additional Land Area Sq. Ft. Needed to Meet LOS: This is calculated for the **Existing 2000** column using worksheet programming formulas as:

$$\text{@IF(LAND AREA SQ. FT. NEEDED TO MEET LOS} > \text{LAND AREA SQ. FT., LAND AREA SQ. FT. NEEDED TO MEET LOS} - \text{LAND AREA SQ. FT., 0)}$$

which means that, if the existing supply of land area square feet is more than that needed to meet LOS, there is no existing deficiency, and for the **Needed 2020** column as:

$$[(\text{LAND AREA SQ. FT. NEEDED TO MEET LOS}_{2020}) - (\text{LAND AREA SQ. FT.})]$$

Additional Acres Needed to Meet LOS: This is **Additional Land Area Sq. Ft. Needed to Meet LOS** divided by 43,560 square feet. In the **Existing 2000** column, this figure shows the land area needed to meet the adopted LOS. In the **Needed 2020** column, this figure reflects the additional land area needed to accommodate growth from 2000 to 2020 less the existing supply in 2000.

In Table 6-4, similar calculations are made only substituting beds for facility square feet. If data are available to the user, square feet could be used instead of beds, or in addition to beds.

The result of these calculations is an estimate of future public safety facility space and land-use needs.

GENERAL GOVERNMENT ADMINISTRATION, COMMUNITY CENTER, RECREATION CENTER, AND LIBRARY FACILITIES

The facility and land-use needs of general government administration tend to expand with increasing community size, until about 1 million residents where it begins to fall, as shown in Table 6-5 (similar tabulation of more recent data has not been made). However, these figures include workers employed in community services for which separate facility and associated land-use needs are estimated elsewhere. For this reason, local planners in Yukon County have inventoried general government facility and associated land-use needs after first accounting for facility and land-use needs already considered. Local planners then worked with elected officials to formalize an LOS standard for general government administration facility and associated land-use expansion through the planning horizon.

Table 6-5
Observed Government Employment Nationwide

Population Range	Full-Time Employees Per 1,000 Population[a]
< 50,000	10.9
50,000-99,999	10.3
100,000-199,999	11.2
200,000-299,999	11.6
300,000-499,999	14.1
500,000-999,999	19.7
1,000,000	15.0

a. U.S. Bureau of the Census (March 1988). Figures are for total, full-time municipal employees.

Like public safety facilities, there are no national standards for general government administration facilities or community centers (focusing on social service delivery and enrichment programs), nor are there any comparative statistics available across different communities. Lacking benchmarks, Yukon County planners inventoried such facilities to establish current LOS standards and worked with officials to decide an appropriate

LOS standard to guide future facility planning. These results are reported in Table 6-6 for general government facilities, Table 6-7 for community centers, and Table 6-8 for recreation centers. The calculations are the same as those for public safety facilities (except that daytime functional population from Table 5-3 is used as the basis for LOS standards for community and recreation centers).

Table 6-6
General Government Facility Space and Land-Use Needs

Measure	Existing 2000	Needed 2020
24/7 Functional Population	519,671	749,535
Facility Space		
Facility Sq. Ft.	250,000	
Sq. Ft. Per Functional Resident	0.48	
Adopted Facility Sq. Ft. Per Functional Resident	0.90	
Facility Sq. Ft. Needed to Meet LOS	467,704	674,582
Additional Facility Sq. Ft. Needed to Meet LOS	217,704	424,582
Land Area		
Land Area Acres	20.00	
Land Area Sq. Ft.	871,200	
Land Area Sq. Ft. Per Functional Resident	1.68	
Adopted Land Area Sq. Ft. Per Functional Resident	3.50	
Land Area Sq. Ft. Needed to Meet LOS	1,818,849	2,623,373
Land Area Acres Needed to Meet LOS	41.76	60.22
Additional Land Area Sq. Ft. Needed to Meet LOS	947,659	1,752,173
Additional Acres Needed to Meet LOS	21.76	40.22

Table 6-7
Community Center Space and Land-Use Needs

Measure	Existing 2000	Needed 2020
Daytime Functional Population	530,089	749,535
Facility Space		
Facility Sq. Ft.	200,000	
Sq. Ft. Per Functional Resident	0.38	
Adopted Facility Sq. Ft. Per Functional Resident	0.75	
Facility Sq. Ft. Needed to Meet LOS	397,567	562,151
Additional Facility Sq. Ft. Needed to Meet LOS	197,567	362,151
Land Area		
Land Area Acres	25.00	
Land Area Sq. Ft.	1,089,000	
Land Area Sq. Ft. Per Functional Resident	2.05	
Adopted Land Area Sq. Ft. Per Functional Resident	4.00	
Land Area Sq. Ft. Needed to Meet LOS	2,120,355	2,998,141
Land Area Acres Needed to Meet LOS	48.68	68.83
Additional Land Area Sq. Ft. Needed to Meet LOS	1,031,355	1,909,141
Additional Acres Needed to Meet LOS	23.68	43.83

Fortunately for libraries, there are some generally recommended standards to guide facility planning. Some nationally recommended standards are reported in Table 6-9. There are also some national benchmarks. In 1996, there were 2.8 books per capita in public libraries throughout the nation with a range of 5.2 in Maine to 1.5 in Tennessee (National Center for Education Statistics, March 2001). Many states have their own benchmarks. Florida, for example, ranks libraries by a number of factors such as books per capita (1.8 in 2001 with a range of 3.6 in Alachua County to 0.6 in Hialeah among large

service areas) and square feet of space per capita (0.4 in 2001 with a range of 0.7 in Brevard County to less than 0.2 in Hialeah among large service areas).[2] Many states have their own standards that guide state library funding support. In the case of Yukon County, planners inventoried library facilities for their holdings, building space, and land area, and worked with library officials to establish LOS standards to guide library facility planning. This is reported in Table 6-10 and is calculated using the same approach described above for other facilities.

Table 6-8
Recreation Center Space and Land-Use Needs

Measure	Existing 2000	Needed 2020
Daytime Functional Population	530,089	749,535
Facility Space		
Facility Sq. Ft.	150,000	
Sq. Ft. Per Functional Resident	0.28	
Adopted Facility Sq. Ft. Per Functional Resident	0.55	
Facility Sq. Ft. Needed to Meet LOS	291,549	412,244
Additional Facility Sq. Ft. Needed to Meet LOS	141,549	262,244
Land Area		
Land Area Acres	15.00	
Land Area Sq. Ft.	653,400	
Land Area Sq. Ft. Per Functional Resident	1.23	
Adopted Land Area Sq. Ft. Per Functional Resident	2.40	
Land Area Sq. Ft. Needed to Meet LOS	1,272,213	1,798,885
Land Area Acres Needed to Meet LOS	29.21	41.30
Additional Land Area Sq. Ft. Needed to Meet LOS	618,813	1,145,485
Additional Acres Needed to Meet LOS	14.21	26.30

Table 6-9
Recommended Library Facility Standards

Community Population	Public Library Association[a]		Wheeler & Goldhor[b]	
	Building Sq. Ft. Per Capita	Acres Per 1,000 Residents[c]	Building Sq. Ft. Per Capita	Acres Per 1,000 Residents[c]
Under 25,000	0.6	0.06		
Under 10,000			0.70–0.80	0.07
10,000–34,999			0.60–0.65	0.06
35,000–99,999			0.50–0.60	0.05
100,000–199,999			0.40–0.50	0.04
200,000–499,999			0.35–0.40	0.03
500,000			0.3	0.03

a. Public Library Association (1970).
b. Wheeler and Goldhor (1981).
c. Assuming FAR of 0.25.

Table 6-10
Library Facility Space and Land-Use Needs

Measure	Existing 2000	Needed 2020
Daytime Functional Population	530,089	749,535
Volumes		
Volumes	500,000	
LOS Per Functional Resident	0.94	
Adopted LOS Per Functional Resident	2.00	
Volumes Needed to Meet LOS	1,060,178	1,499,071
Additional Volumes Needed to Meet LOS	560,178	999,071
Facility Space		
Facility Sq. Ft.	150,000	
Sq. Ft. Per Functional Resident	0.28	
Adopted Facility Sq. Ft. Per Functional Resident	0.60	
Facility Sq. Ft. Needed to Meet LOS	318,053	449,721
Additional Facility Sq. Ft. Needed to Meet LOS	168,053	299,721
Land Area		
Land Area Acres	12.00	
Land Area Sq. Ft.	522,720	
Land Area Sq. Ft. Per Functional Resident	0.99	
Adopted Land Area Sq. Ft. Per Functional Resident	2.00	
Land Area Sq. Ft. Needed to Meet LOS	1,060,178	1,499,071
Land Area Acres Needed to Meet LOS	24.34	34.41
Additional Land Area Sq. Ft. Needed to Meet LOS	537,458	976,351
Additional Acres Needed to Meet LOS	12.34	22.41

MAJOR COMMUNITY CENTERS

Some facilities are not strictly sensitive to changes in population (such as major league stadia, opera houses, and museums) and should still be counted. In Table 6-11, Yukon County's major community facilities are inventoried and future plans assembled to the extent they are known. Strictly speaking, there are no LOS standards involved, although equating facility size per weighted population can be helpful when benchmarking against other similar communities. We will now review the formulas and implications of Table 6-11.

Daytime Functional Population: This comes from Table 5-3 for 2000 and 2020.

Existing Acres 2000, Existing Facility Sq. Ft. 2000, Planned Acres 2020, and **Planned Facility Sq. Ft. 2020:** These are from local officials for each major community facility. The user may wish to add more major community facilities or relabel those noted here to reflect local conditions.

Existing Acres Per 1,000 Functional Residents and **Planned Acres Per 1,000 Functional Residents:** Calculated as

$$[(\text{EXISTING ACRES 2000}) / (\text{DAYTIME FUNCTIONAL POPULATION}_{2000, 2020})] \times 1{,}000$$

and

$$[(\text{PLANNED ACRES 2020}) / (\text{DAYTIME FUNCTIONAL POPULATION}_{2000, 2020})] \times 1{,}000$$

Existing Facility Sq. Ft. Per Functional Resident and **Planned Facility Sq. Ft. Per Functional Resident:** Calculated as

Table 6-11
Major Community Facility Space and Land-Use Needs

Facility or Measure	Existing Acres 2000	Existing Acres Per 1,000 Functional Residents	Existing Facility Sq. Ft. 2000	Existing Facility Sq. Ft. Per Functional Resident	Planned Acres 2020	Planned Acres Per 1,000 Functional Residents	Planned Facility Sq. Ft. 2020	Planned Facility Sq. Ft. Per Functional Resident
Daytime Functional Population		530,089		530,089		749,535		749,535
Convention Centers	20.00	0.0377	200,000	0.3773	40.00	0.0534	400,000	0.5337
Public Assembly Halls	12.00	0.0226	175,000	0.3301	25.00	0.0334	350,000	0.4670
Other Major Facilities	10.00	0.0189	75,000	0.1415	20.00	0.0267	175,000	0.2335
Total	42.00		450,000		85.00		925,000	

$$[(\text{EXISTING FACILITY SQ. FT. 2000}) / (\text{DAYTIME FUNCTIONAL POPULATION}_{2000, \, 2020})]$$

and

$$[(\text{PLANNED FACILITY SQ. FT. 2020}) / (\text{DAYTIME FUNCTIONAL POPULATION}_{2000, \, 2020})]$$

PARKS AND RECREATIONAL FACILITIES

Parks and recreational facility needs are estimated for local and regional parks, land-extensive uses such as golf courses and greenbelts, and recreation centers. For most of these land uses, LOS standards are recommended by the National Recreation and Parks Association (NRPA), although it advises that the standards are merely advisory and subject to local considerations. NRPA recommendations are adapted for consideration by Yukon County (Table 6-12). These standards apply to publicly owned facilities and are additive to any privately owned

Table 6-12
Recommended Standards for Selected Recreational Facilities

Facility	Acres Per 1,000 Residents[a]
Neighborhood Park	2.00[b]
Community Park	6.50[c]
Regional Park	7.50[d]
Recreation Center	1.50[e]
Golf Course	11.5[f]
Total	

a. Figures adapted from NRPA (1983), unless otherwise noted. The NRPA recommends LOS standards for many more kinds of recreation needs.
b. Midpoint of NRPA's recommended ranges for mini-park and neighborhood park acres per 1,000 residents, rounded to nearest half acre.
c. Midpoint of NRPA's recommended range for community park acres per 1,000 residents.
d. Midpoint of NRPA's recommended range for regional/metropolitan park acres per 1,000 residents.
e. Midpoint of NRPA's recommended range for public swimming pools, multiple recreation courts, and handball courts per 1,000 residents, including adjustment for gross area of enclosed space and rounded to nearest half acre.
f. Author's interpretation of data is number of golfers, golf course size, and percent of new golf courses publicly owned from American Society of Golf Course Architects (circa 1995).

Table 6-13
Park Standards of Selected Cities, Urban Counties, and States, Minimum Acres Per 1,000 Residents

Jurisdiction	Mini-Park	Neighborhood	Community	Regional Acres	Other	Total Acres
Dallas, TX		1.00	1.50	1.50		4.00
Des Moines, IA		1.25	1.25	5.00		7.50
Greensboro, NC	1.50	1.50	2.50	7.50		13.00
Kansas City, MO		6.00	14.00	15.00	20.00	55.00
Los Angeles, CA		2.00	3.33			5.33
Baltimore Co., MD	0.50	5.00	21.00			26.50
Fulton Co., GA		1.00	5.00	5.00		11.00
Hillsborough Co., FL		1.60	1.80	20.00		23.40
Salt Lake Co., UT		1.00	5.00			6.00
Florida	0.50	2.00	2.00	5.00	20.00	29.50
Michigan (Urban)	1.00	2.00	2.50		0.75	6.75
South Carolina	1.50	1.50	3.00	7.00	10.00	33.00

Source: Information collected by the author through the 1990s.

facilities. Table 6-13 offers comparative park standards for selected cities, urban counties, and states.

Yukon County planners inventoried these kinds of facilities to establish current LOS conditions. For parks, recreation centers, and some land-extensive uses, existing LOS conditions are used as a guide for estimating future needs. LOS standards are established in cooperation with park and recreation officials and applied in Table 6-12 for recreation centers, and in Table 6-14 for parks and open space.

The approach to calculating needs for recreation centers is the same used for the facilities reviewed above, except that day-time functional population is used as the LOS basis. For parks and open space, calculations of need are based on the following:

Daytime Functional Population: This comes from Table 5-3 for 2000 and 2020.

Existing Acres 2000: This is from local officials for each parks and open space category. The user may wish to add more parks and open space categories or relabel those noted here to reflect local conditions.

Existing Acres Per 1,000 Functional Residents: Calculated as:

$$[(\text{EXISTING ACRES 2000}) / (\text{DAYTIME FUNCTIONAL POPULATION}_{2000})] \times 1{,}000$$

Table 6-14
Parks and Open Space Land-Use Needs

Facility or Measure	Existing Acres 2000	Existing Acres Per 1,000 Functional Residents	LOS Acres Per 1,000 Functional Residents	Existing Demand	Excess (Deficient) Supply	Acres Needed or Planned 2020	New Acres Needed 2020
Daytime Functional Population		530,089		530,089		749,535	
Neighborhood Park	300.00	0.5659	1.25	662.61	(362.61)	936.92	636.92
Community Park	1,200.00	2.2638	5.50	2,915.49	(1,715.49)	4,122.44	2,922.44
Regional Park	1,400.00	2.6411	5.00	2,650.44	(1,250.44)	3,747.68	2,347.68
Subtotal Park	2,900.00			6,228.54	(3,328.54)	8,807.04	5,907.04
Golf Course, Public	900.00	1.6978	4.50	2,385.40	(1,485.40)	3,372.91	2,472.91
Special Use	150.00	0.2830				400.00	250.00
Conservancy/Greenbelt	500.00	0.9432				1,000.00	500.00
Subtotal Open Space	1,550.00			2,385.40		4,772.91	3,222.91
Total	4,450.00			8,613.94	(3,328.54)	13,579.95	9,129.95

LOS Acres Per 1,000 Functional Residents: This is the locally adopted LOS standard for parks and open space. For large or special purpose land uses such as greenbelts, conservation areas, or other special use areas, LOS policies are not practical, but the figures are used to estimate acres of such land per 1,000 daytime functional residents in Table 6-11.

Existing Demand: This is calculated for only those parks and open space uses that have an adopted LOS standard as:

[(LOS ACRES PER 1,000 FUNCTIONAL RESIDENTS)
× (DAYTIME FUNCTIONAL POPULATION$_{2000}$)] × 1,000

Excess (Deficient) Supply: This indicates the extent to which existing parks and open space uses for which LOS standards have been established are sufficient. If they are not, there is an existing deficiency. It is calculated as:

[(EXISTING ACRES 2000) − (EXISTING DEMAND)]

Acres Needed or Planned 2020: This is

[(LOS ACRES PER 1,000 FUNCTIONAL RESIDENTS)
× (DAYTIME FUNCTIONAL POPULATION$_{2020}$)] × 1,000

for those parks and open space uses for which LOS standards have been adopted or otherwise planned based on information from parks and open space officials.

New Acres Needed 2020: This is simply

[(ACRES NEEDED OR PLANNED 2020) − (EXISTING ACRES 2000)]

for each parks and open space use category.

PRIVATE LAND-EXTENSIVE LAND USES

Private land-extensive land uses include such features as golf courses, polo fields, and hunting plantations. They are usually immune from future demand assessment because locally knowledgeable people do not know the nature of future demand. Unless locally knowledgeable sources exist, the user is left to inventory existing conditions and project them into the future, as is done in Table 6-15 based on the following calculation procedure:

Daytime Functional Population: This comes from Table 5-3 for 2000 and 2020.

Existing Acres 2000: This is from local people knowledgeable of private land-extensive land uses or the property assessor. This information may also come from GIS databases.

Existing Acres Per 1,000 Functional Residents: Calculated for each private land-extensive use as:

$$[(\text{EXISTING ACRES 2000}) / (\text{DAYTIME FUNCTIONAL POPULATION}_{2000})] \times 1000$$

Table 6-15
Private Land-Extensive Land-Use Needs

Facility	Existing Acres 2000	Existing Acres Per 1,000 Functional Residents	Acres Needed 2020	New Acres Needed 2020
Daytime Functional Population		530,089	749,535	
Private Golf Courses	1,200.00	2.2638	1,696.78	496.78
Other Private Land-Related	900.00	1.6978	1,272.58	372.58
Total Private Facilities	2,100.00		2,969.36	869.36

Acres Needed 2020: Calculated for each private land-extensive use as:

$$[(\text{EXISTING ACRES PER 1,000 FUNCTIONAL RESIDENTS}) \times (\text{DAYTIME FUNCTIONAL POPULATION}_{2020})]$$

New Acres Needed 2020: Calculated as

$$[(\text{ACRES NEEDED 2020}) - (\text{EXISTING ACRES 2000})]$$

MISCELLANEOUS SUPPORT FACILITIES

Miscellaneous support facilities usually include land-extensive activities such as storage yards, shops with large repair areas, public detention ponds, and wastewater treatment ponds and lagoons. In most cases, such facilities are managed by the community public works department. There is often little relationship between population and the amount of land allocated to these kinds of activities. Users estimating future land-use needs for these facilities must determine from public works officials what their long-term plans require. This usually means acquainting public officials with population, employment, and functional population projections. Quite often, local public works officials have spent little time considering the nature of future land-use needs for these kinds of facilities.

Table 6-16 shows the result of these considerations for Yukon County. The calculation for **Acres Per 1,000 Functional Residents** is:

$$(\text{24/7 FUNCTIONAL POPULATION}_{2000,\ 2020} / \text{TOTAL ACRES}_{2000,\ 2020})$$

Table 6-16
Miscellaneous Support Facility Land-Use Needs

Facility, Land Area	Existing Acres 2000	Planned Additions 2020	Total Acres Planned 2020
Fire Storage, Drill, Practice Yards	45.00	100.00	145.00
Public Works Equipment, Storage Yards	10.00	25.00	35.00
Repair Shops and Associated Yards	10.00	10.00	20.00
Publicly Owned Drainage Ponds	125.00	300.00	425.00
Sand, Gravel, Soil Storage Yards	5.00	15.00	20.00
Landfills	120.00	200.00	320.00
Resource Recovery Facilities	3.00	5.00	8.00
Airports	960.00	1,400.00	2,360.00
Other Public Land in Inventory	15.00	20.00	35.00
Total Acres	1,293.00	2,075.00	3,368.00
24/7 Functional Population	519,671	715,691	
Acres Per 1,000 Functional Residents	2.49	2.90	

RELIGIOUS FACILITIES

Communities vary widely in their use of land for religious facilities. There are no national standards guiding the estimation of land-use needs for religious facilities. As a rule of thumb, developers anticipate a need for one church for about every 2,000 residents.[3] In general, a church of average size requires about 3 acres of land (Hoover and Perry, undated). These two factors suggest a planning standard for long-range, land-use planning purposes of about 1.50 acres per 1,000 residents. Table 6-17 shows the inventory of existing religious facilities and the estimate of future land-use needs for these facilities developed by Yukon County planners. The calculations are as follows:

Permanent Population: This information comes from Table 2-2. This excludes group care and hotel/motel residents. Although many use religious facilities, group care residents often receive services within their residential centers.

Religious Facility Acres: This is based on data from local property tax assessor files.

Table 6-17
Religious Facility Land-Use Needs

Measure	Existing 2000	Needed 2020
Permanent Population	548,668	720,810
Religious Facility Acres	450.00	
Land Area Sq. Ft. Per Permanent Population	35.73	
Religious Facility Acres Needed		591.19
New Acres Needed		141.19

Land Area Sq. Ft. Per Permanent Population: Calculated as

$$[(\text{RELIGIOUS FACILITY ACRES} \times 43{,}560 \text{ SQ. FT. PER ACRE}) / (\text{PERMANENT POPULATION}_{2000})]$$

Religious Facility Acres Needed: Calculated as

$$[(\text{LAND AREA SQ. FT. PER PERMANENT POPULATION}) \times (\text{PERMANENT POPULATION}_{2020}) / (43{,}560 \text{ SQ. FT. PER ACRE})]$$

New Acres Needed: Calculated as

$$[(\text{RELIGIOUS FACILITY ACRES NEEDED} - \text{RELIGIOUS FACILITY ACRES})]$$

SYNTHESIS OF PUBLIC FACILITY SPACE AND LAND-USE NEEDS

Table 6-18 synthesizes public facility space and land-use needs to 2020. This table includes seven numerical columns. The first two summarize and total existing and needed public facility space (or beds) for fire/EMS, police, jail and detention, general government, community center, and recreation center facilities. The next two summarize existing and needed land area for all facilities covered in this chapter. The fifth column shows the new acres needed to be added by the community over the planning horizon; this is calculated as the difference between acres needed in 2020 and acres existing in 2000. The sixth col-

umn reports the assumed gross land adjustment factor for each facility. This adjustment factor helps to account for rights-of-way and utility easements not otherwise addressed in the book. The last column reports gross acres that the comprehensive plan needs to include.

For each facility, gross acres are calculated as:

$$[(\text{ACRES NEEDED 2020}) / (1 / \text{GROSS LAND ADJUSTMENT FACTOR})] + (\text{ACRES NEEDED 2020})$$

All columns are summed at the bottom.

Table 6-18
Summary Public Facility Space and Land-Use Needs

Facility	Existing Space (Beds)	Needed or Planned Space (Beds)	Existing Acres 2000	Acres Needed 2020	New Acres Needed	Gross Land Adjustment Factor	Gross Acres Needed
Public Safety Facilities							
Fire/EMS Facilities	70,000	286,276	10.00	31.08	21.08	25.00%	38.84
Police Facilities	100,000	465,199	15.00	34.29	19.29	25.00%	42.86
Jail and Detention Facilities	1,200	5,368	20.00	98.58	78.58	25.00%	123.23
Government and Leisure Facilities							
General Government Facilities	250,000	674,582	20.00	60.22	40.22	25.00%	75.28
Community Centers	200,000	562,151	25.00	41.30	16.30	25.00%	51.62
Library Facilities	150,000	449,721	12.00	34.41	22.41	25.00%	43.02
Recreation Centers	200,000	412,244	15.00	41.30	26.30	25.00%	51.62

Table 6-18 (continued)
Summary Public Facility Space and Land-Use Needs

Facility	Existing Space (Beds)	Needed or Planned Space (Beds)	Existing Acres 2000	Acres Needed 2020	New Acres Needed	Gross Land Adjustment Factor	Gross Acres Needed
Major Community Facilities							
Convention Centers	200,000	400,000	20.00	40.00	20.00	15.00%	46.00
Public Assembly Halls	175,000	350,000	12.00	25.00	13.00	15.00%	28.75
Other Major Facilities	75,000	175,000	10.00	20.00	10.00	15.00%	23.00
Parks and Open Space							
Neighborhood Parks			300.00	936.92	636.92	20.00%	1,124.30
Community Parks			1,200.00	4,122.44	2,922.44	25.00%	5,153.05
Regional Parks			1,400.00	3,747.68	2,347.68	4.00%	3,897.58
Public Golf Courses			900.00	3,372.91	2,472.91	4.00%	3,507.83
Special Use			150.00	400.00	250.00	4.00%	416.00
Conservancy/Greenbelt			500.00	1,000.00	500.00	4.00%	1,040.00
Private Land-Extensive Land Uses							
Private Golf Courses			1,200.00	1,696.78	496.78	4.00%	1,764.65
Other Private Land-Related			900.00	1,272.58	372.58	4.00%	1,323.49
Miscellaneous Support							
Fire Storage, Drill, Practice Yards			45.00	145.00	100.00	15.00%	166.75
Public Works Equipment, Storage Yards			10.00	35.00	25.00	15.00%	40.25
Repair Shops and Associated Yards			10.00	20.00	10.00	15.00%	23.00
Publicly Owned Drainage Ponds			125.00	425.00	300.00	10.00%	467.50
Sand, Gravel, Soil Storage Yards			5.00	20.00	15.00	10.00%	22.00
Landfills			120.00	320.00	200.00	10.00%	352.00
Resource Recovery Facilities			3.00	8.00	5.00	20.00%	9.60
Airports			960.00	2,360.00	1,400.00	5.00%	2,478.00
Other Public Land in Inventory			15.00	35.00	20.00	20.00%	42.00

Table 6-18 (continued)
Summary Public Facility Space and Land-Use Needs

Facility	Existing Space (Beds)	Needed or Planned Space (Beds)	Existing Acres 2000	Acres Needed 2020	New Acres Needed	Gross Land Adjustment Factor	Gross Acres Needed
Religious							
Religious Facilities			450.00	591.19	141.19	25.00%	738.98
Summary							
Total Land Acres, Acres			8,452.00	20,934.67	12,482.67	10.30%	23,091.20
Total Space, Sq. Ft.	1,420,000	3,775,174					
Total Beds	1,200	5,368					

SUMMARY COMMENTS

Many and perhaps most communities do not rationally estimate future facility space and land-use needs. The principle reason is that they do not evaluate current conditions, debate desirable LOS standards, or plan to meet future facility space and land-use needs. Many operate in a crisis mode when needs become apparent and, by that time, appropriate sites for facilities may not exist. The method of assessing current conditions and estimating needs based on desirable LOS standards presented in this chapter is straightforward and may help communities rationally chart their future facility needs.

NOTES

1. See Coleman and Granito (1988), Drabek and Hoetmer (1991), and Garmire (1982) for reviews of fire, emergency medical, and policy facility planning, respectively.
2. Information from http://librarydata.dos.state.fl.us/StatsRankings/2001.
3. Adapted from the ULI (1968, 166) and Hoover and Perry (undated).

REFERENCES

American Society of Golf Course Architects. *Golf Course Development Planning Guide.* Chicago, IL: American Society of Golf Course Architects, circa 1995.

Coleman, Ronny J. and John A. Granito, ed. *Managing Fire Services—Second Edition.* Washington, DC: International City/County Management Association, 1988.

Drabek, Thomas E. and Gerard J. Hoetmer. *Emergency Management: Principles and Practice for Local Government.* Washington, DC: International City/County Management Association, 1991.

Garmire, Bernard. *Local Government Police Management—Second Edition.* Washington, DC: International City/County Management Association, 1982.

Hoover, Robert C. and Everett L. Perry. *Church and City Planning.* New York, NY: Bureau of Research and Survey, National Council of Churches of Christ in the U.S.A., undated.

International City/County Management Association. *The Municipal Year Book 2003.* Washington, DC: International City/County Management Association, 2003.

___. *The Municipal Year Book 1992.* Washington, DC: International City/County Management Association, 1992.

National Center for Education Statistics. *Public Library Trends Analysis, Fiscal Years 1992-1996—Statistical Analysis Report.* Washington, DC: U.S. Department of Education, Office of Educational Research and Improvement, March 2001.

National Recreation and Parks Association, *Recreation, Park and Open Space Standards and Guidelines.* Alexandria, VA: National Recreation and Parks Association, 1983.

Public Library Association. *Interim Standards for Small Public Libraries.* Chicago, IL: American Library Association, 1970.

Urban Land Institute. *The Community Builders Handbook.* Washington, DC: Urban Land Institute, 1968.

U.S. Bureau of the Census. *City Employment in 1986*, GE-86-No. 2. Washington, DC: U.S. Department of Commerce, March 1988.

Wheeler, Joseph L. and Herbert Goldhor. *Fact Book of the American Public Library.* Champaign, IL: University of Illinois School of Library and Information Science, 1981.

7

Educational Facility Space and Land-Use Needs

OVERVIEW

Educational facilities include publicly and privately operated day-care centers, nursery schools, kindergartens, elementary schools, secondary schools, technical schools, junior and senior colleges, and universities. Each state establishes its own standards for public elementary and secondary schools. There is a wide range of standards used by the states to establish school size. Table 7-1 reviews standards for land area by school type for 48 of the 50 states.

An important planning consideration is the effect of changing student generation rates on the need, especially for elementary and secondary schools, both public and private. Table 7-2 shows trends in student generation rates from 1970 to 2020. Note that during those 50 years, student generation rates will have dropped by about half nationally. Figures will vary among communities, however, so localized estimates will be needed. They may be estimated from projections of population by age that are typically provided at the county level by state population centers, regional planning agencies, MPOs, and private data providers such as Woods and Poole Economics.

For many other kinds of educational facilities, there are few and even unclear relationships between population size and land area needed. This is especially true for senior colleges and universities, and for private schools because they have few, if any, state standards applicable to land area.

Note that only the most routine approach is used to estimate land-use and facility needs. Not considered is the growing role of charter schools in meeting local needs. If charter schools are becoming a significant local educational option, and if their land-use and facility needs are significantly different from main-line schools, then perhaps a new land-use category for educational facilities may need to be added by the user.

Table 7-1
New School Facility Land Area Requirements by State

State	Grades K-6	Grades K-8	Grades 7-8	Grades 7-9	Grades 9-12
Alabama		5 acres + 1 acre / 100 students	10 acres + 1 acre / 100 students		30 acres + 1 acre / 100 students
Alaska		10 acres + 1 acre / 100 students	20 acres + 1 acre / 100 students		30 acres + 1 acre / 100 students
Arizona		8-18 acres	18-36 acres		30-70 acres
Arkansas	No land area minimum	No land area minimum	No land area minimum	No land area minimum	No land area minimum
California	450 students = 9.6 acres 750 students = 13.8 acres 1,200 students = 17.6 acres		600 students = 17.4 acres 900 students = 20.9 acres 1,200 students = 23.1 acres		1,200 students = 33.5 acres 1,800 students = 44.5 acres 2,400 students = 52.7 acres
Colorado	No land area minimum	No land area minimum	No land area minimum	No land area minimum	No land area minimum
Delaware	No land area minimum	No land area minimum	No land area minimum	No land area minimum	No land area minimum
Florida	Site standards, no minimum	Site standards, no minimum	Site standards, no minimum	Site standards, no minimum	Site standards, no minimum
Georgia		5 acres + 1 acre / 100 students	12 acres + 1 acre / 100 students		20 acres + 1 acre / 100 students
Hawaii		No land area minimum	No land area minimum		No land area minimum
Idaho		5 acres + 1 acre / 100 students	300 students = 10 acres 400 students = 15 acres 500+ students = 20 + 1 / 100 students		< 400 students = 20 acres < 800 students = 25 acres 800+ students = 30 + 1 / 100 students
Illinois	5 acres + 1 acre / 100 students			15 acres + 1 acre / 100 students	20 acres + 1 acre / 100 students
Indiana	7 acres + 1 acre / 100 students	7 acres + 1 acre / 100 students	15 acres + 1 acre / 100 students	15 acres + 1 acre / 100 students	20 acres + 1 acre / 100 students
Iowa	No land area minimum	No land area minimum	No land area minimum	No land area minimum	No land area minimum
Kansas	No land area minimum	No land area minimum	No land area minimum	No land area minimum	No land area minimum
Kentucky	5 acres + 1 acre / 100 students	5 acres + 1 acre / 100 students	10 acres + 1 acre / 100 students	10 acres + 1 acre / 100 students	10 acres + 1 acre / 100 students
Louisiana	No land area minimum	No land area minimum	No land area minimum	No land area minimum	No land area minimum
Maine	5 acres + 1 acre / 100 students, minimum 20 acres + 1 acre / 100 students, maximum	5 acres + 1 acre / 100 students, minimum 20 acres + 1 acre / 100 students, maximum	10 acres + 1 acre / 100 students, minimum 25 acres + 1 acre / 100 students, maximum	10 acres + 1 acre / 100 students, minimum 25 acres + 1 acre / 100 students, maximum	15 acres + 1 acre / 100 students, minimum 30 acres + 1 acre / 100 students, maximum
Maryland	No land area minimum	No land area minimum	No land area minimum	No land area minimum	No land area minimum
Massachusetts	No land area minimum	No land area minimum	No land area minimum	No land area minimum	No land area minimum
Michigan	No land area minimum	No land area minimum	No land area minimum	No land area minimum	No land area minimum

Table 7-1 (continued)
New School Facility Land Area Requirements by State

State	Grades K-6	Grades K-8	Grades 7-8	Grades 7-9	Grades 9-12
Minnesota	10-15 acres + 1 / 100 students	25-35 acres + 1 / 100 students	25-35 acres + 1 / 100 students	25-35 acres + 1 / 100 students	K-12 <800 students, 35-40 acres + 1 / 100 students 2,000+ students, 60 acres + 1 / 100 students
Mississippi	5 acres + 1 acre / 100 students, minimum	5 acres + 1 acre / 100 students, minimum	5 acres + 1 acre / 100 students, minimum	5 acres + 1 acre / 100 students, minimum	15 acres + 1 acre / 100 students, minimum
Missouri	10 acres + 1 acre / 100 students, minimum	10 acres + 1 acre / 100 students, minimum	20 acres + 1 acre / 100 students, minimum	20 acres + 1 acre / 100 students, minimum	30 acres + 1 acre / 100 students, minimum
Montana	No land area minimum	No land area minimum	No land area minimum	No land area minimum	No land area minimum
Nebraska	No land area minimum	No land area minimum	No land area minimum	No land area minimum	No land area minimum
Nevada	No land area minimum	No land area minimum	No land area minimum	No land area minimum	No land area minimum
New Hampshire	5 acres + 1 acre / 100 students	5 acres + 1 acre / 100 students	10 acres + 1 acre / 100 students	10 acres + 1 acre / 100 students	15 acres + 1 acre / 100 students
New Jersey	No land area minimum	No land area minimum	No land area minimum	No land area minimum	No land area minimum
New Mexico	No land area minimum	No land area minimum	No land area minimum	No land area minimum	No land area minimum
New York	3 acres + 1 acre / 100 students	3 acres + 1 acre / 100 students	3 acres + 1 acre / 100 students	3 acres + 1 acre / 100 students	10 acres + 1 acre / 100 students
North Carolina	10 acres + 1 acre / 100 students		15 acres + 1 acre / 100 students		30 acres + 1 acre / 100 students
North Dakota	No land area minimum	No land area minimum	No land area minimum	No land area minimum	No land area minimum
Ohio	10 acres + 1 acre / 100 students	10 acres + 1 acre / 100 students	20 acres + 1 acre / 100 students	20 acres + 1 acre / 100 students	35 acres + 1 acre / 100 students
Oklahoma	10 acres + 1 acre / 100 students	10 acres + 1 acre / 100 students	20 acres + 1 acre / 100 students	20 acres + 1 acre / 100 students	30 acres + 1 acre / 100 students
Oregon	No land area minimum	No land area minimum	No land area minimum	No land area minimum	No land area minimum
Pennsylvania	No land area minimum	No land area minimum	No land area minimum	No land area minimum	No land area minimum
Rhode Island	10 acres + 1 acre / 100 students	10 acres + 1 acre / 100 students	20 acres + 1 acre / 100 students	20 acres + 1 acre / 100 students	30 acres + 1 acre / 100 students
South Carolina	10 acres + 1 acre / 100 students	10 acres + 1 acre / 100 students	20 acres + 1 acre / 100 students	20 acres + 1 acre / 100 students	30 acres + 1 acre / 100 students
South Dakota	No land area minimum	No land area minimum	No land area minimum	No land area minimum	No land area minimum
Tennessee	No land area minimum	No land area minimum	No land area minimum	No land area minimum	No land area minimum
Texas	No land area minimum	No land area minimum	No land area minimum	No land area minimum	No land area minimum
Utah	10 acres + 1 acre / 100 students	20 acres + 1 acre / 100 students	20 acres + 1 acre / 100 students	20 acres + 1 acre / 100 students	30 acres + 1 acre / 100 students
Vermont	No land area minimum	No land area minimum	No land area minimum	No land area minimum	No land area minimum

Table 7-1 (continued)
New School Facility Land Area Requirements by State

State	Grades K-6	Grades K-8	Grades 7-8	Grades 7-9	Grades 9-12
Virginia	4 acres + 1 acre / 100 students	4 acres + 1 acre / 100 students	10 acres + 1 acre / 100 students	10 acres + 1 acre / 100 students	10 acres + 1 acre / 100 students
Washington	No land area minimum		5 acres + 1 acre / 100 students	5 acres + 1 acre / 100 students	5 acres + 1 acre / 100 students
West Virginia	K-4, 5 acres + 1 / 100 students > 240	5-9, 11 acres + 1 / 100 st > 600 stnd		15 acres + 1 acre / 100 students > 800	
Wyoming	4 acres + 1 acre / 100 students	4 acres + 1 acre / 100 students	10 acres + 1 acre / 100 students	10 acres + 1 acre / 100 students	< 400 students = 20 acres < 800 students = 25 acres > 800 students = 30 acres

Source: Adapted from Lawrence et al. (May 2003). Where no grades are given by the state (only elementary, middle, and high, or E & S specified), standards are spread across all relevant categories above.

Table 7-2
National Student Generation Rate Trends

Year	Grades K-5	Grades 6-8	Grades 9-12	Total
1970	0.3113	0.3259	0.3006	0.9379
1980	0.2054	0.2256	0.2612	0.6922
1990	0.1958	0.1864	0.1925	0.5747
2000	0.1924	0.1933	0.1934	0.5790
2010	0.1700	0.1761	0.1920	0.5381
2020	0.1737	0.1716	0.1741	0.5194

Source: Calculated by the author.

PUBLIC EDUCATIONAL FACILITY SPACE AND LAND-USE NEEDS

Estimating public educational facility space and land-use needs is done in two calculation tables. The first (Table 7-3) estimates future net and gross acres needed for public elementary and secondary schools, and public post-secondary schools in the following way:

Table 7-3
Public Educational Facility Land-Use Needs

Educational Facility	Public Students 2000	Estimated Student Distribution 2020	Public Students 2020	Adopted Facility Sq. Ft. Per Student Station	FAR	Land Area Sq. Ft. Per Student Station	Existing Land 2000	Existing Land Demand 2000	Acres Needed or Planned 2020	New Land Needed	Gross Acre Adjust-ment Factor	Gross Acres Needed	Sq. Ft. Land Area Per Permanent Resident in 2020 Based on 720,810 Permanent Residents
Public E & S Schools	110,000		155,000										
Grades K-5 (Elementary School)	34,680	35.0%	54,250	100.00	0.2000	500.00	460.00	398.07	622.70	224.63	15.00%	732.59	37.63
Grades 6-8 (Middle School)	29,113	30.0%	46,500	115.00	0.1750	657.14	385.00	439.20	701.50	262.30	12.50%	801.71	42.39
Grades 9-12 (High School)	35,457	35.0%	54,250	130.00	0.1500	866.67	760.00	705.45	1,079.35	373.90	10.00%	1,199.28	65.23
Auxiliary Facilities				3.25	0.2500	13.00	30.00	32.83	46.26	13.43	25.00%	61.68	
Total Public E & S Schools	99,250	100.0%	155,000				1,635.00		2,403.55	860.84		2,733.58	145.25
Public Post-secondary Education													
Junior/Community College	3,640	15.75%	7,200			1,210.00	40.00		200.00	160.00	15.00%	235.29	12.09
Technical School	3,850	16.66%	6,550			997.56	40.00		150.00	110.00	15.00%	176.47	9.06
Senior College	4,740	20.51%	8,600			2,026.05	150.00		400.00	250.00	12.50%	457.14	24.17
University	10,880	47.08%	17,800			1,957.75	0.00		800.00	800.00	10.00%	888.89	48.35
Total Public Post-secondary Education	23,110	100.00%	40,150				230.00		1,550.00	1,320.00		1,757.80	93.67
Total Students	122,360		195,150				1,865.00		3,953.55	2,180.84		4,491.38	238.92

Public Students 2000: This is the total of all public elementary and secondary students plus students, public and private post-secondary students. These data come from public school districts and private education providers.

Estimated Student Distribution 2020: This is the assumed distribution of public school students based on estimations provided by local public school districts.

Public Students 2020: This figure comes from population-by-age group data provided by standard projection services, MPOs, utility companies, and state population centers. The public school total is net of the total estimated students in 2020. This assumes that the ratio of public to total students will remain constant through the planning period. Public school students for each grade category is based on the distribution noted in the **Estimated Student Distribution 2020** column.

Adopted Facility Sq. Ft. Per Student Station: This is the LOS standard adopted or used for planning purposes by local public school districts.

FAR: This is the FAR standard adopted or used for planning purposes by local public school districts. Figures here are assumed and need to reflect local situations.

Land Area Sq. Ft. Per Student Station: For public elementary and secondary schools, this is calculated as:

$$[(LAND\ AREA\ SQ.\ FT.\ PER\ STUDENT\ STATION) / (FAR)]$$

For public and private post-secondary schools, this is calculated as:

$$[(ACRES\ NEEDED\ OR\ PLANNED\ 2020)\\ \times (43{,}560\ SQ.\ FT.\ PER\ ACRE)] / (PUBLIC\ STUDENTS\ 2020)$$

Existing Land 2000: This figure is from local public school districts.

Existing Land Demand 2000: Calculated as

$$\{[(LAND\ AREA\ SQ.\ FT.\ PER\ STUDENT\ STATION)\\ \times (PUBLIC\ STUDENTS\ 2000)] / (43{,}560\ SQ.\ FT.\ PER\ ACRE)\}$$

Acres Needed or Planned 2020: For public and elementary and secondary schools, this is calculated as

$$\{[(LAND\ AREA\ SQ.\ FT.\ PER\ STUDENT\ STATION)\\ \times (PUBLIC\ STUDENTS\ 2020)] / (43{,}560\ SQ.\ FT.\ PER\ ACRE)\}$$

New Land Needed: Calculated as

$$[(ACRES\ NEEDED\ OR\ PLANNED\ 2020) - (EXISTING\ LAND\ 2000)]$$

Gross Acre Adjustment Factor: This is the planning assumption for the amount of total developed land that is used for roads, drainage, utility easements, and other property-serving purposes. It is based on local planning knowledge and planning targets (the higher the factor, the less efficient will land be used and the more costly development becomes).

Gross Acres Needed: Calculated as

$$[(ACRES\ NEEDED\ OR\ PLANNED\ 2020)\\ / (1 - GROSS\ ACRE\ ADJUSTMENT\ FACTOR)]$$

The last column, **Sq. Ft. Land Area Per Permanent Resident in 2020 Based on 720,810 Permanent Residents**, will be used later (in Chapter 11) to estimate the impacts of unanticipated development. The number of permanent residents will of course be tailored to the local situation; the number used in this column refers to Table 2-2.

PUBLIC ELEMENTARY AND SECONDARY EDUCATIONAL FACILITY SPACE NEEDS

Although many school districts have planners who estimate future educational facility space and land-use needs, most do not. This section introduces some basic elements of elementary and secondary educational facility space needs assessment for use in comprehensive plans. If the local school district has school facility planners, the user should rely on those professionals. Table 7-4 (the second calculation table) lays out a general way in which to estimate future educational facility space needs.

Public E & S Students 2000: This is from the **Public Students 2000** column in Table 7-3 for elementary and secondary students.

Existing Student Stations 2000: This is from local school district officials.

Scheduling Efficiency Ratio: This is the figure used by local school systems to provide flexibility in scheduling classrooms and other spaces as needed to meet needs that arise at any given point in time. The figures should be available from local school district officials.

Existing Usable Student Stations 2000: Calculated as

(EXISTING STUDENT STATIONS 2000) × (SCHEDULING EFFICIENCY RATIO)

Surplus (Deficient) Student Stations: Calculated as

[(EXISTING USABLE STUDENT STATIONS 2000)
− (PUBLIC E & S STUDENTS 2000)]

Table 7-4
Public Elementary and Secondary Educational Facility Space Needs

Facility Feature	Grades K-5	Grades 6-8	Grades 9-12	Auxiliary Facilities
Public E & S Students 2000	34,680	29,113	35,457	
Existing Student Stations 2000	41,500	40,000	45,000	
Scheduling Efficiency Ratio	87.50%	85.00%	82.50%	
Existing Usable Student Stations 2000	36,313	34,000	37,125	
Surplus (Deficient) Student Stations	1,633	4,887	1,668	
Public E & S Students 2020	54,250	46,500	54,250	
Planned Student Stations Needed 2020	62,000	54,706	65,758	
New Student Stations Needed	25,688	20,706	28,633	
Existing Facility Sq. Ft. 2000	3,633,750	3,847,500	4,950,000	432,000
Existing Sq. Ft. Per Student Station 2000	87.56	96.19	110.00	3.42
Adopted Sq. Ft. Per Student Station	100.00	115.00	130.00	3.25
Facility Sq. Ft. Needed 2000	3,468,000	3,347,995	4,609,410	411,125
Excess (Deficient) Facility Sq. Ft. 2000	165,750	499,505	340,590	20,875
Facility Sq. Ft. Needed 2020	6,200,000	6,291,176	8,548,485	503,750
New Facility Sq. Ft. Needed	2,566,250	2,443,676	3,598,485	71,750

where a negative number (in brackets) indicates there are more students than usable student stations.

Public E & S Students 2020: This is from the column **Estimated Students 2020** in Table 7-3.

Planned Student Stations Needed 2020: Calculated as

[(PUBLIC E & S STUDENTS 2020) / (SCHEDULING EFFICIENCY RATIO)]

New Student Stations Needed: This is simply the difference between **Planned Student Stations Needed 2020** and **Existing Usable Student Stations 2000**.

Existing Facility Sq. Ft. 2000: This comes from local school district officials.

Existing Sq. Ft. Per Student Station 2000: Calculated as

[(EXISTING FACILITY SQ. FT. 2000) / (EXISTING STUDENT STATIONS 2000)]

Adopted Sq. Ft. Per Student Station: This is based on the LOS standard used by the local school district.

Facility Sq. Ft. Needed 2000: Calculated as

[(PUBLIC E & S STUDENTS 2000) × (ADOPTED SQ. FT. PER STUDENT STATION)]

Excess (Deficient) Facility Sq. Ft. 2000: This is the difference between **Existing Facility Sq. Ft. 2000** and **Facility Sq. Ft. Needed 2000** where a negative number (in brackets) indicates an insufficient supply of space to meet demand.

Facility Sq. Ft. Needed 2020: Calculated as

[(PUBLIC E & S STUDENTS 2020) × (ADOPTED SQ. FT. PER STUDENT STATION)]

New Facility Sq. Ft. Needed: This indicates the total amount of new facility space needed to meet demands in 2020, assuming there is no replacement to current facilities. It is simply the difference between **Facility Sq. Ft. Needed 2020** and **Existing Facility Sq. Ft. 2000**.

For auxiliary facilities, the calculations are similar from the row **Existing Facility Sq. Ft. 2000** except that the number of students or student stations involved is actually all public elementary and secondary students, not students by grade category.

PRIVATE EDUCATIONAL FACILITY LAND-USE NEEDS

Estimating the land-use needs for private elementary and secondary and post-secondary schools is done in Table 7-5 using the following calculations:

Table 7-5
Private Educational Facility Land-Use Needs

Facility Feature	Year 2000	Year 2020
Private Elementary and Secondary Education		
Private Students 2000	11,975	
Permanent Population	548,668	720,810
Students Per Permanent Resident	0.0218	0.0218
Private Students 2020		15,732
Elementary and Secondary Land, Acres	260.00	341.57
Private Post-secondary Education		
Existing and Planned Land, Acres	0	0
Existing and Planned Students	0	0
Summary of Private Educational Facility Land-Use Needs		
Total Private Students	11,975	15,732
Total Acres	260.00	341.57
Gross Land Adjustment Factor		25.00%
Planned Acres Needed 2020		455.43

Private Students 2000: This comes from the census for 2000. For non-census years, these figures may be available from local school districts, state departments of education, or associations of private schools.

Permanent Population: This figure comes from Table 2-2.

Students Per Permanent Resident: Calculated as

$$[(\text{PRIVATE STUDENTS 2000}) / (\text{PERMANENT POPULATION}_{2000})]$$

Private Students 2020: Calculated as

$$[(\text{STUDENTS PER PERMANENT RESIDENT}_{2000}) \times (\text{PERMANENT POPULATION}_{2020})$$

Elementary and Secondary Land, Acres: This figure is based on the current year data from inventory of private schools or from the local property assessor. The figure for future demand is calculated as:

$$[(\text{PRIVATE STUDENTS 2020}) / (\text{PRIVATE STUDENTS 2000})] \times (\text{PRIVATE SCHOOL LAND})$$

Existing and Planned Land, Acres: For many counties, including growing suburban ones, there are no private post-secondary educational facilities in the traditional college campus sense. There may be private vocational facilities in stand-alone buildings or as a part of others. There may be private extension or executive educational facilities but these tend to be in office buildings or office and business parks. The space needs for these kinds of facilities are subsumed in the office space and land area calculations. This is assumed to be the case in Yukon County, where there are no existing or planned private post-secondary educational facilities. Zeros are thus reported in the **Year 2000** and **Year 2020** columns for this row entry.

Existing and Planned Students: This is the estimate of existing and projected students in conventional private post-secondary campus settings. This figure is used later to estimate utility impacts.

Total Private Students: For 2000, this is calculated as the sum of **Private Students 2000** in the **Private Elementary and Secondary Education** section plus **Existing and Planned Students** in the **Private Post-secondary Education** section of the **Year 2000** column. For 2020, this is calculated as the **Private Students 2020** in the **Private Elementary and Secondary Education** section plus **Existing and Planned Students** in the **Year 2020** column. This figure is used in Chapter 8.

Total Acres: This is simply the sum of the elementary and secondary and post-secondary land areas in acres.

Gross Land Adjustment Factor: This figure is the amount of total developed land that is used for roads, drainage, utility easements, and other property-serving purposes. This is based on local planning knowledge and planning targets.

Planned Acres Needed 2020: Calculated as

$$[(\text{TOTAL ACRES}) / (1 - \text{GROSS LAND ADJUSTMENT FACTOR})]$$

Two other tables are generated: one estimating student generation rates for elementary and secondary schools and the other for post-secondary educational facilities (Table 7-6 and Table 7-7, respectively). Although they are merely for informational purposes here, they do come into play when estimating the land-use and facility impacts associated with unanticipated changes in the comprehensive plan, such as for a 100-acre office park (see Chapter 11).

Table 7-6
Elementary and Secondary School Student Generation Rates

Permanent Residential Land-Use Category	Student Generation Rate 2020	Student Generation Public K-5 2020	Student Generation Public 6-8 2020	Student Generation Public 9-12 2020	Private Student Generation Rate 2020
1-5 Acres Per Unit	0.4500	0.1575	0.1350	0.1575	0.0582
1-2 Units Per Net Acre	0.4500	0.1575	0.1350	0.1575	0.0582
3-5 Units Per Net Acre	0.4500	0.1575	0.1350	0.1575	0.0572
6-8 Units Per Net Acre	0.4500	0.1575	0.1350	0.1575	0.0572
9-14 Units Per Net Acre	0.2100	0.0735	0.0630	0.0735	0.0482
15+ Units Per Net Acre	0.1500	0.0525	0.0450	0.0525	0.0451

Table 7-7
Post-secondary Student Generation

Post-secondary Land-Use Category	Students 2000	Student Generation Rate 2020
Daytime Functional Population		749,535
Junior/Community College	7,200	0.0096
Technical School	6,550	0.0087
Senior College	8,600	0.0115
University	17,800	0.0237

SUMMARY OBSERVATIONS

In recent years, a debate has emerged over the land area requirements of public schools. Most states require such large campuses that sufficient land cannot be acquired near where students actually live, either because tracts of sufficient size are not available or they are too expensive. Many state standards thus force local school districts to acquire land and locate schools many miles away from students using them, which can lead to perverse outcomes. Some communities that attempt to achieve more compact development forms are thwarted in their efforts when the local school district purchases land for future schools far away from where communities otherwise want development to occur. If state standards for land area can be relaxed, resulting in school campuses that are based on smaller sites than current rules require, the ability of both school districts and local planning officials to match schools with where people live is made much easier. This is being done statewide in Maryland as part of its "smart growth" policy. The user is advised to consult with local and state education officials to determine standards that affect land-use and facility planning.

REFERENCES

DeChiara, Joseph and Lee Koppelman. *Urban Planning and Design Criteria— Third Edition.* New York, NY: Van Nostrand Reinhold, 1981.

Lawrence, Barbara Kent and Janell Weihs. Scottsdale, AZ: Council of Educational Facility Planners, International, May 2003 (untitled).

Water and Wastewater Utility Land-Use Needs

OVERVIEW

Utilities include water and wastewater systems, electrical and natural gas grids, telephone systems, cable systems, and drainage facilities and ways. Land-use needs for electrical and natural gas grids, telephone systems, cable systems, and drainage ways are assumed within the gross acre adjustment factor to net land-use needs. Land area for water and wastewater lines are assumed as well. Land-use needs for private utilities yards and offices (normally electrical, gas, cable, and telephone) are assumed within the Transportation, Communication, and Utilities (TCU) employment land-use category (see Chapter 4). Special land-use needs for some drainage facilities are assumed within the miscellaneous facility category (see Chapter 6). Here, the facility and land-use needs for only water and wastewater systems are considered.

Water systems are customarily composed of source facilities (usually wells and/or surface water intakes), treatment plants, pumps, and storage facilities. In this chapter, the demand for treated water for domestic consumption is considered along with land needed to support major water system elements such as treatment plants but not lines.

Wastewater systems are usually composed of pumping stations, treatment plants, and sometimes irrigation land (to meet federal tertiary treatment standards). In this chapter, the demand for wastewater treatment is considered along with land needed to support major system elements such as the treatment plant and land for irrigation but not lines. Not all land uses need water and wastewater utility services. In this analysis, all land uses need water services, but the category of residential land uses ranging from 1-5 acres per unit does not need wastewater services, presumably because septic systems are used. (The bane of septic systems is known widely and we do not encourage dependency on such here.)

Although demand for domestic water and wastewater treatment varies by land use, region (arid areas need more treated water, while wet areas need more wastewater treatment because of inflow and infiltration of stormwater), conservation efforts, and age of system (older wastewater systems are more porous than newer ones and thus bring in stormwater during storms, while older water systems simply lose water in transmission), some general consumption information is useful for planning purposes.

Table 8-1 shows water consumption requirements for a range of land uses, while Table 8-2 does the same for wastewater treatment requirements for the same land uses. Where possible, the user should use locally developed data on average daily and peak consumption per unit of impact. This is usually available from local public works departments or consulting engineers.

Table 8-1
Water Consumption By Land Use

Land Use	Unit of Measure	Water Flow, GPD
Airports	Passenger	5
	Employee	25
Apartments	< 3 Bedroom	180
	3+ Bedroom	280
	Clubhouse	500
	Laundry Unit	500
Community Halls	Maximum Seat	10
Bar, Tavern	Seat	25
Campground	Space	180
Car Wash	Bay	900
Church	Seat	5
Coin Laundry	Machine	500
Commercial Laundry	Machine	800
Country Club	Resident Member	125
	Nonresident Member	25
Fast Food	Seat	40
Hospital	Bed	250
Light Industrial	Employee	25
	Shower	40
Motel, Hotel	Unit with Restaurant	125
	Unit without Restaurant	90
Nursing Home	Bed	150
	Employee	25

Table 8-1 (continued)
Water Consumption By Land Use

Land Use	Unit of Measure	Water Flow, GPD
Office	1,000 Sq. Ft.	125
	Employee	25
Police/Fire Station with Kitchen	Resident Employee	90
	Nonresident Employee	25
Residence, Single Family	Unit	280
Restaurant	Seat	5
	Employee	25
Retail	1,000 Sq. Ft.	60
School	Student	25
	Cafeteria Seat	5
	Gymnasium Seat	5
Service Station	Daily Car	12
	Employee	25
Shopping Center	1,000 Sq. Ft.	125
Swimming Pool	Swimmer	25
	Employee	32
Theater	Seat	5
Theater, Drive-In	Space	10
Warehouse	1,000 Sq. Ft.	60

Source: Adapted from *Environmental Health Planning Guide* and *Environmental Health Practice in Recreational Areas* (Public Health Service, undated). No warranty is made that the figures reported in this table reflect the consumption characteristics of any given local government.

Table 8-2
Wastewater Treatment By Land Use

Land Use	Unit of Measure	Wastewater Flow, GPD[a]
Airports	Passenger	5
	Employee	24
Apartments	< 3 Bedroom	162
	3+ Bedroom	252
	Clubhouse	400
	Laundry Unit	475
Community Halls	Maximum Seat	10
Bar, Tavern	Seat	24
Campground	Space	144
Car Wash	Bay	760
Church	Seat	5
Coin Laundry	Machine	475
Commercial Laundry	Machine	760
Country Club	Resident Member	100
	Nonresident Member	20
Fast Food	Seat	38
Hospital	Bed	238
Light Industrial	Employee	24
	Shower	38
Motel, Hotel	Unit with Restaurant	119
	Unit without Restaurant	86
Nursing Home	Bed	143
	Employee	24
Office	1,000 Sq. Ft.	119
	Employee	24

Table 8-2 (continued)
Wastewater Treatment By Land Use

Land Use	Unit of Measure	Wastewater Flow, GPD[a]
Police/Fire Station with Kitchen	Resident Employee	86
	Nonresident Employee	24
Residence, Single Family	Unit	224
Restaurant	Seat	5
	Employee	24
Retail	1,000 Sq. Ft.	572
School	Student	24
	Cafeteria Seat	5
	Gymnasium Seat	5
Service Station	Daily Car	11
	Employee	24
Shopping Center	1,000 Sq. Ft.	119
Swimming Pool	Swimmer	24
	Employee	30
Theater	Seat	5
Theater, Drive-In	Space	10
Warehouse	1,000 Sq. Ft.	57

a. Wastewater flow is based on approximately 80% of water flow for single-family residential, community and country clubs, and campground uses; 90% for apartment use; and 95% for all other uses. No warranty is made that this table reflects the consumption characteristics of any given community.

Source: Adapted from *Environmental Health Planning Guide* and *Environmental Health Practice in Recreational Areas* (Public Health Service, undated). No warranty is made that the figures reported in this table reflect the consumption characteristics of any given local government.

The first two calculation tables—Table 8-3 for water and Table 8-4 for wastewater—estimate treatment needs using the following approach:

Land-Use Unit: This is the unit of development that will require water and/or wastewater service.

Total Impact Units 2000: This information comes from the **Total Residential** row in the **Occupied Units 2000** column of Table 3-3, the **Total Urban-Related Employees** in the **2000** column of Table 2-3, and the sum of **Total Students** in the **Public Students 2000** column of Table 7-3 and the **Existing and Planned Students** figure in the **Year 2000** column of Table 7-5.

Total Impact Units 2020: This information comes from the **Total Residential** row in the **Occupied Units Needed 2020** column of Table 3-6, the **Total Urban-Related Employees** in the **2020** column of Table 2-3, and the sum of **Total Students** in the **Public Students 2020** column of Table 7-3 and the **Existing and Planned Students** figure in the **Year 2020** column of Table 7-5.

Employee In-Place Percent: This information is adapted from *Environmental Health Planning Guide* (Public Health Service, undated).

Demand Per Unit: These are the assumed levels of consumption per day by land use. The figures shown in this example are high relative to national averages but are within reason for low-density suburban areas with inflow and infiltration problems.

MGD Water/Sewer Demand 2000: For residential land uses and students, it is calculated as

$$[(\text{TOTAL IMPACT UNITS 2000}) \times (\text{DEMAND PER UNIT})] / 1,000,000$$

while for employment-based land uses, it is calculated as:

$$[(\text{TOTAL IMPACT UNITS 2000}) \times (\text{EMPLOYEE IN-PLACE PERCENT}) \times (\text{DEMAND PER UNIT})] / 1,000,000$$

MGD Water/Sewer Demand 2020: For residential land uses and students, it is calculated as

$$[(\text{TOTAL IMPACT UNITS 2020}) \times (\text{DEMAND PER UNIT})] / 1,000,000$$

while for employment-based land uses, it is calculated as

$$[(\text{TOTAL IMPACT UNITS 2020}) \times (\text{EMPLOYEE IN-PLACE PERCENT}) \times (\text{DEMAND PER UNIT})] / 1,000,000$$

Table 8-3
Water Treatment Demand

Land Use	Land-Use Unit	Total Impact Units 2000	Total Impact Units 2020	Employee In-Place Percent	Demand Per Unit	MGD Water Demand 2000	MGD Water Demand 2020
Residential							
Acreage Residential, 1-5 Acres	Residential Unit	13,697	10,485	na	450.00	6.1637	4.7180
Detached Urban Units	Residential Unit	145,516	164,354	na	400.00	58.2064	65.7418
Attached Units	Residential Unit	65,229	113,141	na	250.00	16.3073	28.2852
Group Care	Bed, Unit	8,500	15,546	na	150.00	1.2750	2.3319
Hotel/Motel	Room	55,980	70,000	na	125.00	6.9975	8.7500
Subtotal Residential		288,922	373,526			81.9523	101.0769
Employment							
Construction	Employee	12,400	15,300	25.00%	45.00	0.1395	0.1721
Manufacturing	Employee	22,300	25,500	100.00%	45.00	1.0035	1.1475
TCU	Employee	10,000	19,800	100.00%	45.00	0.4500	0.8910
Wholesale	Employee	20,000	23,600	100.00%	45.00	0.9000	1.0620
Retail	Employee	31,600	46,500	100.00%	25.00	0.7900	1.1625
FIRE	Employee	15,500	24,700	80.00%	25.00	0.3100	0.4940
Services	Employee	55,200	82,100	80.00%	25.00	1.1040	1.6420
Government	Employee	25,800	37,900	80.00%	25.00	0.5160	0.7580
Subtotal Employment		192,800	275,400			5.2130	7.3291
Education	Student	134,335	210,882		25.00	3.3584	5.2721
Total						90.5237	113.6781

Table 8-4
Wastewater Treatment Demand

Land Use	Land-Use Unit	Total Impact Units 2000	Total Impact Units 2020	Employee In-Place Percent	Demand Per Unit	MGD Sewer Demand 2000	MGD Sewer Demand 2020
Residential							
Acreage Residential, 1-5 Acres	Residential Unit	na	na	na	na	na	na
Detached Urban Units	Residential Unit	145,516	164,354	na	300.00	43.6548	49.3063
Attached Units	Residential Unit	65,229	113,141	na	200.00	13.0458	22.6281
Group Care	Bed, Unit	8,303	15,546	na	143.00	1.1873	2.2231
Hotel/Motel	Room	52,341	70,000	na	86.00	4.5014	6.0200
Subtotal Residential		271,389	363,041			57.8879	74.1576
Employment							
Construction	Employee	12,400	15,300	25.00%	35.00	0.1085	0.1339
Manufacturing	Employee	22,300	25,500	100.00%	35.00	0.7805	0.8925
TCU	Employee	10,000	19,800	100.00%	35.00	0.3500	0.6930
Wholesale	Employee	20,000	23,600	100.00%	35.00	0.7000	0.8260
Retail	Employee	31,600	46,500	100.00%	20.00	0.6320	0.9300
FIRE	Employee	15,500	24,700	80.00%	20.00	0.2480	0.3952
Services	Employee	55,200	82,100	80.00%	20.00	0.8832	1.3136
Government	Employee	25,800	37,900	80.00%	20.00	0.4128	0.6064
Subtotal Employment		192,800	275,400			4.1150	5.7906
Education	Student	122,360	195,150		24.00	3.2240	5.0612
Total						65.2269	85.0093

The third calculation table, Table 8-5, estimates the extent to which capacity needs to be added to water and wastewater systems to accommodate future demand in the following way:

Capacity, MGD 2000: This comes from local water/wastewater agency sources.

MGD Demand 2000: The figure for **Water Supply and Treatment** comes from the **Total** row of the **MGD Water Demand 2000** column of Table 8-3, while the figure for **Wastewater Treatment** comes from the **Total** row of the **MGD Sewer Demand 2000** column of Table 8-4.

Excess (Deficient) Capacity, MGD 2000: Calculated as

[(DEMAND, MGD 2000) – (CAPACITY, MGD 2000)]

MGD Demand 2020: For water supply and treatment, this entry is from the **Total** row of the **MGD Water Demand 2020** column of Table 8-3, while the figure for **Wastewater Treatment** comes from the **Total** row of the **MGD Sewer Demand 2020** column of Table 8-4.

New Capacity Needed, MGD 2020: Calculated as

[(CAPACITY NEEDED, MGD 2020) – (CAPACITY, MGD 2000)]

In Table 8-6, the need for new acres to accommodate future water and wastewater facility needs is estimated.

Existing Acres 2000: This information is from local water supply and treatment agencies.

Planned Land Additions 2020: This information is from local water supply and treatment agencies.

Planned Acres Needed 2020: Calculated as

Table 8-5
Capacity of Water and Wastewater Facilities

Facility	Capacity, MGD 2000	MGD Demand 2000	Excess (Deficient) Capacity, MGD 2000	MGD Demand 2020	New Capacity Needed, MGD 2020
Water Supply and Treatment	95.00	90.5237	4.4763	113.6781	18.6781
Wastewater Treatment	65.00	65.2269	(0.2269)	85.0093	20.0093

Table 8-6
Water and Wastewater Land-Use Needs

Facility, Land Area	Existing Acres 2000	Planned Land Additions 2020	Planned Acres Needed 2020	Gross Acre Adjustment Factor	Total Gross Acres Needed
Water Supply and Treatment Facility Land	100.00	40.00	140.00	10.00%	155.56
Wastewater Treatment Facility Land	100.00	60.00	160.00	10.00%	177.78
Wastewater Irrigation Fields	200.00	100.00	300.00	10.00%	333.33

[(EXISTING ACRES 2000) + (PLANNED LAND ADDITIONS 2020)]

Gross Acre Adjustment Factor: Planning assumption for the amount of total developed land that is used for roads, drainage, utility easements, and other property-serving purposes. This is based on local planning knowledge and planning targets.

Total Gross Acres Needed: Calculated as

[(PLANNED ACRES NEEDED 2020)
/ (1 – GROSS ACRE ADJUSTMENT FACTOR)]

SUMMARY OBSERVATIONS

In general, compact development leads to less water and wastewater consumption. In contrast, extensive areas of low-density development lead to considerably higher levels of consumption because of larger yards (consuming higher amounts of water) and more exposure to leakage (affecting both water and wastewater lines). Moreover, capital costs per unit of development rise with declining density; to maintain sufficient pressure, more pumps and larger lines are needed to push or collect water from longer distances, for example. While some may worry that old urban systems need to be upgraded to serve higher levels of development, chances are that they will need to be upgraded anyway. Water and wastewater systems can shape development patterns, but only when there is a clear vision of the development pattern that is desirable.

REFERENCES

Public Health Service. *Environmental Health Planning Guide.* Washington, DC: U.S. Government Printing Office, undated.
___. *Environmental Health Practice in Recreational Areas.* Washington, DC: U.S. Government Printing Office, undated.

Summary Land-Use Needs and Market Factor Adjustment

OVERVIEW

This chapter puts together the land-use estimates developed from the previous chapters. It also accounts for one important consideration: There should be an adjustment to the overall demand for land that provides for appropriate market flexibility. Let us consider this now.

One of the issues involved in comprehensive land-use planning is the extent to which plans should incorporate a surplus or market factor adjustment. Good land-use planning practice estimates the need for land by general land-use category. When communities include vastly more land in their plans than is needed based on data and analysis, those plans lead to urban sprawl. Too much excess land can indicate that urban sprawl is not being discouraged, yet too little may unreasonably thwart flexibility. This section reviews how one determines an appropriate "market factor" adjustment consistent with good planning, and applies the factor appropriate to Yukon County.

In general, most local plans should have 25% more land area than needed to be developed by the end year of a 20-year planning horizon, or a 10-year supply of vacant, buildable land at the beginning of a short-term, five-year planning horizon. These figures have three implications:

1. They provide the urban land market with just enough supply that monopolistic pricing behavior among landowners should be dampened, if not prevented, yet not too much land where urban sprawl is the result.

2. They provide prospective developers with reasonably adequate choices of sites and locations.

3. They give the planning system the flexibility it needs to adjust land-use designations in later years as experience dictates and needs change.

Since this book is about estimating land-use needs over the long term, this chapter will focus on the rationale behind the 25% excess land factor for the 20-year planning horizon.

First, a word about the five-year land factor. The Twin Cities (Minneapolis–St.Paul) area has had a regional urban service boundary for about three decades. Conceptually, the boundary is adjusted every five years to assure a 10-year supply of vacant land provided with the full range of urban services. Thus, in the fifth year, there is another five years' supply. Available evidence indicates that this approach achieves the objective of managing urban sprawl and providing the land market with reasonable flexibility (Nelson and Duncan, 1995).

With regard to long-range planning, it is important to understand that, although a land-use plan may allocate 25% more land area than needed to accommodate development at the end of a planning horizon, the plan itself should be revised at least every five years. This provides an adequate supply of land in the long term. Mathematically, if a community is growing at a constant rate such that it will double every 20 years, and the plan is revised every five years to accommodate development over the next 20 years, the community will never have less than twice the amount of vacant land needed to accommodate development during any five-year period. Interestingly, this is equivalent to the Twin Cities' formula.

What is the analytic foundation for the 25% factor? There are few comprehensive studies of the distribution of land uses among American cities. Three studies are most commonly cited as representative of land-use distributions reflecting, in general, reasonably competitive urban land markets. Despite their age, they are the only studies available that address this issue.

Niedercorn and Hearle (1964) found that vacant land accounted for 20.7% of the mean proportion of land in the 48 largest U.S. cities. Using data published by Manvel (1968), Hartshorn (1991) estimated that among cities over 100,000 population, the mean proportion of vacant land among U.S. cities was 22.3% and, for cities over 250,000, it was 12.5%. Assuming cities used in these studies could have been considered built out at the time (as most were), this is one indicator of the ratio of vacant to built land at the end of a planning horizon. New development is dissuaded from locating in built-out cities and therefore finds suburban locations.

Northam (1971) used data from Manvel (1968) and the University of Oregon's Bureau of Municipal Research and Service (circa 1968) to estimate vacant land characteristics of cities at various sizes. Northam's analysis provides valuable insights into what one may consider the "natural" vacant land rates for cities of different sizes. The national data for 106 cities include cities ranging in population from 100,000 to more than 1 million. The Oregon sample includes data on 33 cities ranging in size from less than 2,500 to 50,000. One should consider the planning and development environment of the 1960s so that the data can be placed in contemporary context:

- The 1960s were an era in which the vast majority of cities were not subject to the kind of growth management that is now being employed in many parts of the nation.

- Since federal and state aid for infrastructure improvements (roads, water and wastewater systems, and mass transit systems) was more plentiful then than now, one may reasonably assume that cities could expand with relatively low local costs to meet local development demands. Indeed, because subsidized infrastructure financing can lead to higher vacant land figures than may be expected otherwise, the Northam study may overestimate the "natural" vacancy rates of growing cities.

- The Oregon data predate Oregon's statewide land-use planning policies and thus reflect vacant land conditions in the absence of statewide planning policies.

The results of Northam's study are summarized in Table 9-1.

Table 9-1
Vacant Land Area as a Percent of Total City Area

City Population	Average Vacant Land Rate as a Percent Total City Land Area
Largest 106 Cities (1970)	
Over 1,000,000	8.7%
500,000–1,000,000	23.9%
250,000–500,000	18.6%
100,000–250,000	27.4%
Cities over 100,000	19.7%
Oregon Cities (1966)	
10,000–50,000	30.5%
2,500–10,000	36.7%
Less than 2,500	53.8%
Cities less than 50,000	37.9%

Source: Adapted from Northam (1971).

In general, as city size increases, its natural vacant land supply decreases. Total vacant buildable land in a larger city can be many times that of a smaller city. Northam concludes that the variation in amount of vacant land in the large city becomes greater as a function of lower population size. As urban population rises, vacant land in the urban center decreases.

However, Northam does not consider vacant land that is buildable. He also lumps rapidly growing cities in with those that were essentially built out at the time of his study. Moreover, since some cities have mountains or oceans that prevent expansion of urban development, vacant land figures for those cities may be less than average. Going to the original data and adapting Northam's findings, I developed Table 9-2 to make these adjustments. It shows the percent of buildable land that is vacant for all fast-growing cities reported in Manvel (1968).

Table 9-2 offers interesting insights. First, these cities have higher natural vacant land rates than other cities—37% compared to 20% among cities over 100,000 population. Second, these cities have an average supply of vacant "buildable" land that is 31% of the total buildable land supply. Third, since these figures are for a given year of analysis, one can reasonably conclude that the natural vacant buildable rate for rapidly growing urban areas with few impediments is in the magnitude of one-third of its buildable land supply (i.e., for any given year, such cities may need a supply of vacant buildable land that is equal to about one-third of the city buildable land area). It is important to note that this rate is for the present year and not for future years.

Table 9-2
Vacant Buildable Land to Total Buildable Land Among Fast-Growing Cities with Few Development Constraints

City	Total Acres Vacant Land	Percent of City Area	Percent of Vacant Land Buildable	Adjusted Percent Vacant Land Buildable
Albuquerque, NM	22,000	51%	95%	48%
Beaumont, TX	31,363	68%	84%	57%
Dallas, TX	75,517	41%	62%	25%
Denver, CO	7,000	11%	99%	11%
Fresno, CA	3,169	20%	100%	20%
Houston, TX	127,994	47%	95%	45%
Indianapolis, IN	150,180	48%	60%	29%
Kansas City, MO	13,116	36%	100%	36%
Los Angeles, CA	29,408	10%	100%	10%
Miami, FL	2,830	13%	100%	13%
Phoenix, AZ	76,729	49%	67%	33%
Sacramento, CA	18,610	31%	80%	25%
St. Petersburg, FL	9,672	27%	100%	27%
San Antonio, TX	37,132	34%	85%	29%
San Diego, CA	107,537	54%	95%	51%
San Jose, CA	39,630	57%	62%	35%
Spokane, WA	10,245	37%	82%	30%
Tucson, AZ	17,840	37%	98%	36%
Average[a]		37%		31%

a. Not weighted.

Source: Northam (1971), adapted from Table IV, pp. 352-3; Manvel (1968).

In terms of planning, one may be persuaded to allocate land such that, at the end of a planning horizon, no more than one-third of the remaining land area is buildable (i.e., in the last year of the planning horizon, there would be one-third more buildable land than developed). However, doing this will create far greater excess capacity in earlier years. This can lead to urban sprawl unless the actual build-out is managed to assure continuous development patterns.

The Northam data also indicate that not all cities or urban areas should have the same excess land factor. Larger cities and urban areas need less excess land as a percent of total buildable land. Adapting Northam (1971) and Manvel (1968), Table 9-3 shows the excess land factor applied to different population sizes for land-use estimating purposes.

These figures are higher than indicated for the range of urban area sizes reported in the referenced studies. Large areas will be the most land intensive, while small areas will be the least land intensive. The figures are really factors for the last year in a planning horizon.

The preceding tables can be used to derive final estimates of land-use requirements. The result of the market factor adjustment is that land area estimated for land-use planning purposes is considerably in excess of land area estimated to be actually developed and occupied. In most situations, there will be about twice as much development capacity in land allocated to development in the early years of a 20-year planning horizon than will be developed. Indeed, one could apply a rule of thumb that would double the forecast of occupied gross acres needed to accommodate future development over 20 years.

Table 9-3
Excess Land Factors Applied to Different Population Categories

County Size in End Year of Planning Horizon	Category Name	Excess Buildable Land Factor
Less than 100,000	Small	30%
100,000-1,000,000	Moderate	25%
More than 1,000,000	Large	15%

Source: Calculated by author.

Not all land needed for development over a planning horizon is necessarily buildable (i.e., possessing water, sewer, and other public facilities and services) in the first, fifth, or even tenth year. Rather, phasing of buildable land would be prudent to properly manage growth as it occurs in the short term and to avoid excessive investments in infrastructure.

The question for the short term is: How much vacant buildable land should be available to accommodate development? Based on the referenced studies, the buildable land supply should range from about 15% to 30% of total buildable land during any given year (see Table 9-3), depending on the size of the county or comparable land area. Any more and sprawl is not discouraged because public facilities may not be maximized relative to the location of vacant land and the need to revitalize or develop urban areas; any less and there is the potential for noncompetitive pricing behavior among landowners.

For Yukon County, which falls in the middle range of Table 9-3, the appropriate market factor adjustment would be 25%. There are two modifications, however. The first is with respect to rural residential land uses. These land uses consume vast amounts of land and, unless properly located, will undermine resource operations and threaten the efficient expansion of urban development. The allocation of land for these land uses must therefore be more rigorous and arguably less generous than for other purely urban land uses. A market factor of 10% is used for Yukon County.

Second, the market factor for publicly owned land uses may also need to be lower for several reasons:

- Unlike the private sector, the public sector generally has more flexibility in acquiring land it needs, whether through direct negotiations with landowners of needed sites or through eminent domain.
- Sometimes the public sector has access to land that it can use to trade for that which it needs.

- The public sector may negotiate with private developers for public facility land sites as part of large development projects; this can be achieved either through developer proffers (such as school, park, and fire station sites), transfer of development densities, or compensatory mechanisms (such as credits for impact fees otherwise due).

It is for these reasons that the market factor for publicly owned land uses is reduced to 10% in the case of Yukon County.

The compilation of net and gross land-use needs for all land-use categories presented, plus the appropriate market factor adjustment, are shown in Table 9-4.

Table 9-4
Summary of Land-Use Needs

Land Use	Existing Acres	Acres Needed or Planned	New Net Acres Needed	Gross Acres Needed	Market Factor Adjustment	Planned Acres Needed	Percent of Net Existing Urban Land	Percent of Net Planned Urban Land	Percent of Gross Planned Urban Land	Percent of Net New Urban Land
Residential										
Rural Residential										
1-5 Acres Per Unit	20,584.00	18,426.40	(2,157.60)	20,473.78	10.00%	22,521.16				
Urban										
1-2 Units Per Net Acre	37,721.00	34,746.51	(2,974.49)	43,433.14	25.00%	54,291.43				
3-5 Units Per Net Acre	11,288.00	14,776.07	3,488.07	19,701.42	25.00%	24,626.78				
6-8 Units Per Net Acre	3,450.00	7,452.28	4,002.28	10,646.11	25.00%	13,307.63				
9-14 Units Per Net Acre	3,960.00	6,533.68	2,573.68	10,051.81	25.00%	12,564.76				
15+ Units Per Net Acre	955.00	2,080.21	1,125.21	3,467.02	25.00%	4,333.77				
Subtotal Urban	57,374.00	65,588.74	8,214.74	87,299.50		109,124.37	60.87%	55.17%	58.84%	33.36%
Group Care										
Nursing Home Beds	224.00	254.92	30.92	424.86	25.00%	424.86				
Assisted Living Units	196.00	502.68	306.68	837.79	25.00%	837.79				
Subtotal Group Care	420.00	757.59	337.59	1,262.65		1,262.65	0.45%	0.64%	0.68%	1.37%
Hotel/Motel										
Low Rise (1-3 Floors)	722.00	951.18	229.18	1,585.30	25.00%	1,585.30				
Mid Rise (4-7 Floors)	315.00	401.19	86.19	729.44	25.00%	729.44				
High Rise (8+ Floors)	193.00	291.18	98.18	582.37	25.00%	582.37				
Subtotal Hotel/Motel	1,230.00	1,643.55	413.55	2,897.10		2,897.10	1.31%	1.38%	1.56%	1.68%
Employment										
Industrial										
Construction	20.00	133.14	113.14	166.43	25.00%	221.90				
Manufacturing	250.00	1,551.10	1,301.10	1,938.88	25.00%	2,585.17				
TCU	200.00	662.70	462.70	828.37	25.00%	1,104.50				

Table 9-4 (continued)
Summary of Land-Use Needs

Land Use	Existing Acres	Acres Needed or Planned	New Net Acres Needed	Gross Acres Needed	Market Factor Adjustment	Planned Acres Needed	Percent of Net Existing Urban Land	Percent of Net Planned Urban Land	Percent of Gross Planned Urban Land	Percent of Net New Urban Land
Wholesale Trade	900.00	1,454.60	554.60	1,818.25	25.00%	2,424.34				
Subtotal Industrial	1,370.00	3,801.54	2,431.54	4,751.93		6,335.91	1.45%	3.20%	3.42%	9.87%
Retail Trade										
Neighborhood	800.00	1,172.53	372.53	1,803.90	25.00%	2,405.19				
Community	620.00	934.36	314.36	1,334.80	25.00%	1,779.74				
Regional	315.00	449.47	134.47	599.29	25.00%	799.06				
Super Regional	172.00	240.79	68.79	300.98	25.00%	401.31				
Subtotal Retail Trade	1,907.00	2,797.15	890.15	4,038.98		5,385.30	2.02%	2.35%	2.90%	3.61%
Office										
General Office	800.00	2,421.34	1,621.34	3,026.67	25.00%	4,035.56				
Office Park	200.00	554.34	354.34	739.11	25.00%	985.49				
Suburb Multilevel	40.00	106.34	66.34	151.92	25.00%	202.56				
Subtotal Office	1,040.00	3,082.01	2,042.01	3,917.70		5,223.60	1.10%	2.59%	2.82%	8.29%
Public Facilities										
Public Safety										
Fire/EMS	10.00	31.08	21.08	38.84	25.00%	51.79				
Police	15.00	34.29	19.29	42.86	25.00%	57.15				
Jails, Detention	20.00	98.58	78.58	123.23	25.00%	164.30				
Subtotal Public Safety	45.00	163.95	118.95	204.93		273.24	0.05%	0.14%	0.15%	0.48%
Government, Community, Recreation, Library										
General Government	20.00	60.22	40.22	75.28	25.00%	100.37				
Community Center	25.00	41.30	16.30	51.62	25.00%	68.83				
Recreation Center	15.00	41.30	26.30	51.62	25.00%	68.83				
Library	12.00	34.41	22.41	43.02	25.00%	57.36				

Table 9-4 (continued)
Summary of Land-Use Needs

Land Use	Existing Acres	Acres Needed or Planned	New Net Acres Needed	Gross Acres Needed	Market Factor Adjustment	Planned Acres Needed	Percent of Net Existing Urban Land	Percent of Net Planned Urban Land	Percent of Gross Planned Urban Land	Percent of Net New Urban Land
Subtotal Government, Community, Recreation, Library	72.00	177.23	105.23	221.54		295.39	0.08%	0.15%	0.16%	0.43%
Parks and Open Space										
Neighborhood Park	300.00	936.92	636.92	1,124.30	25.00%	1,499.07				
Community Park	1,200.00	4,122.44	2,922.44	5,153.05	25.00%	6,870.74				
Regional Park	1,400.00	3,747.68	2,347.68	3,897.58	10.00%	4,330.65				
Public Golf Course	900.00	3,372.91	2,472.91	3,507.83	10.00%	3,897.58				
Subtotal Parks and Open Space	3,800.00	12,179.95	8,379.95	13,682.77		16,598.04	4.03%	10.25%	8.95%	34.03%
Private Land-Extensive										
Private Golf Course	1,200.00	1,696.78	496.78	1,764.65	10.00%	1,960.72				
Other Private Land-Extensive	900.00	1,272.58	372.58	1,323.49	10.00%	1,470.54				
Subtotal Private Land-Extensive	2,100.00	2,969.36	869.36	3,088.13		3,431.26	2.23%	2.50%	1.85%	3.53%
Major Community Centers										
Convention Centers	20.00	40.00	20.00	46.00	10.00%	51.11				
Public Assembly Halls	12.00	25.00	13.00	28.75	10.00%	31.94				
Other Major Facilities	10.00	20.00	10.00	23.00	10.00%	25.56				
Subtotal Major Community Centers	42.00	85.00	43.00	97.75		108.61	0.04%	0.07%	0.06%	0.17%
Miscellaneous										
Fire Storage, Drill, Practice Yards	45.00	100.00	55.00	166.75	10.00%	185.28				
Public Works Equipment, Storage Yards	10.00	25.00	15.00	40.25	10.00%	44.72				
Repair Shops and Associated Yards	10.00	10.00	0.00	23.00	10.00%	25.56				
Publicly Owned Drainage Ponds	125.00	300.00	175.00	467.50	10.00%	519.44				
Sand, Gravel, Soil Storage Yards	5.00	15.00	10.00	22.00	10.00%	24.44				
Landfills	120.00	200.00	80.00	352.00	10.00%	391.11				

Table 9-4 (continued)
Summary of Land-Use Needs

Land Use	Existing Acres	Acres Needed or Planned	New Net Acres Needed	Gross Acres Needed	Market Factor Adjustment	Planned Acres Needed	Percent of Net Existing Urban Land	Percent of Net Planned Urban Land	Percent of Gross Planned Urban Land	Percent of Net New Urban Land
Resource Recovery Facilities	3.00	5.00	2.00	9.60	10.00%	10.67				
Airports	960.00	1,400.00	440.00	2,478.00	10.00%	2,753.33				
Other Public Land in Inventory	15.00	20.00	5.00	42.00	10.00%	46.67				
Subtotal Miscellaneous	1,293.00	2,075.00	782.00	3,601.10		4,001.22	1.37%	1.75%	2.16%	3.18%
Religious										
Religious Facility	450.00	591.19	141.19	738.98	25.00%	985.31	0.48%	0.50%	0.53%	0.57%
Educational Facilities										
Public and Private E & S										
Grades K-5	460.00	622.70	162.70	732.59	25.00%	976.79				
Grades 6-8	385.00	701.50	316.50	801.71	25.00%	1,068.95				
Grades 9-12	760.00	1,079.35	319.35	1,199.28	25.00%	1,599.04				
Auxiliary	30.00	46.26	16.26	61.68	25.00%	82.24				
Private E & S	260.00	341.57	81.57	455.43	25.00%	607.24				
Subtotal Public and Private E & S	1,895.00	2,791.39	896.39	3,250.69		4,334.26				
Post-secondary, Public and Private										
Junior/Community College	40.00	200.00	160.00	235.29	10.00%	261.44				
Technical School	40.00	150.00	110.00	176.47	10.00%	196.08				
Senior College	150.00	400.00	250.00	457.14	10.00%	507.94				
University	0.00	800.00	800.00	888.89	10.00%	987.65				
Subtotal Post-secondary, Public and Private	230.00	1,550.00	1,320.00	1,757.80		1,953.11				
Subtotal Education	2,125.00	4,341.39	2,216.39	5,008.49		6,287.37	2.25%	3.65%	3.39%	9.00%
Water and Wastewater Utilities										
Water Supply and Treatment Facility Land	100.00	40.00	(60.00)	155.56	10.00%	172.84				

Table 9-4 (continued)
Summary of Land-Use Needs

Land Use	Existing Acres	Acres Needed or Planned	New Net Acres Needed	Gross Acres Needed	Market Factor Adjustment	Planned Acres Needed	Percent of Net Existing Urban Land	Percent of Net Planned Urban Land	Percent of Gross Planned Urban Land	Percent of Net New Urban Land
Wastewater Treatment Facility Land	100.00	60.00	(40.00)	177.78	10.00%	197.53				
Wastewater Irrigation Fields	200.00	100.00	(100.00)	333.33	10.00%	370.37				
Subtotal Water and Wastewater Utilities	400.00	200.00	(200.00)	666.67		740.74	0.42%	0.17%	0.40%	−0.81%
Total Facility and Support Land-Use Needs	8,202.00	18,441.67	10,239.67	22,301.87		26,433.81				
Grand Total All Land Uses	94,252.00	118,880.06	24,628.06	151,952.00	18.07%	185,471.28	78.16%	84.50%	87.86%	108.76%
Overall Share, Roads, Utilities, Easements, Etc.				21.76%						

SUMMARY OBSERVATIONS

The overall effect of Yukon County's land-use planning to 2020 will result in important shifts mostly among residential land uses. From Chapter 2 we saw that, during the 1990s, new residential development averaged 2.6 units per net acre for urban land. Between 2000 and 2020, however, Yukon County's plan calls for a density of 9.5 new units per net acre.

Why the dramatic change in the density of new residential development in this example? Perhaps Yukon County's vision is for more compact urban development. Perhaps its landscape is constrained by natural features or publicly owned land, or the desire to preserve open space important for agriculture, forestry, and other rural uses. Perhaps it is a combination of these and other factors. Yet, the distribution of population living in detached units in 2020 will be about the same as that observed in 2000, about 64%.

As a consequence, although the total share of Yukon County's land area devoted to residential land uses will remain high (falling only from 60.9% in 2000 to 58.8% in 2020), the share of new land developed for residential purposes will be just 32.9%. The reason is that much of the existing residential land base—principally rural residential tracts—will be converted to higher density residential uses or other uses altogether.

The overall plan calls for the development of about 24,000 new acres of land to accommodate about 170,000 new permanent residents and 90,000 new jobs between 2000 and 2020. Without planning that anticipates land-use needs, this figure could be doubled easily. The next chapter (Chapter 10) discusses the cost implications of growth to 2020 for Yukon County.

REFERENCES

Bureau of Municipal Research and Service. *Planning Bulletin No. 2.* Eugene, OR: University of Oregon, circa 1968.

Hartshorn, Truman A. *Interpreting the City: An Urban Geography.* New York, NY: John Wiley & Sons, 1991.

Manvel, Allen D. "Land Use in 106 Large Cities." *Three Land Research Studies,* Study No. 2, Research Report No. 12. Washington, DC: National Commission on Urban Problems, 1968.

Nelson, Arthur C. and James B. Duncan. *Growth Management Principles and Practice.* Chicago, IL: American Planning Association, 1995.

Niedercorn, J.H. and E.F.R. Hearle. "Recent Land Use Trends in 48 Large American Cities." *Land Economics* 40:105-110, 1964.

Northam, Ray M. "Vacant Urban Land in the American City." *Land Economics* 47:345-355, 1971.

Capital Facility
Cost Implications

OVERVIEW

We now come to the cost to provide the facilities needed to accommodate development projected to occur between 2000 and 2020. This exercise is rarely, if ever, done in land-use and facility planning. It need not be complicated, as shown in the simple calculations in Table 10-1. Here, costs per unit of facility expansion and land are provided by officials or others who know those costs. They need not be precise nor should they be considered the final word on costs since that can only be known when facilities are actually built. However, they should be reasonably based on recent or current construction costs and costs experienced by similar communities.

Table 10-1 shows more than just the bottom line cost to meet facility and associated land-use needs by 2020. Examine, for instance, the column headed "Value of Excess (Deficient) Capacity." There are some facilities that can presently serve more people than is demanded, such as water and wastewater treatment in the example of Yukon County. This is normal since such facilities must have more supply than demand, otherwise there would be water shortages and sewer connection moratoria.

On the other hand, there are some facilities for which demand exceeds supply, thus indicating a deficiency in service delivery relative to demand. Sometimes this deficiency may be artificially created through policy that raises the desirable LOS above that which is already delivered, such as with parks and golf courses in the case of Yukon County. Striving to achieve better LOS conditions is laudable, but it can bring some consternation if the cost of bringing the community to its desired level is costly—in the case of parks, over $100 million. The public may not actually feel the undersupply of parks since they only know and use what is available.

There are some facilities for which demand is greater than supply and the resulting deficiency is truly felt, however. This would be the situation with schools (although not presently in Yukon County, except for some shortfall in land area for Grades 6-8 schools). Such conditions would need to be addressed.

What does it cost to meet future facility and associated land-use needs? In the case of Yukon County, about $3.6 billion. This does not include transportation that, again, is not addressed here because of its high degree of sensitivity to the pattern of development, nor is the cost to extend water and waste lines, pumps, and other distribution systems included.

What does it cost per new resident based on the facilities included here? This may not be a fair question because employment-based land uses that bring in new employees also impose costs. The functional population figures help us consider cost implications for residents and all development. Based on new residents only, the cost would appear to be about $19,458, again excluding transportation impacts. The figures per new 24/7 and daytime functional resident are about $18,447 and $16,478, respectively (see Table 10-1).

We can also view this cost on the basis of a detached dwelling unit. With a projected household size of 2.75, the cost exceeds $50,000. This is a high but not unreasonable figure considering all facilities, even though it does not include the cost of transportation facilities (which may raise costs about another quarter to a third).

Table 10-1
Capital Facility Cost Estimates

Facility	Existing Facility Capacity	Existing Facility Demand	Excess (Deficient) Capacity	Cost Per Unit	Value of Excess (Deficient) Capacity	Capacity Needed 2020	Facility Capacity Expansion Needed (Excess Capacity)	Estimated Facility Cost
Fire/EMS								
Building Sq. Ft.	70,000	207,869	(137,869)	$221.00	($30,468,939)	286,276	216,276	$47,797,083
Land Area, Net Acres	10.00	19.83	(9.83)	$45,000.00	($442,126)	31.08	21.08	$948,375
Police								
Building Sq. Ft.	100,000	337,786	(237,786)	$192.00	($45,654,973)	465,199	365,199	$70,118,235
Land Area, Net Acres	15.00	20.79	(5.79)	$45,000.00	($260,551)	34.29	19.29	$868,051
Jails, Detention								
Maximum Security Beds	500	1,559	(1,059)	$52,000.00	($55,068,716)	2,147	1,647	$85,647,793
Minimum Security Beds	500	1,559	(1,059)	$38,000.00	($40,242,523)	2,147	1,647	$62,588,772
Juvenile Detention Beds	200	780	(580)	$29,000.00	($16,820,000)	1,074	874	$25,332,558
Jail, Detention Land, Acres	20.00	72	(51.58)	$45,000.00	($2,321,103)	98.58	78.58	$3,536,101
General Government								
Building Sq. Ft.	250,000	467,704	(217,704)	$125.00	($27,213,016)	674,582	424,582	$53,072,716
Land Area, Net Acres	20.00	60.22	(40.22)	$45,000.00	($1,810,096)	60.22	40.22	$1,810,096
Community Center								
Building Sq. Ft.	200,000	397,567	(197,567)	$175.00	($34,574,158)	562,151	362,151	$63,376,502
Land Area, Net Acres	25.00	48.68	(23.68)	$45,000.00	($1,065,450)	68.83	43.83	$1,972,253
Recreation Center								
Building Sq. Ft.	150,000	291,549	(141,549)	$190.00	($26,894,282)	412,244	262,244	$49,826,434
Land Area, Net Acres	15.00	29.21	(14.21)	$45,000.00	($639,270)	41.30	26.30	$1,183,352
Library								
Volumes	500,000	1,060,178	(560,178)	$21.50	($12,043,819)	1,499,071	999,071	$21,480,016
Building Sq. Ft.	150,000	318,053	(168,053)	$112.50	($18,905,995)	449,721	299,721	$33,718,630

Table 10-1 (continued)
Capital Facility Cost Estimates

Facility	Existing Facility Capacity	Existing Facility Demand	Excess (Deficient) Capacity	Cost Per Unit	Value of Excess (Deficient) Capacity	Capacity Needed 2020	Facility Capacity Expansion Needed (Excess Capacity)	Estimated Facility Cost
Land Area, Net Acres	12.00	24.34	(12.34)	$45,000.00	($555,225)	34.41	22.41	$1,008,627
Major Community Center Facilities								
Convention Centers, Building Sq. Ft.	200,000	na	na	$182.00	na	na	400,000	$72,800,000
Convention Centers, Net Acres	20.00	na	na	$45,000.00	na	na	40.00	$1,800,000
Public Assembly Halls, Building Sq. Ft.	175,000	na	na	$166.00	na	na	350,000	$58,100,000
Public Assembly Halls, Net Acres	12.00	na	na	$45,000.00	na	na	25.00	$1,125,000
Other Major Facilities, Building Sq. Ft.	75,000	na	na	$168.00	na	na	175,000	$29,400,000
Other Major Facilities, Net Acres	10.00	na	na	$35,000.00	na	na	20.00	$700,000
Parks and Open Space								
Neighborhood Park, Net Acres	300.00	662.61	(362.61)	$45,000.00	($16,317,496)	936.92	636.92	$28,661,358
Community Park, Net Acres	1,200.00	2,915.49	(1,715.49)	$45,000.00	($77,196,983)	4,122.44	2,922.44	$131,509,976
Regional Park, Net Acres	1,400.00	2,650.44	(1,250.44)	$15,000.00	($18,756,662)	3,747.68	2,347.68	$35,215,144
Public Golf Course, Net Acres	900.00	2,385.40	(1,485.40)	$10,000.00	($14,853,997)	8,807.04	7,907.04	$79,070,393
Special Use	150.00	na	na	$15,000.00	na	na	400.00	$6,000,000
Conservancy/Greenbelt	500.00	na	na	$10,000.00	na	na	1,000.00	$10,000,000
Miscellaneous								
Fire Storage, Drill, Practice Yards, Net Acres	45.00	na	na	$25,000.00	na	100.00	55.00	$1,375,000
Public Works Equipment, Storage Yards, Net Acres	10.00	na	na	$25,000.00	na	25.00	15.00	$375,000
Repair Shops and Associated Yards, Net Acres	10.00	na	na	$25,000.00	na	10.00	0.00	$0

Table 10-1 (continued)
Capital Facility Cost Estimates

Facility	Existing Facility Capacity	Existing Facility Demand	Excess (Deficient) Capacity	Cost Per Unit	Value of Excess (Deficient) Capacity	Capacity Needed 2020	Facility Capacity Expansion Needed (Excess Capacity)	Estimated Facility Cost
Publicly Owned Drainage Ponds, Net Acres	125.00	na	na	$15,000.00	na	300.00	175.00	$2,625,000
Sand, Gravel, Soil Storage Yards, Net Acres	5.00	na	na	$15,000.00	na	15.00	10.00	$150,000
Landfills, Net Acres	120.00	na	na	$15,000.00	na	200.00	80.00	$1,200,000
Resource Recovery Facilities, Net Acres	3.00	na	na	$30,000.00	na	5.00	2.00	$60,000
Airports, Net Acres	960.00	na	na	$25,000.00	na	1,400.00	440.00	$11,000,000
Other Public Land in Inventory, Net Acres	15.00	na	na	$25,000.00	na	20.00	5.00	$125,000
Educational Facilities								
Grades K-5 Building Sq. Ft.	3,633,750	3,468,000	165,750	$220.00	$36,465,000	6,200,000	2,566,250	$564,575,000
Grades K-5 Net Acres	460.00	398.07	61.93	$45,000.00	$2,786,777	622.70	162.70	$7,321,694
Grades 6-8 Building Sq. Ft.	3,847,500	3,347,995	499,505	$240.00	$119,881,200	6,291,176	2,443,676	$586,482,353
Grades 6-8 Net Acres	385.00	439.20	(54.20)	$45,000.00	($2,438,843)	701.50	316.50	$14,242,296
Grades 9-12 Building Sq. Ft.	4,950,000	4,609,410	340,590	$265.00	$90,256,350	8,548,485	3,598,485	$953,598,485
Grades 9-12 Net Acres	760.00	705.45	54.55	$35,000.00	$1,909,252	1,079.35	319.35	$11,177,395
Auxiliary Building Sq. Ft.	432,000	411,125	20,875	$175.00	$3,653,125	503,750	71,750	$12,556,250
Auxiliary Net Acres	30.00	32.83	(2.83)	$45,000.00	($127,273)	46.26	16.26	$731,612
Water and Wastewater Utilities								
Water Treatment Facilities, Gallons, MGD	95.00	90.22	4.78	$9.42	$42,166,982	113.68	18.68	$175,947,462
Water Supply and Treatment Facility Land, Net Acres	100.00	na	na	$20,000.00	na	40.00	(60.00)	$0

Table 10-1 (continued)
Capital Facility Cost Estimates

Facility	Existing Facility Capacity	Existing Facility Demand	Excess (Deficient) Capacity	Cost Per Unit	Value of Excess (Deficient) Capacity	Capacity Needed 2020	Facility Capacity Expansion Needed (Excess Capacity)	Estimated Facility Cost
Wastewater Treatment Facilities, Gallons, MGD	65.00	65.23	(0.23)	$14.68	($3,330,855)	85.01	20.01	$293,736,768
Wastewater Treatment Facility Land, Net Acres	100.00	na	na	$20,000.00	na	60.00	(40.00)	$0
Wastewater Irrigation Fields, Net Acres	200.00	na	na	$20,000.00	na	100.00	(100.00)	$0
Total Impact Cost								$3,615,946,781
Net Value of Excess (Deficient) Capacity					($150,883,665)			
Net Value of Excess (Deficient) Capacity Assigned to New Development								($150,883,665)
Total Facility Capacity Value + Investment Needed for New Development								$3,465,063,116

Analysis			
Cost Per Resident 2020			$4,655
Cost Per New Resident (Excluding Deficiency Amount)			$19,458
24/7 Functional Population and Cost Per 24/7 Functional Resident	715,691		$4,842
New 24/7 Functional Population and Total Cost Per New 24/7 Functional Resident	196,020		$17,677
Net Cost Per New 24/7 Functional Resident			$18,447
Daytime Functional Residents and Total Cost Per Daytime Functional Resident	749,535		$4,623
Daytime Functional Residents and Total Per New Daytime Functional Resident	219,446		$15,790
Net Cost Per New Daytime Functional Resident			$16,478

Not considered here, of course, is the nature of new revenues that new development brings in the form of taxes, user fees, fines, permits, and so forth. It also does not include intergovernmental transfers that rise when communities grow, such as federal and state grant programs, which are based in part on changes in population. At $50,000 per new detached dwelling unit, revenues from all sources would have to average about $4,000 annually to finance capital costs (exclusive of transportation). New revenues generated by new development may be sufficient to finance its capital cost impact on facilities.

Not considered are operations and maintenance costs. These costs can be much more complex to estimate. Still, one could simply take the operation and maintenance budgets of existing functions, divide by existing population or functional population, and multiply those coefficients by change in population and functional population to derive a reasonable estimate. One may find that operation and maintenance expenses can equal or exceed annual average capital costs.

This is the final piece of information Yukon County has developed as part of its effort to estimate land-use and facility needs. It can now consider various ways of addressing these needs, including searching for alternative configurations of development patterns that may reduce land-use needs (especially if the supply of available land is constrained) or capital costs, or both.

Estimating Land-Use and Facility Needs of Unanticipated Development

OVERVIEW

A comprehensive land-use plan should be capable of adequately anticipating land-use and facility needs over the planning horizon and certainly anticipating such needs during interim periods. There are some situations in which this may not hold:

- The first is when a community deliberates annexation of land into incorporated city limits to allow development that was not anticipated in the plan. This situation is as important to counties as it is to cities, especially if annexation extends urban facilities out to formerly undeveloped areas that may now be developed on a scale unforeseen by current plans.
- The second is when a community is presented with a proposal to substantially alter its character, perhaps involving a large, mixed-used development that would result in the community having more development than anticipated in land-use plans.
- The third is when another community undertakes a substantial change in its land-use development patterns that could result in spillover development pressure unforeseen by current plans.
- Finally, a major new economic engine may arrive, such as an automobile factory, research and development facility, federal installation, or the like.

This chapter presents a way in which to estimate land-use and facility impacts associated with unanticipated change in development pressures. It presents a method to estimate the land-use and facility impacts of such unanticipated development or changes to the adopted comprehensive plan.

The method presented here is pioneering. It attempts to account for interactions in land uses, which are difficult to ascertain in the best of circumstances, and does so with numerous simplifying assumptions. Notably, it combines economic base theory and input-output (I-O) analysis to apportion impacts between land uses. Because I-O analysis assumes no impact from change in households in a region, economic base theory is used. The problem is that I-O analysis evaluates the effect that a change in one productive sector of the economy, such as a factory, would have on all others. Since households merely support economic activity, a change in households per se would merely reflect a change somewhere else in the economy. I do not believe this is realistic.

There are numerous examples where a development is purely residential. The new residents bring new jobs—especially in retail, FIRE, and services to the community—but not the other way around. Yet, because there is no I-O multiplier associated with household change per se, there is per se no impact. This is not intuitively correct. I thus use economic base analysis to estimate impacts associated with a change in residential development. Of course, where there are changes in both employment and housing units associated with a development, they both need to be considered, which the approach here does.

There are several other cautionary notes:

- Just because a change was not strictly anticipated in a plan does not mean that the change itself is really different from overall plan outcomes anticipated. For instance, in the annexation example cited above, it may merely displace or rearrange development that would have occurred anyway.

The result may be more development at the annexed location but less development than anticipated elsewhere. Indeed, this is the normal case, so the user must be wary of it.

- Employment projections are usually reasonably good in a short period (perhaps about five years) and not too bad over long periods in areas with a history of steady growth. In reviewing high-quality plans prepared 10 or 20 years ago, I am pleasantly surprised to find that population and employment projections are often very nearly on the mark, although the precise distribution of development may differ substantially. Thus, what might appear to be a change in development pressures associated with a proposal for land-use change may merely reflect a change in the distribution in development, not development per se.

- Using a simple formula (share of total workers living in the area who also work in the area), I apportion new households associated with new employment to local or nonlocal communities. There will be situations where a higher or lower percentage of households associated with new development will actually locate in the community. Related to this is the assumption that new households, and indeed new jobs, will be distributed in the same proportion as the plan anticipates for all new residential and employment development over the planning horizon. This may be unrealistic. If a low-skill, high-labor demand industry moves in, most workers will gravitate toward higher density and smaller housing units than the plan may otherwise assume.

The user should consider the impact estimates to be broad indicators of change, not precise change. The user will need to use judgment, perhaps including that of others, to refine some impact estimates. Nonetheless, the method presented in this chapter is a point of departure for assessing the impacts of unanticipated change in development in a way that is reasonably simple.

BASIC IMPACT COEFFICIENTS

We begin with a review of and modifications to basic impact coefficients, which are presented in Table 11-1. Because new development, whether residential or employment, will not always be fully occupied, this table produces "effective" residential units and employment per acre. The result is *less* impact per acre of development since it adjusts development for vacancy. The following calculations are made:

Land-Use Unit: This is the unit of development that will be used to estimate impacts of unanticipated land uses.

Persons Per Occupied Unit: For residential land uses, this figure is the **Assumed Household Size 2020** from Table 3-6. The employment coefficient is calculated as:

$$[(1{,}000 / \text{GROSS SQ. FT. PER EMPLOYEE})]$$

with the employment figure from Table 4-6.

Vacancy Rate 2020: The residential figure is from Table 3-7 while the employment figure is from Table 4-2.

Effective Persons Per Unit: Calculated as

$$[(\text{PERSONS PER OCCUPIED UNIT}) \times (1 - \text{VACANCY RATE 2020})]$$

Table 11-1
Basic Impact Coefficients for Unanticipated Change in Land-Use and Facility Needs

Private Land-Use Category	Land-Use Unit	Persons Per Occupied Unit	Vacancy Rate 2020	Effective Persons Per Unit	Employees Per Net Acre	In-Place Employee Percent	Residential Units and Effective Employment Per Net Acre	Planned Residents, Employees Per Net Acre
Residential								
Permanent Residential								
1-5 Acres Per Unit	Residential Unit	2.7500	3.00%	2.6675	na	na	0.5000	1.3338
1-2 Units Per Acre	Residential Unit	2.7500	3.00%	2.6675	na	na	1.7500	4.6681
3-5 Units Per Acre	Residential Unit	2.7000	3.00%	2.6190	na	na	4.5000	11.7855
6-8 Units Per Acre	Residential Unit	2.7000	3.00%	2.6190	na	na	7.5000	19.6425
9-14 Units Per Acre	Residential Unit	2.3500	6.00%	2.2090	na	na	12.7500	28.1648
15+ Units Per Acre	Residential Unit	2.2000	6.00%	2.0680	na	na	25.5000	52.7340
All Permanent Residential	Residential Unit	2.5456	4.25%	2.4375				
Group Care								
Residential								
Nursing Homes	Bed	1.7500	2.00%	1.7150	na	na	32.0000	54.8800
Assisted Living	Residential Unit	1.2500	2.00%	1.2250	na	na	24.0000	29.4000
Employment								
Nursing Homes	Bed	0.2963	na	0.2963	na	na	32.0000	9.4808
Assisted Living	Residential Unit	0.2963	na	0.2963	na	na	24.0000	7.1106
Hotel/Motel								
Residential								
Low Rise (1-3 Floors)	Room	1.9000	6.50%	1.7765	na	na	45.0000	79.9425
Mid Rise (4-7 Floors)	Room	1.9000	6.50%	1.7765	na	na	60.0000	106.5900
High Rise (8+ Floors)	Room	1.9000	6.50%	1.7765	na	na	75.0000	133.2375

Table 11-1 (continued)
Basic Impact Coefficients for Unanticipated Change in Land-Use and Facility Needs

Private Land-Use Category	Land-Use Unit	Persons Per Occupied Unit	Vacancy Rate 2020	Effective Persons Per Unit	Employees Per Net Acre	In-Place Employee Percent	Residential Units and Effective Employment Per Net Acre	Planned Residents, Employees Per Net Acre
Employment								
Low Rise (1-3 Floors)	Room	0.2529	na	0.2529	na	na	45.0000	11.3786
Mid Rise (4-7 Floors)	Room	0.2529	na	0.2529	na	na	60.0000	15.1714
High Rise (8+ Floors)	Room	0.2529	na	0.2529	na	na	75.0000	18.9643
Employment								
Industrial								
Construction	1,000 Sq. Ft.	3.4712	5.00%	3.2976	28.7287	25.00%	7.1822	28.7287
Manufacturing	1,000 Sq. Ft.	1.6409	5.00%	1.5589	16.4399	100.00%	16.4399	16.4399
TCU	1,000 Sq. Ft.	3.6100	5.00%	3.4295	29.8778	100.00%	29.8778	29.8778
Wholesale Trade	1,000 Sq. Ft.	1.4325	5.00%	1.3609	16.2244	100.00%	16.2244	16.2244
Retail Trade								
Neighborhood	1,000 Sq. Ft.	1.5833	5.00%	1.5042	15.8631	100.00%	15.8631	15.8631
Community	1,000 Sq. Ft.	1.4902	5.00%	1.4157	14.9300	100.00%	14.9300	14.9300
Regional	1,000 Sq. Ft.	1.3971	5.00%	1.3272	20.6910	100.00%	20.6910	20.6910
Super Regional	1,000 Sq. Ft.	1.3039	5.00%	1.2387	19.3116	100.00%	19.3116	19.3116
Office								
General Office	1,000 Sq. Ft.	2.8536	4.67%	2.7204	46.9498	80.00%	37.5599	46.9498
Office Park	1,000 Sq. Ft.	2.8536	4.67%	2.7204	46.9498	80.00%	37.5599	46.9498
Suburban Multilevel	1,000 Sq. Ft.	2.9750	4.67%	2.8362	46.9498	80.00%	37.5599	46.9498

Employees Per Net Acre: This comes from only Table 4-6 because it is not applicable to residential land uses.

In-Place Employee Percent: This information is from Table 4-6.

Residential Units and Effective Employment Per Net Acre: The residential figures are from the **Plan New Unit Net Density 2020** column of Table 3-7. The employment figures are calculated as follows:

[(EMPLOYEES PER ACRE) × (IN-PLACE EMPLOYEE PERCENT)]

Planned Residents, Employees Per Net Acre: The employment figure is from the column:

(EMPLOYEES PER NET ACRE)

while the residential figure is calculated as:

[(EFFECTIVE PERSONS PER UNIT)
× (RESIDENTIAL UNITS AND EFFECTIVE EMPLOYMENT PER NET ACRE)]

We now proceed to economic multiplier analysis to aid ultimately in estimating direct, indirect, and induced impacts of unanticipated land-use changes.

ECONOMIC BASE RESIDENTIAL CHANGE COEFFICIENT

Economic base analysis is used to develop employment coefficients associated with unanticipated change in residential development. Economic base analysis disaggregates local employment into "basic" and "nonbasic" parts (see Klosterman 1990). A basic employee is one who produces a good or service that is "exported" out of the region. Automobile workers are obvious examples of basic employees. Not so obvious would be a local brain surgeon whose practice attracts patients from outside the region to her. Although employees in manufacturing may customarily be considered basic, this is also not always the case. Tofu production is considered a manufacturing process, but tofu firms typically serve only the immediate community and there is very little exporting of it to areas outside the region.

Nonbasic workers would be those who provide goods and services for local consumption (e.g., dental offices, grocery stores, and repair shops). There seems to be a bias in economic development literature to advance basic over nonbasic employment opportunities, however. This is shortsighted because oftentimes there are not enough nonbasic employees to meet local needs. Some local dollars that should have been spent locally are "leaked" to other regions. Good economic development strategies attempt to eliminate such leakage.

Care should be taken, however, to be sure the "region" is not too small or too large. For the nation as a whole, the vast majority of workers produce goods and services for domestic consumption. The nation is too large to be considered a region, but states are not. On the other hand, regions that are defined too narrowly will have skewed relationships among economic activities. If the region is defined as a very small county surrounded by other small counties, a used car dealership there could be considered "basic" when in fact it serves essentially a local market. Although there are no firm rules on the ideal size of regions for economic base analysis (or for I-O analysis), I prefer census regions, states, metropolitan statistical areas (and consolidated ones over primary ones in relevant situations), and BEA "Economic Areas."

Economic base analysis is useful in estimating the potential impact of a change in resident population. If a region adds a number of households that were not anticipated and not related to other economic activities, such as retirement communities, how many employees will be needed to support them? Table 11-2 estimates the nonbasic employment coefficient per permanent resident. Simply speaking, if we know how people are moving into the region, this coefficient can be used to estimate the number of employees they would support. The calculations leading to this are as follows:

Local Employment 2020: This is from the individual employment sector rows corresponding to the **2020** column of Table 2-3.

National Employment 2020: These figures come from the BEA of the U.S. Department of Commerce or standard projection services. National figures from the BEA (1999) are used in this example.

Location Quotient 2020: The location quotient indicates the presence of basic (LQ > 1.0) employees within an economic sector. By implication, this also indicates the presence of leakage (LQ < 1.0) and is calculated as:

$$\{[(\text{LOCAL EMPLOYMENT 2020}_{\text{EMPLOYMENT LAND-USE CATEGORY}})$$
$$/ (\text{TOTAL EMPLOYMENT}_{\text{LOCAL EMPLOYMENT 2020}})]$$
$$/ [(\text{NATIONAL EMPLOYMENT 2020}_{\text{EMPLOYMENT LAND-USE CATEGORY}})$$
$$/ (\text{TOTAL EMPLOYMENT}_{\text{NATIONAL EMPLOYMENT 2020}})]\}$$

Basic Employment 2020: In Lotus, Excel, and Quatro, the formula is written as follows:

$$@\text{IF}(\text{LOCATION QUOTIENT 2020}_{\text{EMPLOYMENT LAND-USE CATEGORY}})$$
$$< 1, 0, [(\text{LOCAL EMPLOYMENT 2020}_{\text{EMPLOYMENT LAND-USE CATEGORY}})$$
$$- ((1 / (\text{LOCATION QUOTIENT 2020}_{\text{EMPLOYMENT LAND-USE CATEGORY}})$$
$$\times (\text{LOCAL EMPLOYMENT 2020}_{\text{EMPLOYMENT LAND-USE CATEGORY}}))]$$

Table 11-2
Basic and Nonbasic Employment

Land-Use Category	Local Employment 2020	National Employment 2020	Location Quotient 2020	Basic Employment 2020
Construction	15,300	7,705,500	1.0017	26
Manufacturing	25,500	19,681,900	0.6536	0
TCU	19,800	7,310,600	1.3664	5,309
Wholesale Trade	23,600	7,534,900	1.5801	8,664
Retail	46,500	26,351,600	0.8902	0
FIRE	24,700	11,868,200	1.0500	1,175
Services	82,100	43,892,023	0.9437	0
Government	37,900	20,896,400	0.9150	0
Group Care	4,700	2,633,177	0.9005	0
Hotel/Motel	17,700	2,364,400	3.7767	13,013
Total Employment	297,800	150,238,700		28,188

Analysis	
Basic Employment Percent	9.47%
Nonbasic Employment Percent	90.53%
Nonbasic Employment	269,612
Permanent Population	720,810
Nonbasic Employment Per Permanent Resident	0.3740

which means essentially that if local employment in any given employment category is more than needed to serve local economic needs, the difference is considered export base employment. (All other employment is considered "nonbasic" and essentially serves local needs.)

Permanent Population: This comes from Table 2-2 for the future year of reference.

Nonbasic Employment Per Permanent Resident: Calculated as

$$[(\text{NONBASIC EMPLOYMENT}) / (\text{PERMANENT POPULATION})]$$

The nonbasic employee coefficient will be used in the manner shown later.

EMPLOYMENT CHANGE COEFFICIENTS

What if new, unanticipated development employs workers, whether basic or nonbasic? What will be the impact on other economic sectors and on households attracted to the community? The employment impact can be estimated using employment multipliers generated from I-O analysis (see U.S. BEA 1997). I-O multipliers account for interindustry relationships within regions. The analysis is based on an accounting framework called the I-O table. The I-O table shows, for each industry, industrial distributions of inputs purchased and outputs sold between industries. One calculation of the I-O process leads to direct-effect employment multipliers by economic sectors. For example, the national direct-effect employment multiplier for motor vehicles and equipment is 7.4625 (i.e., for each job in this sector, a total of 7.4625 jobs are created), one for itself and 6.4625 for all others. On the other hand, the national direct-

effect employment multiplier for personal services (e.g., hair salons and barbers) is just 1.7871, one for itself and 0.7871 for others.

I-O tables are useful to trace implications of changes in the regional economy; they are not very useful for estimating land-use and facility needs. The direct-effect employment multipliers, however, are useful in a general sense, which is developed here. In 1992, the BEA published direct-effect employment multipliers for all states, which are reported in Table 11-3 (along with the national multipliers, which were acquired separately by the author).

There is one important limitation to these multipliers, however: We do not know which industries are affected by a change in one of the other industries. For example, how are the other 6.4625 jobs created from motor vehicle employment or the 0.7871 from personal services distributed? Although the BEA produces I-O tables for regions of any configuration, it does not do so with direct-effect employment multipliers.

The approach used here is to assume that the distribution of additional jobs attracted is similar to the distribution of new jobs anticipated in the land-use plan. The underlying assumption is that the region will only attract those firms that are a good fit with it and the spinoff impacts will be distributed roughly proportionately to the region's employment makeup.

Remember that the objective of this analysis is to estimate approximate magnitudes of impact, not to calculate precise impacts. The user, perhaps working with others knowledgeable of the local economy, can refine the estimates of impact to make them more realistic given local conditions.

These calculations are reported in Table 11-2.

Table 11-3
Employment Multipliers

Industrial Sector	National Employment Multiplier 1992	National Employment (000s) 1987	Regional Employment Multiplier 1992	Regional Employment (000s) 1987
Construction				
New Construction	3.4920	2,094	2.3326	52.1
Maintenance and Repair Construction	2.6864	2,904	1.9281	63.7
Weighted Average	3.0239		2.1101	
Total Construction		4,998		115.8
Manufacturing				
Food and Kindred Products and Tobacco	7.2701	1,678	3.9367	63.2
Textile Mill Products	3.8110	725	3.1244	109.8
Apparel	2.7801	1,100	2.0758	69.2
Paper and Allied Products	5.0271	679	3.7730	32.2
Printing and Publishing	3.0814	1,507	2.3076	41.7
Chemicals and Petroleum Refining	7.8156	1,191	3.2515	20.7
Rubber and Leather Products	3.1143	967	2.1060	19.5
Lumber and Wood Products and Furniture	3.4259	1,258	2.6011	50.5
Stone, Clay and Glass Products	3.3687	582	2.3776	22.3
Primary Metal Products	4.9144	749	2.9742	15.8
Fabricated Metal Products	3.6716	1,407	2.3426	21.5
Machinery, Except Electrical	3.8944	2,023	2.2320	27.0
Electric and Electronic Equipment	3.6710	2,084	2.4632	32.3

Table 11-3 (continued)
Employment Multipliers

Industrial Sector	National Employment Multiplier 1992	National Employment (000s) 1987	Regional Employment Multiplier 1992	Regional Employment (000s) 1987
Motor Vehicles and Equipment	7.4625	865	3.8412	18.7
Transportation Equipment, Except Motor Vehicles	3.9897	1,183	2.6577	30.8
Instruments and Related Products	3.4526	696	2.1189	6.5
Miscellaneous Manufacturing Industries	3.4199	370	2.3743	7.2
Weighted Average	4.4003		2.8319	
Total Manufacturing		19,064		588.9
TCU				
Transportation	2.7994	3,167	2.2105	128.0
Communication	3.1078	1,293	2.3289	45.9
Electric, Gas, Water and Sanitary Services	8.1695	925	4.0769	28.7
Weighted Average	3.7959		2.5017	
Total TCU		5,385		202.6
Wholesale Trade				
Weighted Average	2.5722		2.1492	
Total Wholesale Trade		5,872		229.3
Retail Trade				
Retail Trade	1.8038	13,178	1.5537	412.1
Eating and Drinking Places	1.8097	6,127	1.4869	176.8
Weighted Average	1.8057		1.5336	
Total Retail Trade		19,305		588.9

Table 11-3 (continued)
Employment Multipliers

Industrial Sector	National Employment Multiplier 1992	National Employment (000s) 1987	Regional Employment Multiplier 1992	Regional Employment (000s) 1987
FIRE				
Finance	3.2392	3,889	2.3738	86.4
Insurance	3.5191	1,418	2.7686	63.9
Real Estate	7.2635	1,242	5.8404	92.6
Weighted Average	4.0630		3.7992	
Total FIRE		6,549		242.9
Services				
Personal Services	1.7871	1,147	1.4297	65.3
Business Services	2.2868	5,172	1.9051	196.6
Miscellaneous Services	2.3019	22,321	1.7726	278.6
Weighted Average	2.2786		1.7794	
Total Services		28,640		540.5
Health Services	2.1645	6,828	1.8223	160.0
Hotels and Lodging Places and Amusements	2.1871	1,147	1.6697	72.7
Office Related (FIRE, Services)	2.6107	35,189	2.4056	783.4

Table 11-3 modifies the BEA's direct-effect employment multipliers to fit into the land-use categories used for planning purposes. Adjustments are made for both the nation and state within which Yukon County is located only to show how effects differ based on two different regions. The state multipliers are used to calculate impacts as will be shown. The calculations contained in this table include:

Industrial Sector: These are the economic categories developed by the BEA for its 39-industry multiplier analysis, adjusted for this land-use impact analysis as follows: eating- and drinking-based employment moved from services to retail trade; hotel, motel and amusement moved out of services into its own category; and health care services also moved out of services into its own category.

National or **Regional Employment Multiplier 1992:** These are the national and regional (state) employment multipliers based on the BEA's *Regional Input-Output Multipliers II (RIMSII)* model refined in 1992.

National or **Regional Employment (000s) 1987:** This is the national and regional (state) employment in 1987, the BEA's base year for I-O analysis.

Weighted Average: Where land uses are composed of several multiple economic categories, a weighting approach is used. It is imperfect but nonetheless suitable for estimating a reasonable magnitude of land-use impact associated with unanticipated change in otherwise planned development. The calculation for FIRE, for example, is:

$$\{[(\text{NATIONAL EMPLOYMENT MULTIPLIER 1992}_{\text{FINANCE}})$$
$$\times (\text{NATIONAL EMPLOYMENT (000s) 1987}_{\text{FINANCE}})]$$
$$+ [(\text{NATIONAL EMPLOYMENT MULTIPLIER 1992}_{\text{INSURANCE}})$$
$$\times (\text{NATIONAL EMPLOYMENT (000s) 1987}_{\text{INSURANCE}})]$$
$$+ [(\text{NATIONAL EMPLOYMENT MULTIPLIER 1992}_{\text{REAL ESTATE}})$$
$$\times (\text{NATIONAL EMPLOYMENT (000s) 1987}_{\text{REAL ESTATE}})]\}$$
$$/ [(\text{NATIONAL EMPLOYMENT (000s)}_{\text{FINANCE}})$$
$$+ (\text{NATIONAL EMPLOYMENT (000s)}_{\text{INSURANCE}})$$
$$+ (\text{NATIONAL EMPLOYMENT (000s)}_{\text{REAL ESTATE}})]$$

In the case of office parks or office development where no particular distribution of employment among BEA industrial categories is known, an overall weighted multiplier representing all major office land uses may be used. This is calculated as:

$$\{[(\text{NATIONAL EMPLOYMENT MULTIPLIER 1992}_{\text{FIRE WEIGHTED AVERAGE}})$$
$$\times (\text{NATIONAL EMPLOYMENT (000s) 1987}_{\text{FIRE TOTAL}})]$$
$$+ [(\text{NATIONAL EMPLOYMENT MULTIPLIER 1992}_{\text{SERVICES WEIGHTED AVERAGE}})$$
$$\times (\text{NATIONAL EMPLOYMENT (000s) 1987}_{\text{SERVICES TOTAL}})]\}$$
$$/ [(\text{NATIONAL EMPLOYMENT (000s) 1987}_{\text{FIRE TOTAL}})$$
$$+ (\text{NATIONAL EMPLOYMENT (000s) 1987}_{\text{SERVICES TOTAL}})]$$

The result of these calculations is a set of assumptions that can be used to estimate employment and household impacts associated with unanticipated land-use changes.

HOUSEHOLD AND EMPLOYMENT CAPTURE

We need to consider one more thing before looking at the impact of unanticipated land-use changes. There are three forms of impact: direct, indirect, and induced.

"Direct" impact means the acres, housing units, and jobs proposed. A 100-acre proposal for new residential units might include 1,000 townhouses housing 2,000 people, for example; another 100 acres for an office park might support 3,000 workers. These are examples of direct impact. The new townhouses will house people who need services such as shopping, receiving medical assistance, or having their cars serviced. This is the "indirect" impact associated with the initial change, but the indirect workers will need other workers to support their needs. This is the "induced" impact.

The same cycle of direct begetting indirect begetting induced impacts is seen with the 100-acre office park example. The prior discussion described how one estimates the direct and induced demand through the use of multipliers for employment-based

land uses and total new jobs per resident for new residential population. The remaining questions are:

1. How many new jobs supported by the change will be located locally?
2. How many new households supported by those jobs will choose to live locally? They will certainly work and live somewhere but, especially in large metropolitan areas, not all will choose to live in the same county or planning area where they work.

One common way to estimate both figures is to reduce total new jobs and associated households supported by the percent of workers who commute into the local area for employment. If 40% of the workers commute in, then 60% of the workers would appear to live locally, and hence 60% of the new jobs and associated households created by the unanticipated change is "captured" locally. Usually, the smaller the planning area, the lower the capture rate.

How is this issue addressed here? First of all, there should be the option for one to estimate total impacts regardless of where they are all felt. Table 11-4 in the workbook allows for an assumption on the capture rate for jobs and households. It can be the rate internally calculated by the worksheet (discussed below) or one selected by the user. Both analyses are recommended, so a range of impacts can be assessed during the decision-making process addressing the proposed change in the comprehensive plan.

How does one estimate the job and household capture rate? A common way is to take the ratio of the percent of in-commuting minus 1 from the most recent census, and either use it as the capture rate or assume a different figure at the end of the plan-

Table 11-4
Employment Ratio Adjustments

Adjustment Factor	Adjustment Figure
Employment Per Resident, Residents Per Employee	
Nonbasic Employment Per Permanent Resident	0.3740
Residents Per Nursing Home Employee	5.7885
Residents Per Assisted Living Employee	4.1347
Residents Per Hotel/Motel Employee	7.0257
Employment Capture	
National Average Workers Per Household, 2020	1.60
Households, 2020	283,000
Workers in Households, 2020	452,800
Employees, 2020	298,100
Percent Workers Captured, 2020	65.83%
Percent Capture Assumption if Different from Calculation	0.00%
Percent Capture Assumption	65.83%

ning horizon. This approach does not adjust for people living in the planning area who commute out. A different approach is simpler in that it uses the ratio of jobs in the planning area to total jobs in the planning area's households.

We know nationally that the typical household has about 1.60 workers and this figure may not change much over the next two decades. (This figure indicates part-time and temporary workers.) If a planning area will have 100,000 households at the end of the planning horizon, it will have about 160,000 workers living there (including part-time and temporary workers). If the planning area is projected to have 120,000 jobs by the end of the planning horizon, it has a jobs-housing balance of

0.75 (meaning that, in theory, 75% of the workers living in the planning area work there as well). This is obviously not the case but it does suggest that, at a ratio of 1.00, there is a balance between in-commuting and out-commuting. This is the ratio used to assume the percent of new jobs and households created by an unanticipated land-use change that will remain in the planning area. The formula is:

$$\{(EMPLOYEES, 2020) / [(HOUSEHOLDS, 2020)$$
$$\times (NATIONAL\ AVERAGE\ WORKERS\ PER\ HOUSEHOLD\ 2020)]\}$$

However, the adjustment figure cannot be greater than 1.00, otherwise there would be more jobs and households locating in the planning area than the total jobs and household impacts caused by an unanticipated land-use change.

EXAMPLE OF CHANGE IN 100 ACRES OF RESIDENTIAL DEVELOPMENT, 6-8 UNITS PER NET ACRE

Let us now see how all this works with a simple example. Suppose there is a proposal to add 100 net acres of residential land with a density of 6 to 8 units per acre to the inventory of urban land contained in the Yukon County land-use plan, and this represents unanticipated development (i.e., the proposal does not shift development that would have occurred elsewhere to the proposed site). What is the impact of this proposed change on the residential and employment land area needed?

Consider that the 100 acres would average about 7.50 units per acre (based on planning assumptions in worksheet Table 3-7) and generate about 750 new housing units. This equates to about 1,964 new residents (based on Table 11-1). From worksheet Table 11-4, we know that each resident is associated with 0.3740 jobs (from **Nonbasic Employment Per Permanent Resident**) which, in this case, equates to about 734 new jobs. Not all those jobs will actually locate in Yukon County, so we adjust this figure by 65.8% (from **Percent Workers Captured, 2020**) as reported in Table 11-4, bringing the total to about 483.69 jobs as seen in Table 11-6 (from **Total New Employees**). We can assume that those jobs will be distributed proportionately with that anticipated in Yukon County's land-use plan, and will lead to associated increases in land needed for employment land uses.

Two tables are needed to calculate total impact. The first (Table 11-5) focuses on residential land-use impacts; the second (Table 11-6) addresses employment land-use impacts.

Table 11-5: Residential Land-Use Impacts

Calculations for this table include:

New Acres: This is the net acres added to community that were not anticipated in the plan. (Acres added to group care and hotel/motel land uses are the same in the residential and employment components.) If added area includes land for roads, utilities, easements, etc., the gross acre figure should be adjusted to net acres with the gross land adjustment factor reflected in the appropriate column.

New Residential Units: Calculated as

$$[(NEW\ ACRES) \times (PLAN\ NEW\ UNIT\ NET\ DENSITY\ 2020)]$$

where PLAN NEW UNIT NET DENSITY 2020 comes from Table 3-7 and also reported as part of the **Residential Units and Effective Employment Per Net Acre** column for residential land uses in Table 11-1.

New Residents (Adjusted For Unit Vacancy): Calculated as

$$[(NEW\ RESIDENTIAL\ UNITS) \times (EFFECTIVE\ PERSONS\ PER\ UNIT)]$$

where EFFECTIVE PERSONS PER UNIT comes from the **Effective Persons Per Unit** column in Table 11-1. This calculation adjusts total housing units added to those occupied after considering vacancies.

New Local Employees Generated From New Residents With Local Adjustment: Calculated as

$$[(NEW\ RESIDENTS\ (ADJUSTED\ FOR\ UNIT\ VACANCY)) \times (NONBASIC\ EMPLOYMENT\ PER\ PERMANENT\ RESIDENT) \times (PERCENT\ CAPTURE\ ASSUMPTION)]$$

where both NONBASIC EMPLOYMENT PER PERMANENT RESIDENT and PERCENT CAPTURE ASSUMPTION come from Table 11-4.

Indirect Households Generated From New Local Employees: Calculated as

$$[(NEW\ LOCAL\ EMPLOYEES\ GENERATED\ FROM\ NEW\ RESIDENTS\ WITH\ LOCAL\ ADJUSTMENT) / (NATIONAL\ AVERAGE\ WORKERS\ PER\ HOUSEHOLD,\ 2020)]$$

where NATIONAL AVERAGE WORKERS PER HOUSEHOLD, 2020 comes from Table 11-4.

Plan Percent Residents 2020: This apportions new households by the planned distribution of new residents as reported in Table 3-6.

Additional Residential Units Needed to Support Resident Change: This calculation shows the number of housing units needed by type based on this unanticipated change.

Table 11-5
Impact of Unanticipated Change, 100-Acre Plan Change for 6-8 Units Per Acre—Residential Component

Land-Use Category	New Acres	New Residential Units	New Residents (Adjusted For Unit Vacancy)	New Local Employees Generated From New Residents With Local Adjustment	Indirect Households Generated From New Local Employees	Plan Percent Residents 2020	Additional Residential Units Needed to Support Resident Change	Residential Units Needed to Support New Employment Households Captured	Total Residential Unit Change	Total Resident Change	Net Acre Change	Gross Acre Adjustment Factor	Gross Acre Change
Permanent Residential													
1-5 Acres Per Unit	0.00	0.00	0.00	0.00	0.00	4.00%	4.53	0.00	4.53	12.09	9.07	10.00%	10.07
1-2 Units Per Acre	0.00	0.00	0.00	0.00	0.00	20.00%	22.67	0.00	22.67	60.46	12.95	20.00%	16.19
3-5 Units Per Acre	0.00	0.00	0.00	0.00	0.00	20.00%	23.09	0.00	23.09	60.46	5.13	25.00%	6.84
6-8 Units Per Acre	100.00	750.00	1,964.25	483.69	302.31	18.00%	20.78	0.00	770.78	2,018.67	102.77	30.00%	146.81
9-14 Units Per Acre	0.00	0.00	0.00	0.00	0.00	23.00%	31.48	0.00	31.48	69.53	2.47	35.00%	3.80
15+ Units Per Acre	0.00	0.00	0.00	0.00	0.00	13.00%	19.00	0.00	19.00	39.30	0.75	40.00%	1.24
Subtotal Permanent Residential	100.00	750.00	1,964.25	483.69	302.31	98.00%	121.54	0.00	871.54	2,260.51	133.13		184.96
Group Care													
Nursing Homes	0.00	.				45.00%			15.46	26.51	na	na	na
Assisted Living	0.00					55.00%			10.31	12.63	na	na	na
Subtotal Group Care	0.00					100.00%			25.77	39.14			
Hotel/Motel Units													
Low Rise (1-3 Floors)	0.00					50.00%			56.85	100.99	na	na	na
Mid Rise (4-7 Floors)	0.00					25.00%			28.42	50.50	na	na	na
High Rise (8+ Floors)	0.00					25.00%			28.42	50.50	na	na	na
Subtotal Hotel/Motel Units	0.00					100.00%			113.70	201.98			

The formula for this calculation is:

[(PLAN PERCENT RESIDENTS 2020)
× (INDIRECT HOUSEHOLDS GENERATED FROM NEW LOCAL EMPLOYEES)]
/ (EFFECTIVE PERSONS PER UNIT)

where EFFECTIVE PERSONS PER UNIT comes from the **Effective Persons Per Unit** column in Table 11-1.

Residential Units Needed to Support New Employment Households Captured: This is determined through the following calculation:

[(TOTAL EMPLOYEES FROM EMPLOYMENT CHANGE)
× (PERCENT CAPTURE ASSUMPTION)]
/ (NATIONAL AVERAGE WORKERS PER HOUSEHOLD, 2020)

where TOTAL EMPLOYEES FROM EMPLOYMENT CHANGE is from Table 11-6. (As these two tables are interactive to generate impact figures from both residential and nonresidential development, numbers from one are used in the other. The user can consider them essentially one large table; however, for presentation purposes, it was believed that dividing them made the analysis easier.) NATIONAL AVERAGE WORKERS PER HOUSEHOLD, 2020 comes from Table 11-4

Total Residential Unit Change: Calculated as

[(NEW RESIDENTIAL UNITS) + (ADDITIONAL RESIDENTIAL
UNITS NEEDED TO SUPPORT RESIDENT CHANGE)
+ (RESIDENTIAL UNITS NEEDED TO SUPPORT NEW
EMPLOYMENT HOUSEHOLDS CAPTURED)]

Total Resident Change: This is an estimate of total direct, indirect, and induced resident impact associated with the unanticipated residential land-use change.

Net Acre Change: This is calculated as the total housing units needed by each residential type divided by density for each type.

Gross Acre Adjustment Factor and **Gross Acre Change:** This is calculated consistent with the residential land-use assumptions in Chapter 3.

Table 11-5 shows the residential impact figures. Because no employment-based land-use changes are proposed, some columns in this table are blanks or duplicate other numbers.

Table 11-6: Employment-Based Land-Use Impacts

Let us now consider employment-based land-use impacts associated with this unanticipated change in residential development.

There are only three considerations addressed here and they all lead to an estimate of employment-based land-use needs associated with this unanticipated change in residential land uses. They are:

Indirect Employees From Residential Change: This is from Table 11-6.

Net Acre Change: This is calculated as the total housing units needed by each residential type divided by density for each type.

Gross Acre Adjustment Factor and **Gross Acre Change:** This is calculated consistent with the residential land-use assumptions in Chapter 3.

The table is reported in its entirety, even though most columns remain blank in this example. The next example will fill these columns out. We will review the meaning and formulas of columns as needed then.

Table 11-6
Impact of Unanticipated Change, 100-Acre Plan Change for 6-8 Units Per Acre—Employment-Based Component

Land-Use Category	New Acres	Employment Multiplier	Direct Employees	Indirect Employees Based on Employment Change With Local Adjustment	Percent Indirect Employment Distribution	Indirect Employees From Employment Change	Total Employees From Employment Change	Indirect Employees From Residential Change	Total New Employees	Net Acre Change	Gross Acre Adjustment Factor	Gross Acre Change
Group Care												
Nursing Homes	0.00	1.8223	0.00	0.00	0.95%	0.00	0.00	4.58	4.58	0.14	40.00%	0.24
Assisted Living	0.00	1.8223	0.00	0.00	0.63%	0.00	0.00	3.05	3.05	0.13	40.00%	0.21
Hotel/Motel Units												
Low Rise (1-3 Floors)	0.00	1.6697	0.00	0.00	2.97%	0.00	0.00	14.37	14.37	0.32	40.00%	0.53
Mid Rise (4-7 Floors)	0.00	1.6697	0.00	0.00	1.49%	0.00	0.00	7.19	7.19	0.12	45.00%	0.22
High Rise (8+ Floors)	0.00	1.6697	0.00	0.00	1.49%	0.00	0.00	7.19	7.19	0.10	50.00%	0.19
Industrial												
Construction	0.00	2.1101	0.00	0.00	5.14%	0.00	0.00	24.85	24.85	3.46	20.00%	4.33
Manufacturing	0.00	2.8319	0.00	0.00	8.56%	0.00	0.00	41.42	41.42	2.52	20.00%	3.15
TCU	0.00	2.5017	0.00	0.00	6.65%	0.00	0.00	32.16	32.16	1.08	20.00%	1.35
Wholesale Trade	0.00	2.1492	0.00	0.00	7.92%	0.00	0.00	38.33	38.33	2.36	20.00%	2.95
Retail Trade												
Neighborhood	0.00	1.5336	0.00	0.00	6.25%	0.00	0.00	30.21	30.21	1.90	35.00%	2.93
Community	0.00	1.5336	0.00	0.00	4.68%	0.00	0.00	22.66	22.66	1.52	30.00%	2.17
Regional	0.00	1.5336	0.00	0.00	3.12%	0.00	0.00	15.11	15.11	0.73	25.00%	0.97
Super Regional	0.00	1.5336	0.00	0.00	1.56%	0.00	0.00	7.55	7.55	0.39	20.00%	0.49
Office												
General Office	0.00	2.4056	0.00	0.00	31.58%	0.00	0.00	152.77	152.77	4.07	20.00%	5.08
Office Park	0.00	2.4056	0.00	0.00	12.15%	0.00	0.00	58.76	58.76	1.56	25.00%	2.09
Suburban Multilevel	0.00	2.4056	0.00	0.00	4.86%	0.00	0.00	23.50	23.50	0.63	30.00%	0.89
Employment Impact	0.00		0.00	0.00	100.00%	0.00	0.00	483.69	483.69	21.02		27.79

Table 11-7 summarizes these land-use impacts but without going into facility impacts; this will be done later with a mixed-use example.

Table 11-7
Summary of Impact for 100-Acre Plan Change for 6-8 Units Per Acre

Summary Factor	Summary Figure
Direct Change in Net Residential Acres	100.00
Indirect Change in Net Residential Acres	33.13
Direct Change in Net Nonresidential Acres	0.00
Indirect Change in Net Nonresidential Acres	21.02
Total Change in Net Residential Acres	133.13
Total Change in Gross Residential Acres	184.96
Total Change in Net Nonresidential Acres	21.02
Total Change in Gross Nonresidential Acres	27.79
Total Net Acre Change	154.16
Total Gross Acre Change	212.75
Direct Resident Change	1,964.25
Indirect Resident Change	296.26
Total Resident Change	2,260.51
Direct Housing Unit Change	750.00
Indirect Housing Unit Change	121.54
Total Housing Unit Change	871.54
Direct Employment Change	0.00
Indirect Employment Change	483.69
Total Employment Change	483.69

EXAMPLE OF CHANGE IN 100 ACRES OF OFFICE PARK DEVELOPMENT

Let us now consider the potential impact of a 100-acre office park development proposed for Yukon County that was not anticipated in the current land-use plan. For example, perhaps the change is associated with a major national firm deciding to relocate its headquarters to an office park that a developer is advocating. Along with the headquarters will come affiliated firms relocating from their current places of business to be near the headquarters. Although the land-use plan would possibly anticipate such employment change (since it is blind as to which kinds of employment are generated), suppose local officials, planners, and users agree that this constitutes an unanticipated change. As in the residential land-use change example, two tables are used here and are reversed for ease of presentation.

Table 11-8: Employment-Based Land-Use Impacts

Using Table 11-1 as a guide, a 100-acre change in office park development will be associated with 4,695 new employees. Another 4,345 employees will be stimulated by it, based on the multiplier calculated from Table 11-2 and adjusting for those jobs created by this change that actually locate outside the planning area. It is assumed that these additional employees will be distributed to other employment land uses based on the land-use plan's assumed distribution of all new employees. This is a simplifying assumption and one that merely gauges the general magnitude of employment-based land-use changes. The process of estimating the distribution of new employment is performed in the following way:

Table 11-8
Impact of Unanticipated Change, 100-Acre Plan Change for Office Park—Employment-Based Component

Land-Use Category	New Acres	Employment Multiplier	Direct Employees	Indirect Employees Based on Employment Change With Local Adjustment	Percent Indirect Employment Distribution	Indirect Employees From Employment Change	Total Employees From Employment Change	Indirect Employees From Residential Change	Total New Employees	Net Acre Change	Gross Acre Adjust- ment Factor	Gross Acre Change
Group Care												
Nursing Homes	0.00	1.8223	0.00	0.00	0.95%	41.14	41.14	0.00	41.14	1.29	40.00%	2.14
Assisted Living	0.00	1.8223	0.00	0.00	0.63%	27.43	27.43	0.00	27.43	1.14	40.00%	1.90
Hotel/Motel Units												
Low Rise (1-3 Floors)	0.00	1.6697	0.00	0.00	2.97%	129.12	129.12	0.00	129.12	2.87	40.00%	4.78
Mid Rise (4-7 Floors)	0.00	1.6697	0.00	0.00	1.49%	64.56	64.56	0.00	64.56	1.08	45.00%	1.96
High Rise (8+ Floors)	0.00	1.6697	0.00	0.00	1.49%	64.56	64.56	0.00	64.56	0.86	50.00%	1.72
Industrial												
Construction	0.00	2.1101	0.00	0.00	5.14%	223.22	223.22	0.00	223.22	31.08	20.00%	38.85
Manufacturing	0.00	2.8319	0.00	0.00	8.56%	372.03	372.03	0.00	372.03	22.63	20.00%	28.29
TCU	0.00	2.5017	0.00	0.00	6.65%	288.87	288.87	0.00	288.87	9.67	20.00%	12.09
Wholesale Trade	0.00	2.1492	0.00	0.00	7.92%	344.31	344.31	0.00	344.31	21.22	20.00%	26.53
Retail Trade												
Neighborhood	0.00	1.5336	0.00	0.00	6.25%	271.36	271.36	0.00	271.36	17.11	35.00%	26.32
Community	0.00	1.5336	0.00	0.00	4.68%	203.52	203.52	0.00	203.52	13.63	30.00%	19.47
Regional	0.00	1.5336	0.00	0.00	3.12%	135.68	135.68	0.00	135.68	6.56	25.00%	8.74
Super Regional	0.00	1.5336	0.00	0.00	1.56%	67.84	67.84	0.00	67.84	3.51	20.00%	4.39
Office												
General Office	0.00	2.4056	0.00	0.00	31.58%	1,372.21	1,372.21	0.00	1,372.21	36.53	20.00%	45.67
Office Park	100.00	2.4056	4,694.98	4,344.74	12.15%	527.77	5,222.76	0.00	5,222.76	139.05	25.00%	185.40
Suburban Multilevel	0.00	2.4056	0.00	0.00	4.86%	211.11	211.11	0.00	211.11	5.62	30.00%	8.03
Employment Impact	100.00		4,694.98	4,344.74	100.00%	4,344.74	9,039.72	0.00	9,039.72	313.85		416.28

New Acres: This is the net acres added to community that were not anticipated in the plan. If added area includes land for roads, utilities, easements, etc., the gross acre figure should be adjusted to net acres with the gross land adjustment factor reflected later.

Employment Multiplier: This figure is from Table 11-2 for either the nation or appropriate region. The choice is a matter of judgment by the user.

Direct Employees: Calculated as

[(PLANNED RESIDENTS, EMPLOYEES PER NET ACRE) × (NEW ACRES)]

where PLANNED RESIDENTS, EMPLOYEES PER NET ACRE comes from Table 11-1.

Indirect Employees Based on Employment Change With Local Adjustment: Calculated as

[(DIRECT EMPLOYEES) × (EMPLOYMENT MULTIPLIER)]
− [(DIRECT EMPLOYEES) × (PERCENT CAPTURE ASSUMPTION)]

where PERCENT CAPTURE ASSUMPTION comes from Table 11-4.

Percent Indirect Employment Distribution: For all employment-based land uses, this is calculated as:

{[(EMPLOYMENT MULTIPLIER) × (DIRECT EMPLOYEES)]
− (DIRECT EMPLOYEES)} × (PERCENT CAPTURE ASSUMPTION)

where PERCENT CAPTURE ASSUMPTION comes from Table 11-4.

Indirect Employees From Employment Change: Calculated as

[(PERCENT INDIRECT EMPLOYMENT DISTRIBUTION)
× (INDIRECT EMPLOYEES BASED ON EMPLOYMENT
CHANGE WITH LOCAL ADJUSTMENT)]

Total Employees From Employment Change: Calculated as

[(DIRECT EMPLOYEES)
+ (INDIRECT EMPLOYEES FROM EMPLOYMENT CHANGE)]

Indirect Employees From Residential Change: Calculated as:

[(NEW LOCAL EMPLOYEES GENERATED FROM NEW RESIDENTS WITH LOCAL
ADJUSTMENT) × (PERCENT INDIRECT EMPLOYMENT DISTRIBUTION)]

where NEW LOCAL EMPLOYEES GENERATED FROM NEW RESIDENTS WITH LOCAL ADJUSTMENT comes from Table 11-9. (As this new office park will "import" households to Yukon County and increase demand for goods and services, this approach estimates those new jobs.)

(**Total New Employees** would be the same since only employment-based land uses would be changed.)

Net Acre Change: Calculated as

[(TOTAL NEW EMPLOYEES)
/ (RESIDENTIAL UNITS AND EFFECTIVE EMPLOYMENT PER NET ACRE)]

where RESIDENTIAL UNITS AND EFFECTIVE EMPLOYMENT PER NET ACRE comes from Table 11-1.

Gross Acre Adjustment Factor: This comes from Table 4-6 or tailored to the change proposed.

Gross Acre Change: Calculated as

[(NET ACRE CHANGE) / (1 − GROSS ACRE ADJUSTMENT FACTOR)]

A revised version of Table 11-6 (now Table 11-8) shows the effect of these calculations.

Table 11-9: Residential Land-Use Impacts

We now consider the relevant residential land-use impacts associated with this unanticipated change in employment-based land uses.

Plan Percent Residents 2020: This figure comes from Table 3-6 for each residential land-use group.

Residential Units Needed to Support New Employment Households Captured: Calculated as

$$\{[(\text{TOTAL EMPLOYEES FROM EMPLOYMENT CHANGE}) \times (\text{PERCENT CAPTURE ASSUMPTION})] / (\text{NATIONAL AVERAGE WORKERS PER HOUSEHOLD, 2020})\} \times (\text{PLAN PERCENT RESIDENTS 2020})$$

where TOTAL EMPLOYEES FROM EMPLOYMENT CHANGE comes from Table 11-8 and where both PERCENT CAPTURE ASSUMPTION and NATIONAL AVERAGE WORKERS PER HOUSEHOLD, 2020 come from Table 11-4.

Net Acre Change: This is calculated as the total housing units needed by each residential type divided by density for each type.

Gross Acre Adjustment Factor and **Gross Acre Change:** This is calculated consistent with the residential land-use assumptions in Chapter 3.

The residential land-use impacts associated with this unanticipated land-use change is shown in Table 11-9. The summary table of residential and employment-based impacts is also displayed in Table 11-10.

Table 11-9
Impact of Unanticipated Change, 100-Acre Plan Change for Office Park—Residential Component

Land-Use Category	New Acres	New Residential Units	New Residents (Adjusted For Unit Vacancy)	New Local Employees Generated From New Residents With Local Adjustment	Indirect Households Generated From New Local Employees	Plan Percent Residents 2020	Additional Residential Units Needed to Support Resident Change	Residential Units Needed to Support New Employment Households Captured	Total Residential Unit Change	Total Resident Change	Net Acre Change	Gross Acre Adjustment Factor	Gross Acre Change
Permanent Residential													
1-5 Acres Per Unit	0.00	0.00	0.00	0.00	0.00	4.00%	0.00	148.78	148.78	396.88	297.56	10.00%	330.63
1-2 Units Per Acre	0.00	0.00	0.00	0.00	0.00	20.00%	0.00	743.91	743.91	1,984.38	425.09	20.00%	531.36
3-5 Units Per Acre	0.00	0.00	0.00	0.00	0.00	20.00%	0.00	743.91	743.91	1,948.30	165.31	25.00%	220.42
6-8 Units Per Acre	0.00	0.00	0.00	0.00	0.00	18.00%	0.00	669.52	669.52	1,753.47	89.27	30.00%	127.53
9-14 Units Per Acre	0.00	0.00	0.00	0.00	0.00	23.00%	0.00	855.50	855.50	1,889.79	67.10	35.00%	103.23
15+ Units Per Acre	0.00	0.00	0.00	0.00	0.00	13.00%	0.00	483.54	483.54	999.96	18.95	40.00%	31.60
Subtotal Permanent Residential	0.00	0.00	0.00	0.00	0.00	98.00%	0.00	3,645.16	3,645.16	8,972.79	1,063.30		1,344.77
Group Care													
Nursing Homes	0.00					45.00%			138.86	238.15	na	na	na
Assisted Living	0.00					55.00%			92.58	113.41	na	na	na
Subtotal Group Care	0.00					100.00%			231.44	351.56			
Hotel/Motel Units													
Low Rise (1-3 Floors)	0.00					50.00%			510.63	907.14	na	na	na
Mid Rise (4-7 Floors)	0.00					25.00%			255.32	453.57	na	na	na
High Rise (8+ Floors)	0.00					25.00%			255.32	453.57	na	na	na
Subtotal Hotel/Motel Units	0.00					100.00%			1,021.26	1,814.27			

Table 11-10
Summary of Impact for 100-Acre Plan Change for Office Park

Summary Factor	Summary Figure
Direct Change in Net Residential Acres	0.00
Indirect Change in Net Residential Acres	1,063.30
Direct Change in Net Nonresidential Acres	100.00
Indirect Change in Net Nonresidential Acres	213.85
Total Change in Net Residential Acres	1,063.30
Total Change in Gross Residential Acres	1,344.77
Total Change in Net Nonresidential Acres	313.85
Total Change in Gross Nonresidential Acres	416.28
Total Net Acre Change	1,377.15
Total Gross Acre Change	1,761.05
Direct Resident Change	0.00
Indirect Resident Change	8,972.79
Total Resident Change	8,972.79
Direct Housing Unit Change	0.00
Indirect Housing Unit Change	3,645.16
Total Housing Unit Change	3,645.16
Direct Employment Change	4,694.98
Indirect Employment Change	4,344.74
Total Employment Change	9,039.72

MIXED LAND-USE DEVELOPMENT IMPACT

Let us now consider a mixed land-use development proposed for Yukon County. Perhaps it is a planned unit development, new community, new town, or other innovative development, but it is not anticipated in the comprehensive plan nor can the proposed development substitute for the development that is already anticipated and planned. Suppose its residential and employment-based land-use features are as shown below. Of course, planned community designs are complex and include public spaces and facilities that may be internalized (i.e., not financed by the local planning area). Suppose, for simplicity, however, that this is not the case with this particular proposal. The next two tables (Table 11-1 and Table 11-12) show the basic residential and employment-based land-use changes proposed.

Table 11-11
Residential Land Uses Proposed

Land-Use Category	Net New Acres
Permanent Residential	
1-5 Acres Per Unit	0.00
1-2 Units Per Net Acre	80.00
3-5 Units Per Net Acre	160.00
6-8 Units Per Net Acre	40.00
9-14 Units Per Net Acre	20.00
15+ Units Per Net Acre	10.00
Subtotal	310.00

Table 11-12
Employment-Based Land Uses Proposed

Land-Use Category	Net New Acres
Group Care	
Nursing Homes	5.00
Assisted Living	10.00
Hotel/Motel Units	
Low Rise (1-3 Floors)	0.00
Mid Rise (4-7 Floors)	10.00
High Rise (8+ Floors)	0.00
Industrial	
Construction	0.00
Manufacturing	40.00
TCU	0.00
Wholesale Trade	10.00
Retail Trade	
Neighborhood	10.00
Community	20.00
Regional	0.00
Super Regional	0.00
Office	
General Office	5.00
Office Park	40.00
Suburban Multilevel	10.00
Employment Impact	160.00

The next three tables (Table 11-13, Table 11-14, and Table 11-15) estimate the impact of this mixed land-use development on Yukon County. The magnitude of the development itself was not anticipated in the comprehensive plan, so local planners want to estimate its impact to inform the planning process of the land-use and capital cost implications, at least as a first impression. Since the detailed calculations involving the purely residential and purely nonresidential examples have already been discussed, we need only to see how the impact of this development impacts on land-use and facility needs.

Table 11-13
Impact of Unanticipated Change, Mixed Land-Use Development Proposal—Residential Component

Land-Use Category	New Acres	New Residential Units	New Residents (Adjusted For Unit Vacancy)	New Local Employees Generated From New Residents With Local Adjustment	Indirect Households Generated From New Local Employees	Plan Percent Residents 2020	Additional Residential Units Needed to Support Resident Change	Residential Units Needed to Support New Employment Households Captured	Total Residential Unit Change	Total Resident Change	Net Acre Change	Gross Acre Adjustment Factor	Gross Acre Change
Permanent Residential													
1-5 Acres Per Unit	0.00	0.00	0.00	0.00	0.00	4.00%	9.54	127.17	136.71	364.69	273.43	10.00%	303.81
1-2 Units Per Acre	80.00	140.00	373.45	91.96	57.48	20.00%	47.72	635.85	823.57	2,196.88	470.61	20.00%	588.27
3-5 Units Per Acre	160.00	720.00	1,885.68	464.35	290.22	20.00%	48.60	635.85	1,404.46	3,678.28	312.10	25.00%	416.14
6-8 Units Per Acre	40.00	300.00	785.70	193.48	120.92	18.00%	43.74	572.27	916.01	2,399.04	122.13	30.00%	174.48
9-14 Units Per Acre	20.00	255.00	563.30	138.71	86.69	23.00%	66.27	731.23	1,052.50	2,324.97	82.55	35.00%	127.00
15+ Units Per Acre	10.00	255.00	527.34	129.86	81.16	13.00%	40.01	413.31	708.32	1,464.80	27.78	40.00%	46.30
Subtotal Permanent Residential	310.00	1,670.00	4,135.47	1,018.35	636.47	98.00%	255.89	3,115.68	5,041.58	12,428.65	1,288.61		1,655.99
Group Care													
Nursing Homes	5.00					45.00%			307.52	527.39	na	na	na
Assisted Living	10.00					55.00%			338.35	414.47	na	na	na
Subtotal Group Care	15.00					100.00%			645.86	941.87			
Hotel/Motel Units													
Low Rise (1-3 Floors)	0.00					50.00%			542.45	963.66	na	na	na
Mid Rise (4-7 Floors)	10.00					25.00%			871.23	1,547.73	na	na	na
High Rise (8+ Floors)	0.00					25.00%			271.23	481.83	na	na	na
Subtotal Hotel/Motel Units	10.00					100.00%			1,684.90	2,993.23			

Table 11-14
Impact of Unanticipated Change, Mixed Land-Use Development Proposal—Employment-Based Component

Land-Use Category	New Acres	Employ-ment Multiplier	Direct Employees	Indirect Employees Based on Employment Change With Local Adjustment	Percent Indirect Employ-ment Distribution	Indirect Employees From Employ-ment Change	Total Employees From Employ-ment Change	Indirect Employees From Resi-dential Change	Total New Employees	Net Acre Change	Gross Acre Adjust-ment Factor	Gross Acre Change
Group Care												
Nursing Homes	5.00	1.8223	47.40	25.66	0.95%	34.06	81.47	9.64	91.11	2.85	40.00%	4.75
Assisted Living	10.00	1.8223	71.11	38.49	0.63%	22.71	93.81	6.43	100.24	4.18	40.00%	6.96
Hotel/Motel Units												
Low Rise (1-3 Floors)	0.00	1.6697	0.00	0.00	2.97%	106.90	106.90	30.26	137.16	3.05	40.00%	5.08
Mid Rise (4-7 Floors)	10.00	1.6697	151.71	66.89	1.49%	53.45	205.16	15.13	220.30	3.67	45.00%	6.68
High Rise (8+ Floors)	0.00	1.6697	0.00	0.00	1.49%	53.45	53.45	15.13	68.58	0.91	50.00%	1.83
Industrial												
Construction	0.00	2.1101	0.00	0.00	5.14%	184.81	184.81	52.32	237.13	33.02	20.00%	41.27
Manufacturing	40.00	2.8319	657.60	793.08	8.56%	308.01	965.61	87.20	1,052.81	64.04	20.00%	80.05
TCU	0.00	2.5017	0.00	0.00	6.65%	239.16	239.16	67.71	306.87	10.27	20.00%	12.84
Wholesale Trade	10.00	2.1492	162.24	122.75	7.92%	285.06	447.31	80.70	528.01	32.54	20.00%	40.68
Retail Trade												
Neighborhood	10.00	1.5336	158.63	55.73	6.25%	224.67	383.30	63.60	446.90	28.17	35.00%	43.34
Community	20.00	1.5336	298.60	104.91	4.68%	168.50	467.10	47.70	514.80	34.48	30.00%	49.26
Regional	0.00	1.5336	0.00	0.00	3.12%	112.33	112.33	31.80	144.14	6.97	25.00%	9.29
Super Regional	0.00	1.5336	0.00	0.00	1.56%	56.17	56.17	15.90	72.07	3.73	20.00%	4.66
Office												
General Office	5.00	2.4056	234.75	217.24	31.58%	1,136.09	1,370.84	321.63	1,692.47	45.06	20.00%	56.33
Office Park	40.00	2.4056	1,877.99	1,737.90	12.15%	436.96	2,314.95	123.70	2,438.65	64.93	25.00%	86.57
Suburban Multilevel	10.00	2.4056	469.50	434.47	4.86%	174.78	644.28	49.48	693.76	18.47	30.00%	26.39
Employment Impact	160.00		4,129.54	3,597.12	100.00%	3,597.12	7,726.66	1,018.35	8,745.01	356.34		475.97

Table 11-15
Summary of Impact for Plan Change for Mixed Land-Use Development

Summary Factor	Summary Figure
Direct Change in Net Residential Acres	310.00
Indirect Change in Net Residential Acres	978.61
Direct Change in Net Nonresidential Acres	160.00
Indirect Change in Net Nonresidential Acres	196.34
Total Change in Net Residential Acres	1,288.61
Total Change in Gross Residential Acres	1,655.99
Total Change in Net Nonresidential Acres	365.34
Total Change in Gross Nonresidential Acres	475.97
Total Net Acre Change	1,644.95
Total Gross Acre Change	2,131.95
Direct Resident Change	4,135.47
Indirect Resident Change	8,293.19
Total Resident Change	12,428.65
Direct Housing Unit Change	1,670.00
Indirect Housing Unit Change	3,371.58
Total Housing Unit Change	5,041.58
Direct Employment Change	4,129.54
Indirect Employment Change	4,615.48
Total Employment Change	8,745.01

COLLATERAL FACILITY AND LAND-USE IMPACTS

The foregoing has considered just residential and employment land-use impacts. What about facility and associated land-use impacts? The general nature of these impacts is reviewed below. It is applied to only the mixed land-use example presented above. Although the mixed land-use development example will likely include collateral facilities and associated lands, the extent to which this is done can be subtracted from the overall impact estimated here to show the net impact on the community.

The calculations begin with a summary of residential, employment, 24/7 and daytime functional population impacts associated. This is done in Table 11-16 using the following calculations:

Total Residential Unit Change: This figure comes from Table 11-13.

Resident, Employee Change: The figure for resident change comes from Table 11-13 under **Total Resident Change**; for employment change, this figure comes from Table 11-14 under **Total New Employees**.

24/7 Functional Population Coefficient and **Daytime Functional Population Coefficient:** This figure is from Table 5-2.

24/7 Functional Population Impact and **Daytime Functional Population Impact:** Calculated as

$$[(\text{RESIDENT, EMPLOYEE CHANGE}) \times (\text{FUNCTIONAL POPULATION COEFFICIENT}_{24/7, \text{ DAYTIME}})]$$

Table 11-16 is then used to estimate facility and land-use impacts of all the public and private facilities or activities in the following tables:

- 24/7 functional population public safety facility space and land-use impact (Table 11-17)

- 24/7 government and daytime community center, recreation center, and library functional population facility space and land-use impact (Table 11-18)
- daytime functional population major community center space and land-use impact (Table 11-19)
- daytime functional population park and open space land-use impact (Table 11-20)
- educational facility space and land-use impact (Table 11-21)
- water and wastewater utility demand impact (Table 11-22)
- water and wastewater utility land-use impact (Table 11-23)
- 24/7 functional population miscellaneous facility land-use impact (Table 11-24)
- summary of land-use impacts (Table 11-25)
- capital facility cost impacts (Table 11-26)

This mixed land-use development will have an impact on capital facilities estimated at about $132.5 million considering all facilities (but excluding transportation impacts), and $133.5 million considering just facilities that are sensitive to growth. This latter cost comes to about $8,100 per 24/7 functional resident and $8,300 per daytime functional resident. The analysis, however, does not consider revenues generated by the development or its collateral economic activities.

Table 11-16
Functional Population Impact

Land Use	Total Residential Unit Change	Resident, Employee Change	24/7 Functional Population Coefficient	24/7 Functional Population Impact	Daytime Functional Population Coefficient	Daytime Functional Population Impact
Residential Impact						
Total Residential Impact	7,372.34	12,428.65		11,858.07		8,507.20
1-5 Acres Per Unit	136.71	364.69	0.6700	244.34	0.5000	182.34
1-2 Units Per Acre	823.57	2,196.88	0.6700	1,471.91	0.5000	1,098.44
3-5 Units Per Acre	1,404.46	3,678.28	0.6700	2,464.44	0.5000	1,839.14
6-8 Units Per Acre	916.01	2,399.04	0.6700	1,607.35	0.5000	1,199.52
9-14 Units Per Acre	1,052.50	2,324.97	0.6700	1,557.73	0.5000	1,162.49
15+ Units Per Acre	708.32	1,464.80	0.6700	981.41	0.5000	732.40
Group Care, Residential						
Nursing Homes	307.52	527.39	0.8333	439.49	1.0000	527.39
Assisted Living	338.35	414.47	0.8333	345.39	1.0000	414.47
Group Care, Employment						
Nursing Homes		91.11	0.4881	44.47	0.9762	88.94
Assisted Living		100.24	0.4881	48.93	0.9762	97.86
Hotel/Motel Units, Residential						
Low Rise (1-3 Floors)	542.45	963.66	0.8333	803.05	0.2500	240.92
Mid Rise (4-7 Floors)	871.23	1,547.73	0.8333	1,289.78	0.2500	386.93
High Rise (8+ Floors)	271.23	481.83	0.8333	401.53	0.2500	120.46
Hotel/Motel Units, Employment						
Low Rise (1-3 Floors)		137.16	0.3714	50.94	0.9762	133.90
Mid Rise (4-7 Floors)		220.30	0.3714	81.82	0.9762	215.05
High Rise (8+ Floors)		68.58	0.3714	25.47	0.9762	66.95

Table 11-16 (continued)
Functional Population Impact

Land Use	Total Residential Unit Change	Resident, Employee Change	24/7 Functional Population Coefficient	24/7 Functional Population Impact	Daytime Functional Population Coefficient	Daytime Functional Population Impact
Employment Land Use						
Total Employment Impact		8,127.62		2,984.64		5,969.28
Industrial						
Construction		237.13	0.0993	23.55	0.1986	47.10
Manufacturing		1,052.81	0.2904	305.69	0.5807	611.38
TCU		306.87	0.3002	92.13	0.6004	184.25
Wholesale Trade		528.01	0.3095	163.44	0.6191	326.88
Retail Trade						
Neighborhood		446.90	1.0018	447.69	2.0035	895.39
Community		514.80	1.0018	515.71	2.0035	1,031.43
Regional		144.14	1.0018	144.39	2.0035	288.78
Super Regional		72.07	1.0018	72.20	2.0035	144.39
Office						
General Office		1,692.47	0.2528	427.89	0.5056	855.78
Office Park		2,438.65	0.2528	616.54	0.5056	1,233.09
Suburban Multilevel		693.76	0.2528	175.40	0.5056	350.80
Total Impact				14,842.71		14,476.48

Table 11-17
24/7 Functional Population Public Safety Facility Space and Land-Use Impact

Private Land-Use Category	Fire/EMS Building Sq. Ft. Per Functional Resident	Fire/EMS Land Sq. Ft. Per Functional Resident	Police Building Sq. Ft. Per Functional Resident	Police Land Sq. Ft. Per Functional Resident	Jail Maximum Beds Per 1,000 Functional Residents	Jail Minimum Beds Per 1,000 Functional Residents	Juvenile Detention Beds Per 1,000 Functional Residents	Jail + Juvenile Detention Land Sq. Ft. Per Functional Resident
LOS	0.40	2.50	0.65	3.00	3.00	3.00	1.50	6.00
Total Demand, Units	6,785.13	40,223.57	10,765.89	48,185.11	48.19	48.19	24.30	95,954.32
Total Demand, Acres		0.92		1.11				2.20
Residential								
1-5 Acres Per Unit	97.74	610.85	158.82	733.02	0.73	0.73	0.37	1,466.04
1-2 Units Per Acre	588.77	3,679.78	956.74	4,415.74	4.42	4.42	2.21	8,831.48
3-5 Units Per Acre	985.78	6,161.11	1,601.89	7,393.33	7.39	7.39	3.70	14,786.67
6-8 Units Per Acre	642.94	4,018.39	1,044.78	4,822.06	4.82	4.82	2.41	9,644.12
9-14 Units Per Acre	623.09	3,894.33	1,012.53	4,673.20	4.67	4.67	2.34	9,346.40
15+ Units Per Acre	392.57	2,453.53	637.92	2,944.24	2.94	2.94	1.47	5,888.48
Group Care								
Nursing Homes	193.59	1,209.91	314.58	1,451.89	1.45	1.45	0.73	2,903.79
Assisted Living	157.73	985.81	256.31	1,182.97	1.18	1.18	0.59	2,365.94
Hotel/Motel Units								
Low Rise (1-3 Floors)	230.26	736.19	290.49	856.64	0.86	0.86	0.50	1,579.39
Mid Rise (4-7 Floors)	369.83	1,182.38	466.56	1,375.85	1.38	1.38	0.80	2,536.65
High Rise (8+ Floors)	115.13	368.09	145.25	428.32	0.43	0.43	0.25	789.70
Industrial								
Construction	18.84	117.76	30.62	141.31	0.14	0.14	0.07	282.62
Manufacturing	244.55	1,528.46	397.40	1,834.15	1.83	1.83	0.92	3,668.30
TCU	73.70	460.64	119.77	552.76	0.55	0.55	0.28	1,105.53
Wholesale Trade	130.75	817.19	212.47	980.63	0.98	0.98	0.49	1,961.26

Table 11-17 (continued)
24/7 Functional Population Public Safety Facility Space and Land-Use Impact

Private Land-Use Category	Fire/EMS Building Sq. Ft. Per Functional Resident	Fire/EMS Land Sq. Ft. Per Functional Resident	Police Building Sq. Ft. Per Functional Resident	Police Land Sq. Ft. Per Functional Resident	Jail Maximum Beds Per 1,000 Functional Residents	Jail Minimum Beds Per 1,000 Functional Residents	Juvenile Detention Beds Per 1,000 Functional Residents	Jail + Juvenile Detention Land Sq. Ft. Per Functional Resident
Retail Trade								
Neighborhood	358.16	2,238.47	582.00	2,686.17	2.69	2.69	1.34	5,372.33
Community	412.57	2,578.57	670.43	3,094.29	3.09	3.09	1.55	6,188.58
Regional	115.51	721.96	187.71	866.35	0.87	0.87	0.43	1,732.70
Super Regional	57.76	360.98	93.85	433.17	0.43	0.43	0.22	866.35
Office								
General Office	342.31	2,139.46	556.26	2,567.35	2.57	2.57	1.28	5,134.70
Office Park	493.24	3,082.72	801.51	3,699.26	3.70	3.70	1.85	7,398.53
Suburban Multilevel	140.32	876.99	228.02	1,052.39	1.05	1.05	0.53	2,104.78

Table 11-18
24/7 Government and Daytime Community Center, Recreation Center, and Library Functional Population Facility Space and Land-Use Impact

Private Land-Use Category	General Government Sq. Ft. Per Functional Resident	General Government Land Sq. Ft. Per Functional Resident	Community Center Sq. Ft. Per Functional Resident	Community Center Land Sq. Ft. Per Functional Resident	Recreation Center Sq. Ft. Per Functional Resident	Recreation Center Land Sq. Ft. Per Functional Resident	Library Volumes Per Functional Resident	Library Building Sq. Ft. Per Functional Resident	Library Land Sq. Ft. Per Functional Resident	Religious Facility Land Sq. Ft. Per Functional Resident
LOS	0.90	3.50	0.75	4.00	0.55	2.40	2.00	0.60	2.00	35.73
Total Demand, Units	13,358.44	51,949.47	10,857.36	57,905.90	7,962.06	34,743.54	28,952.95	8,685.89	28,952.95	289,073.95
Total Demand, Acres		1.19		1.33		0.80			0.66	6.64
Residential										
1-5 Acres Per Unit	219.91	855.19	136.76	729.37	100.29	437.62	364.69	109.41	364.69	6,514.50
1-2 Units Per Net Acre	1,324.72	5,151.69	823.83	4,393.77	604.14	2,636.26	2,196.88	659.07	2,196.88	39,243.52
3-5 Units Per Net Acre	2,218.00	8,625.56	1,379.35	7,356.55	1,011.53	4,413.93	3,678.28	1,103.48	3,678.28	65,706.00
6-8 Units Per Net Acre	1,446.62	5,625.74	899.64	4,798.07	659.73	2,878.84	2,399.04	719.71	2,399.04	42,854.61
9-14 Units Per Net Acre	1,401.96	5,452.07	871.87	4,649.95	639.37	2,789.97	2,324.97	697.49	2,324.97	41,531.63
15+ Units Per Net Acre	883.27	3,434.95	549.30	2,929.59	402.82	1,757.76	1,464.80	439.44	1,464.80	26,166.03
Group Care										
Nursing Homes	435.57	1,693.88	462.25	2,465.34	338.98	1,479.20	1,232.67	369.80	1,232.67	22,019.48
Assisted Living	354.89	1,380.13	384.25	2,049.32	281.78	1,229.59	1,024.66	307.40	1,024.66	18,303.79
Hotel/Motel Units										
Low Rise (1-3 Floors)	768.59	2,988.98	281.11	1,499.25	206.15	899.55	749.63	224.89	749.63	8,607.08
Mid Rise (4-7 Floors)	1,234.43	4,800.57	451.49	2,407.94	331.09	1,444.76	1,203.97	361.19	1,203.97	13,823.76
High Rise (8+ Floors)	384.30	1,494.49	140.56	749.63	103.07	449.78	374.81	112.44	374.81	4,303.54
Industrial										
Construction	21.20	82.43	35.33	188.42	25.91	113.05	94.21	28.26	94.21	na
Manufacturing	275.12	1,069.92	458.54	2,445.53	336.26	1,467.32	1,222.77	366.83	1,222.77	na
TCU	82.91	322.45	138.19	737.02	101.34	442.21	368.51	110.55	368.51	na
Wholesale Trade	147.09	572.03	245.16	1,307.50	179.78	784.50	653.75	196.13	653.75	na

Table 11-18 (continued)
24/7 Government and Daytime Community Center, Recreation Center, and Library Functional Population Facility Space and Land-Use Impact

Private Land-Use Category	General Government Sq. Ft. Per Functional Resident	General Government Land Sq. Ft. Per Functional Resident	Community Center Sq. Ft. Per Functional Resident	Community Center Land Sq. Ft. Per Functional Resident	Recreation Center Sq. Ft. Per Functional Resident	Recreation Center Land Sq. Ft. Per Functional Resident	Library Volumes Per Functional Resident	Library Building Sq. Ft. Per Functional Resident	Library Land Sq. Ft. Per Functional Resident	Religious Facility Land Sq. Ft. Per Functional Resident
Retail Trade										
Neighborhood	402.93	1,566.93	671.54	3,581.56	492.46	2,148.93	1,790.78	537.23	1,790.78	na
Community	464.14	1,805.00	773.57	4,125.72	567.29	2,475.43	2,062.86	618.86	2,062.86	na
Regional	129.95	505.37	216.59	1,155.13	158.83	693.08	577.57	173.27	577.57	na
Super Regional	64.98	252.69	108.29	577.57	79.42	346.54	288.78	86.63	288.78	na
Office										
General Office	385.10	1,497.62	641.84	3,423.14	470.68	2,053.88	1,711.57	513.47	1,711.57	na
Office Park	554.89	2,157.90	924.82	4,932.35	678.20	2,959.41	2,466.18	739.85	2,466.18	na
Suburban Multilevel	157.86	613.89	263.10	1,403.18	192.94	841.91	701.59	210.48	701.59	na

Table 11-19
Daytime Functional Population Major Community Center Space and Land-Use Impact

Land-Use Category	Convention Center Sq. Ft. Per Functional Resident	Convention Center Land Sq. Ft. Per Functional Resident	Public Assembly Facility Sq. Ft. Per Functional Resident	Public Assembly Land Sq. Ft. Per Functional Resident	Other Major Facilities Sq. Ft. Per Functional Resident	Other Major Facilities Land Sq. Ft. Per Functional Resident
LOS, Imputed	0.53	2.32	0.47	1.45	0.23	1.16
Total Demand, Units	7,725.57	33,652.60	6,759.88	21,032.88	3,379.94	16,826.30
Total Demand, Acres		0.77		0.48		0.39
Residential						
1-5 Acres Per Unit	97.31	423.88	85.15	264.93	42.57	211.94
1-2 Units Per Acre	586.20	2,553.48	512.92	1,595.93	256.46	1,276.74
3-5 Units Per Acre	981.48	4,275.33	858.80	2,672.08	429.40	2,137.67
6-8 Units Per Acre	640.14	2,788.45	560.12	1,742.78	280.06	1,394.22
9-14 Units Per Acre	620.38	2,702.37	542.83	1,688.98	271.42	1,351.18
15+ Units Per Acre	390.85	1,702.56	342.00	1,064.10	171.00	851.28
Group Care						
Nursing Homes	328.92	1,432.76	287.80	895.47	143.90	716.38
Assisted Living	273.41	1,190.98	239.24	744.37	119.62	595.49
Hotel/Motel Units						
Low Rise (1-3 Floors)	200.02	871.31	175.02	544.57	87.51	435.65
Mid Rise (4-7 Floors)	321.26	1,399.40	281.10	874.62	140.55	699.70
High Rise (8+ Floors)	100.01	435.65	87.51	272.28	43.76	217.83
Industrial						
Construction	25.14	109.50	22.00	68.44	11.00	54.75
Manufacturing	326.27	1,421.24	285.49	888.28	142.74	710.62
TCU	98.33	428.33	86.04	267.70	43.02	214.16
Wholesale Trade	174.44	759.87	152.64	474.92	76.32	379.93

Table 11-19 (continued)
Daytime Functional Population Major Community Center Space and Land-Use Impact

Land-Use Category	Convention Center Sq. Ft. Per Functional Resident	Convention Center Land Sq. Ft. Per Functional Resident	Public Assembly Facility Sq. Ft. Per Functional Resident	Public Assembly Land Sq. Ft. Per Functional Resident	Other Major Facilities Sq. Ft. Per Functional Resident	Other Major Facilities Land Sq. Ft. Per Functional Resident
Retail Trade						
Neighborhood	477.84	2,081.46	418.11	1,300.91	209.05	1,040.73
Community	550.44	2,397.70	481.63	1,498.56	240.82	1,198.85
Regional	154.11	671.32	134.85	419.57	67.42	335.66
Super Regional	77.06	335.66	67.42	209.79	33.71	167.83
Office						
General Office	456.70	1,989.39	399.61	1,243.37	199.81	994.70
Office Park	658.05	2,866.49	575.80	1,791.55	287.90	1,433.24
Suburban Multilevel	187.21	815.47	163.81	509.67	81.90	407.74

Table 11-20
Daytime Functional Population Park and Open Space Land-Use Impact

Land-Use Category	Neighborhood Park Land Acres Per 1,000 Functional Residents	Community Park Land Acres Per 1,000 Functional Residents	Regional Park Land Acres Per 1,000 Functional Residents	Public Golf Course Land Acres Per 1,000 Functional Residents	Special Use Acres Per 1,000 Functional Residents	Conservancy, Greenbelt Acres Per 1,000 Functional Residents	Private Golf Course Land Acres Per 1,000 Functional Residents	Other Private Land-Related Acres Per 1,000 Functional Residents
LOS	1.25	5.50	5.00	4.50	0.53	1.33	2.26	1.70
Total Demand, Acres	18.10	79.62	72.38	65.14	7.73	19.31	31.83	23.87
Residential								
1-5 Acres Per Unit	0.2279293	1.0028890	0.9117172	0.8205455	0.0973101	0.2432753	0.4127839	0.3095879
1-2 Units Per Acre	1.3730528	6.0414323	5.4922112	4.9429901	0.5861991	1.4654978	2.4866223	1.8649667
3-5 Units Per Acre	2.2989222	10.1152578	9.1956889	8.2761200	0.9814817	2.4537042	4.1633878	3.1225409
6-8 Units Per Acre	1.4993975	6.5973490	5.9975900	5.3978310	0.6401396	1.6003490	2.7154347	2.0365761
9-14 Units Per Acre	1.4531092	6.3936805	5.8124368	5.2311931	0.6203777	1.5509442	2.6316058	1.9737044
15+ Units Per Acre	0.9154975	4.0281890	3.6619900	3.2957910	0.3908545	0.9771362	1.6579818	1.2434863
Group Care								
Nursing Homes	0.7704179	3.3898389	3.0816717	2.7735046	0.3289155	0.8222887	1.3952402	1.0464301
Assisted Living	0.6404132	2.8178179	2.5616527	2.3054874	0.2734124	0.6835309	1.1597993	0.8698495
Hotel/Motel Units								
Low Rise (1-3 Floors)	0.4685170	2.0614747	1.8740679	1.6866611	0.2000245	0.5000613	0.5453780	0.4090335
Mid Rise (4-7 Floors)	0.7524816	3.3109190	3.0099264	2.7089338	0.3212579	0.8031447	0.8759275	0.6569457
High Rise (8+ Floors)	0.2342585	1.0307374	0.9370340	0.8433306	0.1000123	0.2500307	0.2726890	0.2045168
Industrial								
Construction	0.0588798	0.2590710	0.2355191	0.2119672	0.0251376	0.0628440	0.1066323	0.0799742
Manufacturing	0.7642282	3.3626040	3.0569127	2.7512214	0.3262729	0.8156822	1.3840304	1.0380228
TCU	0.2303182	1.0134002	0.9212729	0.8291456	0.0983300	0.2458251	0.4171103	0.3128327
Wholesale Trade	0.4085949	1.7978178	1.6343798	1.4709418	0.1744419	0.4361048	0.7399725	0.5549794

Table 11-20 (continued)
Daytime Functional Population Park and Open Space Land-Use Impact

Land-Use Category	Neighborhood Park Land Acres Per 1,000 Functional Residents	Community Park Land Acres Per 1,000 Functional Residents	Regional Park Land Acres Per 1,000 Functional Residents	Public Golf Course Land Acres Per 1,000 Functional Residents	Special Use Acres Per 1,000 Functional Residents	Conservancy, Greenbelt Acres Per 1,000 Functional Residents	Private Golf Course Land Acres Per 1,000 Functional Residents	Other Private Land-Related Acres Per 1,000 Functional Residents
Retail Trade								
Neighborhood	1.1192364	4.9246400	4.4769454	4.0292509	0.4778369	1.1945924	2.0269564	1.5202173
Community	1.2892868	5.6728621	5.1571474	4.6414326	0.5504368	1.3760920	2.3349207	1.7511905
Regional	0.3609789	1.5883071	1.4439156	1.2995240	0.1541132	0.3852829	0.6537390	0.4903042
Super Regional	0.1804894	0.7941536	0.7219578	0.6497620	0.0770566	0.1926414	0.3268695	0.2451521
Office								
General Office	1.0697302	4.7068127	4.2789206	3.8510286	0.4567012	1.1417530	1.9372998	1.4529748
Office Park	1.5413597	6.7819825	6.1654386	5.5488948	0.6580546	1.6451364	2.7914289	2.0935717
Suburban Multilevel	0.4384951	1.9293783	1.7539803	1.5785823	0.1872072	0.4680181	0.7941222	0.5955916

Table 11-21
Educational Facility Space and Land-Use Impact

Land-Use Category	Grades K-5 Facility Sq. Ft. Per Student	Grades K-5 Land Sq. Ft. Per Student	Grades 6-8 Facility Sq. Ft. Per Student	Grades 6-8 Land Sq. Ft. Per Student	Grades 9-12 Facility Sq. Ft. Per Student	Grades 9-12 Land Sq. Ft. Per Student	Auxiliary Facility Sq. Ft. Per Student	Auxiliary Land Sq. Ft. Per Student	Private Land Sq. Ft. Per Student	Junior, Community College Land Sq. Ft.	Technical School Land Sq. Ft.	Senior College Land Sq. Ft.	University Land Sq. Ft.
LOS	100.00	500.00	115.00	657.14	130.00	866.67	3.25	13.00	341.57	1,210.00	997.56	2,026.05	1,957.75
Total Demand, Sq. Ft.	63,126		62,225		82,064		5,862						
Total Demand, Acres		7.25		8.16		12.56		0.54	2.13	3.41	2.56	6.82	13.65
Residential													
1-5 Acres Per Unit	2,153	10,766	2,122	12,129	2,799	18,662	200	800	2,719	2,119	1,590	4,239	8,478
1-2 Units Per Acre	12,971	64,856	12,786	73,063	16,863	112,418	1,204	4,818	16,378	12,767	9,576	25,535	51,070
3-5 Units Per Acre	22,120	110,601	21,804	124,595	28,756	191,709	2,054	8,216	27,422	21,377	16,033	42,753	85,507
6-8 Units Per Acre	14,427	72,136	14,221	81,263	18,755	125,036	1,340	5,359	17,885	13,942	10,457	27,884	55,769
9-14 Units Per Acre	7,736	38,679	7,625	43,574	10,057	67,044	718	2,873	17,333	13,512	10,134	27,024	54,047
15+ Units Per Acre	3,719	18,593	3,666	20,946	4,834	32,228	345	1,381	10,920	8,513	6,385	17,026	34,051
Group Care													
Nursing Homes	Employment-based daytime functional population									1,034	775	2,068	4,135
Assisted Living	Employment-based daytime functional population									1,137	853	2,275	4,550
Hotel/Motel Units													
Low Rise (1-3 Floors)	Employment-based daytime functional population									1,556	1,167	3,113	6,225
Mid Rise (4-7 Floors)	Employment-based daytime functional population									2,500	1,875	4,999	9,998
High Rise (8+ Floors)	Employment-based daytime functional population									778	584	1,556	3,113

Table 11-21 (continued)
Educational Facility Space and Land-Use Impact

Land-Use Category	Grades K-5 Facility Sq. Ft. Per Student	Grades K-5 Land Sq. Ft. Per Student	Grades 6-8 Facility Sq. Ft. Per Student	Grades 6-8 Land Sq. Ft. Per Student	Grades 9-12 Facility Sq. Ft. Per Student	Grades 9-12 Land Sq. Ft. Per Student	Auxiliary Facility Sq. Ft. Per Student	Auxiliary Land Sq. Ft. Per Student	Private Land Sq. Ft. Per Student	Junior, Community College Land Sq. Ft.	Technical School Land Sq. Ft.	Senior College Land Sq. Ft.	University Land Sq. Ft.
Industrial													
Construction	Employment-based daytime functional population									547	411	1,095	2,190
Manufacturing	Employment-based daytime functional population									7,106	5,330	14,212	28,425
TCU	Employment-based daytime functional population									2,142	1,606	4,283	8,567
Wholesale Trade	Employment-based daytime functional population									3,799	2,850	7,599	15,197
Retail Trade													
Neighborhood	Employment-based daytime functional population									10,407	7,805	20,815	41,629
Community	Employment-based daytime functional population									11,989	8,991	23,977	47,954
Regional	Employment-based daytime functional population									3,357	2,517	6,713	13,426
Super Regional	Employment-based daytime functional population									1,678	1,259	3,357	6,713
Office													
General Office	Employment-based daytime functional population									9,947	7,460	19,894	39,788
Office Park	Employment-based daytime functional population									14,332	10,749	28,665	57,330
Suburban Multilevel	Employment-based daytime functional population									4,077	3,058	8,155	16,309

Table 11-22
Water and Wastewater Utility Demand Impact

Land-Use Category	Impact Unit	Water Demand Per Unit	Water Demand	Waste-water Demand Per Unit	Waste-water Demand
Total Demand, GPD			2,251,001		1,727,061
Residential					
1-5 Acres Per Unit	Residential Unit				
1-2 Units Per Acre	Residential Unit	400	329,430	300	247,072
3-5 Units Per Acre	Residential Unit	400	561,783	300	421,337
6-8 Units Per Acre	Residential Unit	400	366,405	300	274,804
9-14 Units Per Acre	Residential Unit	250	263,125	200	210,500
15+ Units Per Acre	Residential Unit	250	177,079	200	141,663
Group Care					
Nursing Homes	Bed	150	46,128	143	43,975
Assisted Living	Residential Unit	150	50,752	143	48,383
Hotel/Motel Units					
Low Rise (1-3 Floors)	Room	125	67,806	86	46,651
Mid Rise (4-7 Floors)	Room	125	108,903	86	74,925
High Rise (8+ Floors)	Room	125	33,903	86	23,325

Table 11-22 (continued)
Water and Wastewater Utility Demand Impact

Land-Use Category	Impact Unit	Water Demand Per Unit	Water Demand	Waste-water Demand Per Unit	Waste-water Demand
Industrial					
Construction	Employee	45	10,671	35	8,299
Manufacturing	Employee	45	47,377	35	36,848
TCU	Employee	45	13,809	35	10,741
Wholesale Trade	Employee	45	23,760	35	18,480
Retail Trade					
Neighborhood	Employee	25	11,173	20	8,938
Community	Employee	25	12,870	20	10,296
Regional	Employee	25	3,603	20	2,883
Super Regional	Employee	25	1,802	20	1,441
Office					
General Office	Employee	25	42,312	20	33,849
Office Park	Employee	25	60,966	20	48,773
Suburban Multilevel	Employee	25	17,344	20	13,875

Table 11-23
Water and Wastewater Utility Land-Use Impact

Land-Use Category	Water Supply and Treatment Land Sq. Ft. Per 24/7 Functional Resident	Wastewater Treatment Land Sq. Ft. Per 24/7 Functional Resident	Wastewater Irrigation Land Sq. Ft. Per 24/7 Functional Resident
LOS, Imputed	8.52	9.74	18.26
Total Demand, Sq. Ft.	125,126	143,002	268,128
Total Demand, Acres	2.87	3.28	6.16
Residential			
1-5 Acres Per Unit	2,082	2,379	4,461
1-2 Units Per Acre	12,542	14,334	26,876
3-5 Units Per Acre	21,000	23,999	44,999
6-8 Units Per Acre	13,696	15,653	29,349
9-14 Units Per Acre	13,273	15,170	28,443
15+ Units Per Acre	8,363	9,557	17,920
Group Care			
Nursing Homes	4,124	4,713	8,837
Assisted Living	3,360	3,840	7,200
Hotel/Motel Units			
Low Rise (1-3 Floors)	6,843	7,820	14,663
Mid Rise (4-7 Floors)	10,990	12,560	23,550
High Rise (8+ Floors)	3,421	3,910	7,332

Table 11-23 (continued)
Water and Wastewater Utility Land-Use Impact

Land-Use Category	Water Supply and Treatment Land Sq. Ft. Per 24/7 Functional Resident	Wastewater Treatment Land Sq. Ft. Per 24/7 Functional Resident	Wastewater Irrigation Land Sq. Ft. Per 24/7 Functional Resident
Industrial			
Construction	201	229	430
Manufacturing	2,605	2,977	5,582
TCU	785	897	1,682
Wholesale Trade	1,393	1,592	2,984
Retail Trade			
Neighborhood	3,815	4,360	8,175
Community	4,394	5,022	9,417
Regional	1,230	1,406	2,636
Super Regional	615	703	1,318
Office			
General Office	3,646	4,167	7,813
Office Park	5,254	6,004	11,258
Suburban Multilevel	1,495	1,708	3,203

Table 11-24
24/7 Functional Population Miscellaneous Facility Land-Use Impact

Land-Use Category	Fire Storage, Drill, Practice Land Sq. Ft. Per Functional Resident	Public Works Equipment, Land Sq. Ft. Per Functional Resident	Repair Shops and Associated Land Sq. Ft. Per Functional Resident	Publicly Owned Drainage Land Sq. Ft. Per Functional Resident	Sand, Gravel, Soil Storage Land Sq. Ft. Per Functional Resident	Landfills Land Sq. Ft. Per Functional Resident	Resource Recovery Land Sq. Ft. Per Functional Resident	Airport Land Sq. Ft. Per Functional Resident	Other Public Land Sq. Ft. Per Functional Resident
LOS, Imputed	8.83	2.13	1.22	25.87	1.22	19.48	0.49	143.64	2.13
Total Demand, Sq. Ft.	129,595	31,282	17,875	379,848	17,875	286,003	7,150	1,983,692	29,419
Total Demand, Acres	2.98	0.72	0.41	8.72	0.41	6.57	0.16	45.54	0.68
Residential									
1-5 Acres Per Unit	2,156	521	297	6,320	297	4,759	119	26,192	388
1-2 Units Per Net Acre	12,990	3,136	1,792	38,074	1,792	28,668	717	157,780	2,340
3-5 Units Per Net Acre	21,750	5,250	3,000	63,749	3,000	47,999	1,200	264,173	3,918
6-8 Units Per Net Acre	14,185	3,424	1,957	41,578	1,957	31,306	783	172,298	2,555
9-14 Units Per Net Acre	13,747	3,318	1,896	40,294	1,896	30,339	758	166,979	2,476
15+ Units Per Net Acre	8,661	2,091	1,195	25,387	1,195	19,115	478	105,201	1,560
Group Care									
Nursing Homes	4,271	1,031	589	12,519	589	9,426	236	69,517	1,031
Assisted Living	3,480	840	480	10,200	480	7,680	192	56,640	840
Hotel/Motel Units									
Low Rise (1-3 Floors)	7,087	1,711	978	20,773	978	15,641	391	34,605	513
Mid Rise (4-7 Floors)	11,383	2,748	1,570	33,363	1,570	25,120	628	55,579	824
High Rise (8+ Floors)	3,544	855	489	10,386	489	7,820	196	17,303	257
Industrial									
Construction	208	50	29	609	29	459	11	6,766	100
Manufacturing	2,698	651	372	7,907	372	5,954	149	87,819	1,302
TCU	813	196	112	2,383	112	1,794	45	26,466	393
Wholesale Trade	1,442	348	199	4,228	199	3,183	80	46,952	696

Table 11-24 (continued)
24/7 Functional Population Miscellaneous Facility Land-Use Impact

Land-Use Category	Fire Storage, Drill, Practice Land Sq. Ft. Per Functional Resident	Public Works Equipment, Land Sq. Ft. Per Functional Resident	Repair Shops and Associated Land Sq. Ft. Per Functional Resident	Publicly Owned Drainage Land Sq. Ft. Per Functional Resident	Sand, Gravel, Soil Storage Land Sq. Ft. Per Functional Resident	Landfills Land Sq. Ft. Per Functional Resident	Resource Recovery Land Sq. Ft. Per Functional Resident	Airport Land Sq. Ft. Per Functional Resident	Other Public Land Sq. Ft. Per Functional Resident
Retail Trade									
Neighborhood	3,951	954	545	11,581	545	8,720	218	128,613	1,907
Community	4,551	1,099	628	13,340	628	10,044	251	148,154	2,197
Regional	1,274	308	176	3,735	176	2,812	70	41,481	615
Super Regional	637	154	88	1,868	88	1,406	35	20,740	308
Office									
General Office	3,776	912	521	11,068	521	8,334	208	122,925	1,823
Office Park	5,441	1,313	751	15,948	751	12,008	300	177,120	2,627
Suburban Multilevel	1,548	374	214	4,537	214	3,416	85	50,388	747

Table 11-25
Summary of Land-Use Impacts

Land Use	Net Acres	Gross Acre Adjustment Factor	Gross Acres	Net Acres For Growth-Sensitive Facilities	Gross Acres For Growth-Sensitive Facilities
Residential					
1-5 Acres Per Unit	273.43	10.00%	303.81	273.43	303.81
1-2 Units Per Acre	470.61	20.00%	588.27	470.61	588.27
3-5 Units Per Acre	312.10	25.00%	416.14	312.10	416.14
6-8 Units Per Acre	122.13	30.00%	174.48	122.13	174.48
9-14 Units Per Acre	82.55	35.00%	127.00	82.55	127.00
15+ Units Per Acre	27.78	40.00%	46.30	27.78	46.30
Subtotal Residential	1,288.61		1,655.99	1,288.61	1,655.99
Group Care					
Nursing Homes	2.85	40.00%	4.75	2.85	4.75
Assisted Living	4.18	40.00%	6.96	4.18	6.96
Subtotal Group Care	7.02		11.71	7.02	11.71
Hotel/Motel					
Low Rise (1-3 Floors)	3.05	40.00%	5.08	3.05	5.08
Mid Rise (4-7 Floors)	3.67	45.00%	6.68	3.67	6.68
High Rise (8+ Floors)	0.91	50.00%	1.83	0.91	1.83
Subtotal Hotel/Motel	7.63		13.58	7.63	13.58
Industrial					
Construction	33.02	20.00%	41.27	33.02	41.27
Manufacturing	64.04	20.00%	80.05	64.04	80.05
TCU	10.27	20.00%	12.84	10.27	12.84
Wholesale Trade	32.54	20.00%	40.68	32.54	40.68
Subtotal Industrial	139.87		174.84	139.87	174.84

Table 11-25 (continued)
Summary of Land-Use Impacts

Land Use	Net Acres	Gross Acre Adjustment Factor	Gross Acres	Net Acres For Growth-Sensitive Facilities	Gross Acres For Growth-Sensitive Facilities
Retail					
Neighborhood	28.17	35.00%	43.34	28.17	43.34
Community	34.48	30.00%	49.26	34.48	49.26
Regional	6.97	25.00%	9.29	6.97	9.29
Super Regional	3.73	20.00%	4.66	3.73	4.66
Subtotal Retail	73.35		106.55	73.35	106.55
Office					
General Office	45.06	20.00%	56.33	45.06	56.33
Office Park	64.93	25.00%	86.57	64.93	86.57
Suburban Multilevel	18.47	30.00%	26.39	18.47	26.39
Subtotal Office	128.46		169.28	128.46	169.28
Public Safety Facilities					
Fire/EMS	0.92	25.00%	1.23	0.92	1.23
Police	1.11	25.00%	1.47	1.11	1.47
Jails, Detention	2.20	25.00%	2.94	2.20	2.94
Subtotal Public Safety Facilities	4.23		5.64	4.23	5.64
Government, Community, Recreation, Library, Religious Facilities					
General Government	1.19	25.00%	1.59	1.19	1.59
Community Center	1.33	25.00%	1.77	1.33	1.77
Recreation Center	0.80	25.00%	1.06	0.80	1.06
Library	0.66	25.00%	0.89	0.66	0.89
Religious Facility	6.64	25.00%	8.85	6.64	8.85

Table 11-25 (continued)
Summary of Land-Use Impacts

Land Use	Net Acres	Gross Acre Adjustment Factor	Gross Acres	Net Acres For Growth-Sensitive Facilities	Gross Acres For Growth-Sensitive Facilities
Subtotal Government, Community, Recreation, Library, Religious Facilities	10.62		14.16	10.62	14.16
Major Community Facilities					
Convention Centers	0.77	15.00%	0.91	na	na
Public Assembly Halls	0.48	15.00%	0.57	na	na
Other Major Facilities	0.39	15.00%	0.45	na	na
Subtotal Major Community Facilities	1.64		1.93		
Parks and Open Space					
Neighborhood Park	18.10	20.00%	22.62	18.10	22.62
Community Park	79.62	25.00%	106.16	79.62	106.16
Regional Park	72.38	4.00%	75.40	72.38	75.40
Public Golf Course	65.14	4.00%	67.86	65.14	67.86
Special Use	0.53	4.00%	0.56	0.53	0.56
Conservancy/Greenbelt	1.33	4.00%	1.39	1.33	1.39
Private Golf Course	31.83	4.00%	33.16	31.83	33.16
Other Private Land-Related	23.87	4.00%	24.87	23.87	24.87
Subtotal Parks and Open Space	292.81		332.01	292.81	332.01
Educational Facilities					
Public E & S					
Grades K-5	7.25	15.00%	8.52	7.25	8.52
Grades 6-8	8.16	12.50%	9.33	8.16	9.33
Grades 9-12	12.56	10.00%	13.96	12.56	13.96

Table 11-25 (continued)
Summary of Land-Use Impacts

Land Use	Net Acres	Gross Acre Adjustment Factor	Gross Acres	Net Acres For Growth-Sensitive Facilities	Gross Acres For Growth-Sensitive Facilities
Auxiliary	0.54	25.00%	0.72	0.54	0.72
Subtotal Public E & S	28.51		32.53	28.51	32.53
Post-secondary					
Junior/Community College	3.41	15.00%	4.01	na	na
Technical School	2.56	15.00%	3.01	na	na
Senior College	6.82	12.50%	7.80	na	na
University	13.65	10.00%	15.16	na	na
Subtotal Post-secondary	26.44		29.99		
Private Educational Facilities	2.13	25.00%	2.43	2.13	2.43
Subtotal All Educational Facilities	57.08		65.35	30.63	35.36
Water and Wastewater Utilities					
Water Supply and Treatment Facility Land	2.87	10.00%	3.19	na	na
Wastewater Treatment Facility Land	3.28	10.00%	3.65	na	na
Wastewater Irrigation Fields	6.16	10.00%	6.84	na	na
Subtotal Water and Wastewater Utilities	12.31		13.68		
Miscellaneous					
Fire Storage, Drill, Practice Yards	2.98	15.00%	3.50	na	na
Public Works Equipment, Storage Yards	0.72	15.00%	0.84	na	na
Repair Shops and Associated Yards	0.41	15.00%	0.48	na	na

Table 11-25 (continued)
Summary of Land-Use Impacts

Land Use	Net Acres	Gross Acre Adjust- ment Factor	Gross Acres	Net Acres For Growth- Sensitive Facilities	Gross Acres For Growth- Sensitive Facilities
Publicly Owned Drainage Ponds	8.72	10.00%	9.69	na	na
Sand, Gravel, Soil Storage Yards	0.41	10.00%	0.46	na	na
Landfills	6.57	10.00%	7.30	na	na
Resource Recovery Facilities	0.16	20.00%	0.21	na	na
Airports	45.54	5.00%	47.94	na	na
Other Public Land in Inventory	0.68	20.00%	0.84	na	na
Subtotal Miscellaneous	66.18		71.25		
Grand Total	2,089.82		2,635.97	1,983.25	2,519.13

Table 11-26
Capital Facility Cost Impacts

Facility	Growth Impact Units	Cost Per Unit	Total Impact Cost	Impact Cost For Growth- Sensitive Facilities
Fire/EMS				
Building Sq. Ft.	6,785	$221.00	$1,499,513	$1,499,513
Land Area, Net Acres	0.92	$45,000.00	$41,553	$41,553
Police				
Building Sq. Ft.	10,766	$192.00	$2,067,052	$2,067,052
Land Area, Net Acres	1.11	$45,000.00	$49,778	$49,778
Jails, Detention				
Maximum Security Beds	48.19	$52,000.00	$2,505,626	$2,505,626
Minimum Security Beds	48.19	$38,000.00	$1,831,034	$1,831,034
Juvenile Detention Beds	24.30	$29,000.00	$704,715	$704,715
Jail, Detention Land	2.20	$45,000.00	$99,126	$99,126
General Government				
Building Sq. Ft.	13,358	$125.00	$1,669,805	$1,669,805
Land Area, Net Acres	1.19	$45,000.00	$53,667	$53,667
Community Center				
Building Sq. Ft.	10,857	$175.00	$1,900,037	$1,900,037
Land Area, Net Acres	1.33	$45,000.00	$59,820	$59,820
Recreation Center				
Building Sq. Ft.	7,962	$190.00	$1,512,792	$1,512,792
Land Area, Net Acres	0.80	$45,000.00	$35,892	$35,892

Table 11-26 (continued)
Capital Facility Cost Impacts

Facility	Growth Impact Units	Cost Per Unit	Total Impact Cost	Impact Cost For Growth-Sensitive Facilities
Library				
Volumes	28,953	$21.50	$622,488	$622,488
Building Sq. Ft.	8,686	$112.50	$977,162	$977,162
Land Area, Net Acres	0.66	$45,000.00	$29,910	$29,910
Major Community Facilities				
Convention Centers, Building Sq. Ft.	7,725.57	$182.00	$1,406,054	na
Convention Centers, Net Acres	0.77	$45,000.00	$34,765	na
Public Assembly Halls, Building Sq. Ft.	6,759.88	$166.00	$1,122,140	na
Public Assembly Halls, Net Acres	0.48	$45,000.00	$21,728	na
Other Major Facilities, Building Sq. Ft.	3,379.94	$168.00	$567,830	na
Other Major Facilities, Net Acres	0.39	$35,000.00	$13,520	na
Parks and Open Space				
Neighborhood Park, Net Acres	18.10	$45,000.00	$814,302	$814,302
Community Park, Net Acres	79.62	$45,000.00	$3,582,928	$3,582,928
Regional Park, Net Acres	72.38	$15,000.00	$1,085,736	$1,085,736
Public Golf Course, Net Acres	65.14	$10,000.00	$651,441	$651,441
Special Use	0.53	$15,000.00	$8,005	na
Conservancy/Greenbelt	1.33	$10,000.00	$13,342	na

Table 11-26 (continued)
Capital Facility Cost Impacts

Facility	Growth Impact Units	Cost Per Unit	Total Impact Cost	Impact Cost For Growth-Sensitive Facilities
Educational Facilities				
Grades K-5 Building Sq. Ft.	63,126.50	$220.00	$13,887,830	$13,887,830
Grades K-5 Net Acres	7.25	$45,000.00	$326,067	$326,067
Grades 6-8 Building Sq. Ft.	62,224.69	$240.00	$14,933,926	$14,933,926
Grades 6-8 Net Acres	8.16	$45,000.00	$367,324	$367,324
Grades 9-12 Building Sq. Ft.	82,064.45	$265.00	$21,747,079	$21,747,079
Grades 9-12 Net Acres	12.56	$35,000.00	$439,586	$439,586
Auxiliary Building Sq. Ft.	5,861.75	$175.00	$1,025,806	$1,025,806
Auxiliary Net Acres	0.54	$45,000.00	$24,222	$24,222
Water and Wastewater Utilities				
Water Supply and Treatment Facilities, GPD	2,251,001	$9.42	$21,204,427	$21,204,427
Water Supply and Treatment Facility Land, Net Acres	2.87	$20,000.00	$57,450	$57,450
Wastewater Treatment Facilities, GPD	1,727,061	$14.68	$25,353,257	$25,353,257
Wastewater Treatment Facility Land, Net Acres	3.28	$20,000.00	$65,657	$65,657
Wastewater Irrigation Fields, Net Acres	6.16	$20,000.00	$123,107	$123,107

Table 11-26 (continued)
Capital Facility Cost Impacts

Facility	Growth Impact Units	Cost Per Unit	Total Impact Cost	Impact Cost For Growth-Sensitive Facilities
Miscellaneous				
Fire Storage, Drill, Practice Yards, Net Acres	2.98	$25,000.00	$74,377	na
Public Works Equipment, Storage Yards, Net Acres	0.72	$25,000.00	$17,953	na
Repair Shops and Associated Yards, Net Acres	0.41	$25,000.00	$10,259	na
Publicly Owned Drainage Ponds, Net Acres	8.72	$15,000.00	$130,802	na
Sand, Gravel, Soil Storage Yards, Net Acres	0.41	$15,000.00	$6,155	na
Landfills, Net Acres	6.57	$15,000.00	$98,486	na
Resource Recovery Facilities, Net Acres	0.16	$30,000.00	$4,924	na
Airports, Net Acres	45.54	$25,000.00	$1,138,483	na
Other Public Land in Inventory, Net Acres	0.68	$25,000.00	$16,884	na
Total Capital Facility Impact Cost			$126,035,821	$121,350,114
New 24/7 Functional Population and Cost Per New 24/7 Functional Resident	14,843		$8,491	$8,176
New Daytime Functional Population and Cost Per New Daytime Functional Resident	14,476		$8,706	$8,383

SUMMARY DISCUSSION

The analysis posed here is a general way in which to gauge the impact of anticipated development on the community. As my friend and professional colleague, J. Richard Recht, would ask:

- Is this development appropriate at this location?
- Is this development appropriate at this time?
- Is this development appropriate at this scale?
- Is this development appropriately configured?

Good land-use and facility planning should reduce the need for impact assessments of proposed developments since they would have been resolved through the planning and analysis process in the first place. Unfortunately, it is possible that most communities do not have good land-use plans, or any meaningful plans at all. In those situations, the land-use and facility impact approach posed here may help local officials appreciate the implications of proposed new development on their communities.

REFERENCES

Klosterman, Richard E. *Community Analysis and Planning Techniques.* New York, NY: Rowman and Littlefield, 1990.

U.S. Bureau of Economic Analysis. *Regional Economic Impact System.* Washington, DC: U.S. Department of Commerce, 1999.

___. *Regional Input-Output Multipliers II (RIMSII).* Washington, DC: U.S. Bureau of Economic Analysis, 1997.

12

The Canvas Beckons

POSTSCRIPT

This book began with a view to the future and offered ideas on how it may help land-use planners prepare their communities for it. Several chapters suggested how land-use needs are changing. They are changing in important ways indeed. For example, increasing percentages of households appear to prefer cluster and townhouse density residential locations. Although most households would appear to prefer low-density, detached housing options, the shift is evident and showing, and has already changed the urban landscape. For example, most central cities that lost population in the 1980s gained in the 1990s. In some major cities, such as San Francisco and Washington, DC, there are more housing units than ever before, despite populations that are several hundred thousand less than at their peak. Downtown living in some parts of the nation is the hottest niche market with demand far outpacing supply.

Suburbs are also changing. While many and perhaps most suburbs hold to low-density, detached residential development, a growing number are "growing up." All across the country, suburbs that offer a variety of housing options and that mix neighborhood and community-scale shopping with housing are rebounding. Many are the new glamour suburbs that the old trolley car suburbs were a hundred years ago.

Two examples come to mind. Smryna, Georgia, for instance, has replanned its entire downtown and nearby neighborhoods to include a mix of low-rise apartments, townhouses, and condominiums with detached homes, facilitating a greater variety of land uses in many neighborhoods and creating a vibrant center. Its planning has been so successful that housing values have risen more rapidly than in the Atlanta region as a whole. The ULI gave the city its first-ever Award for Excellence to a local government.

The other example is Arlington County, Virginia. Once a backwater suburb, its high-density, transportation-oriented developments, neighborhood conservation scheme (which focuses on achieving a balance between detached and low-rise attached housing), and local-serving retail and service activities have made it into perhaps the nation's poster child for smart growth. In 2003, the Environmental Protection Agency bestowed on Arlington its most coveted smart growth award for government.

Other examples abound throughout suburban America, which is really where the future of American growth, development, and change will take place over the next generation. Not that central cities will be left behind, but as Lang (2003) notes in *The Edgeless City*, MEGA and edge counties will account for perhaps 90% of all growth over the next few decades. Even with the explosion in the demand for downtown housing in such places as diverse as Seattle and Atlanta, I estimate that at best downtown housing will meet only 1% of the nation's housing needs over the next generation. Central cities will collectively meet less than 10% of the nation's housing needs. The greatest challenges and opportunities are in the suburbs.

The nation will double in its population during the 21st century. In the next generation, new construction may be comparable in scale to about 70% of everything in place in 2000. Most planners and the communities for which they work have a nearly unpainted canvas on which to shape the future. From the vacant land that might also be a brownfield to a big-box building that will come down, real estate development in America over the next generation may eclipse that seen in any prior generation.

This book may help planners and communities think about the future in a structured manner. How many housing units and retail spaces are needed? How much space will be needed to accommodate jobs? How must public facilities be expanded to serve new demands? Once we have some answers to these questions, we can consider another: What do emerging studies of changing market preferences tell us about the location, mix, and configuration of future land uses? We can then build scenarios showing future land-use patterns based on current or recent trends and patterns based on future trends. The methods posed in this book may help craft these scenarios.

Still, this book and especially the workbook are a work in progress. It may appear to provide an "off-the-shelf" approach to estimating local land-use and facility needs, but it is only a resource. The worksheets may need to be tailored to local conditions. The list of land uses may need to be changed and types of facilities altered. The planning horizon can also be changed depending on the needs of the user; there may be many horizons.

Above all, perspective is needed. Estimating land-use and facility needs is not precise, although the numbers sometimes make it look that way. We must realize that planning is part science and part art. The "science" part are the numbers broadly indicating the challenge ahead—that is the role of this book and indeed a central role of planners; the "art" part is fitting the numbers to the landscape in ways that help the community achieve its vision—that is the other central role of planners.

REFERENCE

Lang, Robert. *The Edgeless City*. Washington, DC: Brookings Institution, 2003.